Supercharging Sustainability

A BIG-PICTURE OVERVIEW OF
ESG 2.0 AND SUSTAINABLE FINANCE

Bjarni Herrera

WINDERMERE
PRESS

SUPERCHARGING SUSTAINABILITY
A Big Picture Overview of ESG 2.0 and Sustainable Finance
First Edition
Website: bjarniherrera.com

ISBN   978-1-962341-38-7   *Hardcover*
        978-1-962341-37-0   *Paperback*
        978-1-962341-36-3   *Ebook*

Cover design: Sigurdur Atli Sigurdsson (sigurduratli.com)
Glaciers, the majestic ice giants resting on land, symbolise timelessness and the fragile interplay of nature's elements. Yet, Ok, once a proud, although small, glacier in the heart of Iceland, has succumbed to the harsh reality of climate change. No longer can it claim the title of a glacier, reduced instead to a haunting assembly of ice-clad stones and rubble. This transformation is a poignant testament to the urgency of our climate change and other global challenges and the profound impact of human actions on even the most steadfast natural wonders. Is everything OK?

Contents

Reshaping Business for a Better World

Very often, friends, colleagues, and customers have asked me to recommend a good book on sustainability or sustainable finance. There weren't many I could easily recommend to non-experts. Many were on specific topics like life cycle thinking, human rights, or fixed income instruments. Still, it was hard to find a single book that gave a good and comprehensive overview of corporate sustainability and sustainable finance. So, I decided to rise to the challenge and write this book. *Welcome to Supercharging Sustainability: A Big-Picture Overview of ESG 2.0 and Sustainable Finance!*

As corporate sustainability and sustainable finance have become mainstream, their development swift and scope broad, it is essential to understand what they entail and why they matter. I aim to provide people working in corporates and financial markets, at any level, and future talent with a big-picture overview of these topics. I'm conscious of the book's complexity, range of perspectives, a plethora of concepts, and interconnected elements.

We commence our exploration by delving into the global challenges, including climate change, biodiversity loss, inequality, lack of trust, and the relationship between nations. This is so we understand the severity of the challenges. We then explore corporate sustainability and why we must progress from ESG 1.0 to 2.0. We'll also start digging into how best to transform business models to incorporate sustainability and, finally, the role of sustainable finance in how the transition to a sustainable future will be financed!

I aim not to persuade readers to "join" the corporate sustainability (ESG) movement; rather, I present this as a current reality, not an optional approach. I describe that it is happening and aim to provide guidance on engaging with it, and there are many ways to do so, leaving the reasons for action to the reader's discretion. I highlight the risks of inaction, the potential benefits of proactive measures, and the associated costs.

Our initial approach to ESG, termed ESG 1.0, has now evolved into ESG 2.0. This updated version expands to include Prosperity, enhancing the framework with revised standards and regulations that partly address previous shortcomings and issues. Using this knowledge, we'll dig into the framework's Environmental, Social, Governance, and Prosperity pillars to understand the corporate applicability and how companies can manage risks, realise opportunities, and measure progress.

This book relies on academic and popular science, institutional reports, current media, best market practices, and personal anecdotes and experiences. My goal was to capture nuances and provide a balanced overview to allow the reader to investigate further as needed. This is not an academic or scientific book and was written as an informative, quick read to enable further learning, so I sometimes draw conclusions from experience and only a handful of sources.

It was challenging not to be overly EU-centric; acknowledging the EU's pioneering role in sustainability through the Taxonomy and other regulations was essential due to its global influence. The EU's leadership in setting standards that affect worldwide markets and any entity operating within its bounds is undeniable. Similarly, China's leadership in sustainability, despite its complexities, cannot be overlooked. Ultimately, collaboration among major powers is crucial for a unified, sustainable future.

Corporate sustainability and sustainable finance face significant challenges, particularly political backlash and greenwashing. Populism often resists business involvement in environmental and social issues, while superficial efforts lead to greenwashing accusations. Addressing these requires effective communication, education to foster support for sustainability, and a commitment to transparency, stakeholder engagement, and consistent progress reporting.

I would disagree with those who might label this book as "woke" in the context of the "woke capitalism" discussion. Actions like reducing negative environmental impact, respecting human rights, ensuring strong governance, and paying fair taxes are not woke but good business and fundamental responsibilities.

While credible sources were carefully selected when writing this book, absolute accuracy, reliability, and suitability cannot be guaranteed. Geographical variations, diverse company performances, and contextual factors may impact applicability. Views expressed are solely mine unless referenced and may not necessarily reflect the opinions of affiliated organisations. Case studies or discussions on individual companies are intended for illustrative purposes only and aim to spotlight specific organisational aspects rather than portray them as entirely good or bad. The case studies in this book represent snapshots rather than comprehensive analyses.

Legal disputes may be mentioned, often tied to public processes like lawsuits. Still, it's important to note that legal disputes themselves are not negative but often involve parties seeking judicial clarification. Readers should conduct their own research before forming their own opinions and are advised to consult appropriate professionals for advice tailored to their specific situations. I assume no responsibility for any investment decisions based on this book's contents, and nothing herein should be construed as investment advice.

Having got the disclaimers out of the way, the need to build a sustainable society—from our daily lives to our economic system—is well established, and we must move faster to achieve this goal. Failing to do so will inevitably lead to irreversible, perhaps even catastrophic, Earth-system changes, which could challenge our ability to maintain modern society and support good lives. While most agree on the objectives of the sustainability agenda for a better environment and society, conflicting views on the best way forward persist.

Please read this book with a critical mind. You are welcome to agree or disagree with me and the referenced sources or remain neutral—your choice! I hope this book supercharges our sustainability knowledge journey, influences decision-making, facilitates a conversation, and helps form independent opinions based on the best available information. Remember, the devil is in the details!

CHAPTER ONE

Our Global Challenges: The Urgency of Now

The challenges Earth and society face represent risks and opportunities. To manage the risks and unlock the opportunities, we must first understand them. Challenges such as climate change and biodiversity loss profoundly impact the environment, society, and the economy. Social challenges such as inequality, which extends to disparities in climate change impacts, and issues of trust and governance also pose significant obstacles. Moreover, the take-make-waste linear design of the current world economy presents a challenge in creating a sustainable future. The transition to such a future must be just and equitable.This chapter will explore these fundamental sustainability challenges and their implications for businesses, which must be considered when drowning in new standards, regulations, metrics, and integration.

Three Pillars of Sustainability

Before diving into corporate sustainability, there are some fundamentals to cover. The three sustainability pillars (sometimes called dimensions) are the environment, society, and the economy. The environment refers to the natural world (the planet) and its resources, society refers to people and their well-being, and the economy refers to the structures and processes that guide production, distribution, consumption, and economic growth (prosperity).[1] This parallels the first three of the United Nations (UN) Sustainable Development Goals (SDG) 5Ps: people, planet, prosperity, peace, and partnership.

[1] Purvis B, Mao Y, Robinson D. Three pillars of sustainability: in search of conceptual origins. Sustain Sci. 2019;14(3):681-695. doi:10.1007/s11625-018-0627-5

ESG is then the corporate framework and an adaptation of the three pillars and stands for Environmental, Social, Governance, and, recently, Prosperity. Sustainability revolves around meeting present needs without harming future generations.

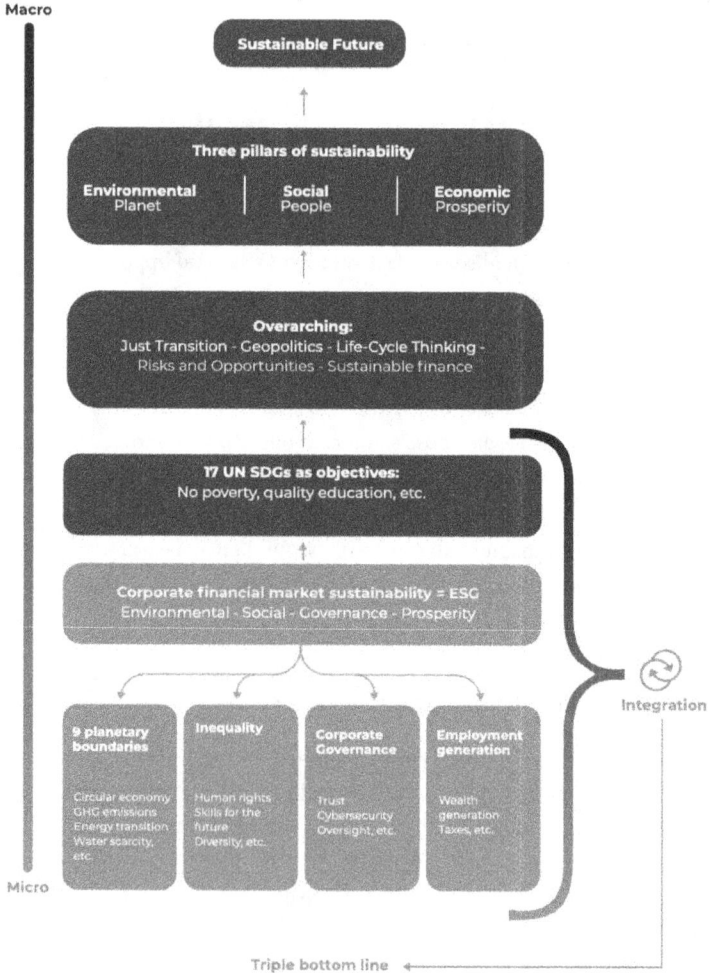

Image 1.1. This is one way to consider the interplay of sustainability, ESG(P), and sustainable finance. Source: Author

Environmental sustainability is the conservation and protection of ecosystems to maintain their resilience, supporting a healthy environment and
society. Climate change, pollution, and resource depletion all compromise
environmental sustainability and strain our planet's natural systems. Biocapacity is central to understanding these challenges—the ability of ecosystems to
produce valuable biological materials and to absorb waste materials generated
by humans.[2] A biocapacity deficit occurs if our consumption of Earth's resources and waste generation exceeds its biocapacity, resulting in an ecological
overshoot and further endangering environmental sustainability.

In 2023, the Earth's Overshoot Day, the day when we used Earth's resources generated in a year, i.e., the ecological footprint based on consumption
patterns, was 2 August.[3] A country's overshoot day is the date on which Earth
Overshoot Day would fall if all of humanity consumed like the people in this
country. Qatar's was 10 February, while Jamaica's was 20 December.[4] This
overshoot has significant implications, such as resource depletion and an
unsustainable ecological footprint, contributing to long-term challenges such
as climate change and biodiversity loss.

---

[2] Nature's regenerative capacity. WWF. wwf.panda.org/discover/knowledge_hub/all_publications/liv-
ing_planet_report_timeline/lpr_2012/demands_on_our_planet/biocapacity
[3] Earth Overshoot Day. Global Footprint Network. footprintnetwork.org/our-work/earth-overshoot-
day
[4] Country overshoot days. Earth Overshoot Day. overshootday.org/newsroom/country-overshot-days

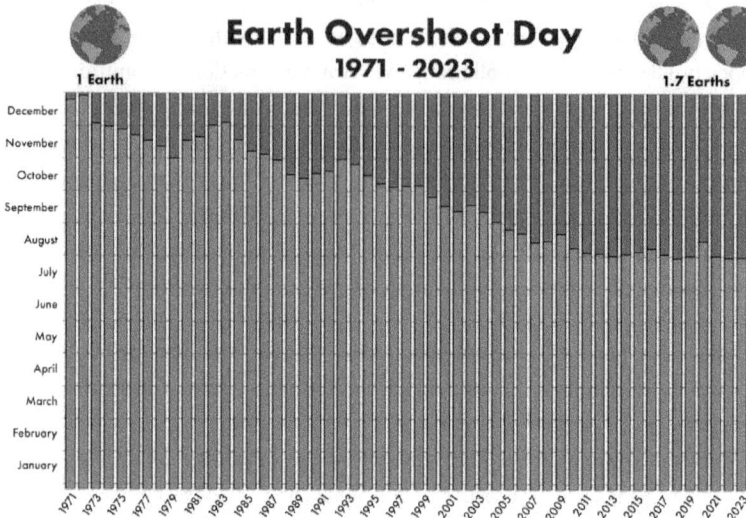

Image 1.2. Resources are finite, unlike money that central banks can print endlessly. Source: Global Footprint Network, footprintnetwork.org, accessed February 2024. National Footprint and Biocapacity Accounts 2023 Edition.

We need a healthy environment for clean air, water, food, and homes free of hazards. Without it, people will get sick or die. The World Health Organization (WHO) estimates that one in four deaths globally are due to unhealthy environments from pollution, chemical exposure, climate change, etc.[5] Environmental sustainability is integral to social and economic sustainability. The environment directly impacts communities, influencing public health and quality of life. Businesses depend on environmental resources, and sustainable practices contribute to long-term economic stability.

Due to its complexity and broadness, there is no universally accepted definition of **social sustainability.** However, simply put, it refers to a resilient and equitable society that meets the needs of all citizens and can be maintained in the future.[6] It also includes identifying and managing positive and negative

[5] An estimated 12.6 million deaths yearly are attributable to unhealthy environments. WHO. Published 15 March 2016. who.int/news/item/15-03-2016-an-estimated-12-6-million-deaths-each-year-are-attributable-to-unhealthy-environments
[6] Hovardas T. Social Sustainability as Social Learning: Insights from Multi-Stakeholder Environmental Governance. Sustainability. 2021;13(14):7744. doi:10.3390/su13147744

business impacts on people and maintaining good relationships and communication with stakeholders.

Our interdependent community requires trust, diversity, learning capacity, and self-organisation.[7] The experience of poverty and inequality, for example, results in a lack of trust within society[8] and hinders economic progress, as citizens are less likely to abide by the law, contribute to the economic vitality, support fellow citizens, and be innovative and creative.[9] Social sustainability influences environmental and economic sustainability by fostering responsible resource management, promoting inclusive decision-making, and furthering equitable economic opportunities.

Economic sustainability means having an economy that supports long-term prosperity and growth, using natural resources efficiently, fairly, and equitably and taking care of people and the planet. This requires businesses to be profitable and consider everyone's needs. The role of growth is debatable.[10] De-growth means deliberately downsizing the economy while advocating for higher prosperity with reduced production and consumption. Abandoning economic growth as an objective has recently increased in popularity in some wealthy countries.[11]

However, seeing that the global economy can agree on such a pathway is difficult. Historically, we have often prioritised economic growth over the environment and society. This has led to problems like deforestation, overfishing, pollution, and labour exploitation. The "treadmill of production" is a concept used to describe this cycle in which we always want more production and consumption, leading to pressure to keep growing the economy.[12]

[7] Missimer M, Robèrt KH, Broman G. A strategic approach to social sustainability—Part 1 J Clean Prod. 2017;140:32, 2017; 140:32-41. doi:10.1016/j.jclepro.2016.03.170

[8] Roca-Puig V. The circular path of social sustainability: An empirical analysis. J Clean Prod. 2019;212:916-924. doi:10.1016/j.jclepro.2018.12.078

[9] Lord KM. Six Ways to Repair Declining Social Trust. SSIR. Published 31 January 2019. ssir.org/articles/entry/six_ways_to_repair_declining_social_trust

[10] Purvis B, Mao Y, Robinson D. Three pillars of sustainability: in search of conceptual origins. Sustain Sci. 2019;14(3):681-695. doi:10.1007/s11625-018-0627-5

[11] Hickel J et al. Degrowth can work - here's how science can help. Nature. Published 12 December 2022. nature.com/articles/d41586-022-04412-x

[12] Curran D. The Treadmill of Production and the Positional Economy of Consumption. Can Rev Sociol Can Sociol. 2017;54(1):28-47. doi:10.1111/cars.12137

Gross domestic product (GDP) has been used, and often misused, as the dominant measure of a country's welfare despite measuring only the monetary value added. For example, cleaning up an oil spill will generally increase GDP because money is exchanged for services, although the spill harms both the environment and society. One of the main alternative metrics, genuine progress indicator (GPI), considers the adverse effects of economic activity, such as crime and environmental damage.[13]

In 2016, GPI was used to compare the progress of seventeen countries, representing over half of the global population and GDP. The results showed that economic welfare when measured by GDP, had not improved since 1978.[14] Economic sustainability encourages responsible corporate practices, which can lead to job creation and social well-being, stable communities, environmental protection, and investments in environmentally friendly technologies and practices. Now that we understand the three pillars of sustainability let us look at how the international community has addressed it through conventions and agreements.

Timeline: From Stockholm in 1972 to Montreal in 2022

The last five decades have seen a tremendous evolution in global attitudes towards sustainability. Many international conferences, treaties, and agreements have been signed and implemented, marking milestones in pursuing sustainable development. Some have succeeded, such as the Montreal Protocol on protecting the ozone layer. Others have not, such as the Millennial Development Goals (MDGs). This overview aims to provide a non-exhaustive timeline of these significant events, outlining the key takeaways and implications—the origin story of where we are today.

1972 - United Nations (UN) Conference on the Human Environment. Also known as the Stockholm Conference, it was the first international meeting

---

[13] Hayes A. Genuine Progress Indicator (GPI): Definition, Formula, Vs. GDP. Investopedia. Published 25 July 2021. investopedia.com/terms/g/gpi.asp
[14] Kubiszewski I et al. Beyond GDP: Measuring and achieving global genuine progress. Ecol Econ. 2013;93:57-68. doi:10.1016/j.ecolecon.2013.04.019

on environmental issues. It produced twenty-six principles and recommendations for global environmental action, leading to the creation of the UN Environment Programme (UNEP), a specialised agency of the UN dedicated to promoting sustainable development and addressing global environmental challenges.[15]

1987 - Montreal Protocol on Substances that Deplete the Ozone Layer. The Montreal Protocol aimed to stop the production and importation of substances like chlorofluorocarbons (CFCs) that damage the ozone layer.[16] It is considered one of the most successful international environmental agreements. The ozone layer has since started to recover, preventing an estimated two million annual deaths from skin cancer.[17]

---

[15] United Nations Conference on the Human Environment, Stockholm 1972. United Nations. un.org/en/conferences/environment/stockholm1972
[16] United Nations. Montreal Protocol on Substances that Deplete the Ozone Layer. Adopted 16 September 1987. treaties.un.org/doc/publication/unts/volume%201522/volume-1522-i-26369-english.pdf
[17] Thirty years on, what is the Montreal Protocol doing to protect the ozone? UNEP. Published 15 November 2019. unep.org/news-and-stories/story/thirty-years-what-montreal-protocol-doing-protect-ozone

From Stockholm to Montreal
Timeline

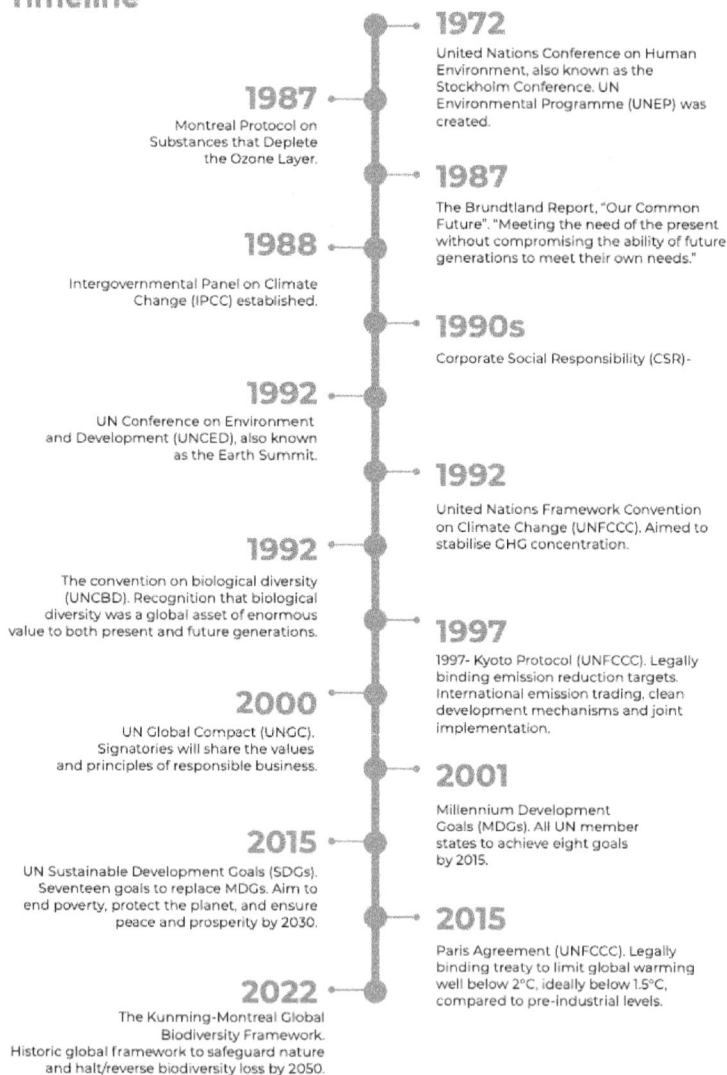

1972
United Nations Conference on Human Environment, also known as the Stockholm Conference. UN Environmental Programme (UNEP) was created.

1987
Montreal Protocol on Substances that Deplete the Ozone Layer.

1987
The Brundtland Report, "Our Common Future". "Meeting the need of the present without compromising the ability of future generations to meet their own needs."

1988
Intergovernmental Panel on Climate Change (IPCC) established.

1990s
Corporate Social Responsibility (CSR)-

1992
UN Conference on Environment and Development (UNCED), also known as the Earth Summit.

1992
United Nations Framework Convention on Climate Change (UNFCCC). Aimed to stabilise GHG concentration.

1992
The convention on biological diversity (UNCBD). Recognition that biological diversity was a global asset of enormous value to both present and future generations.

1997
1997- Kyoto Protocol (UNFCCC). Legally binding emission reduction targets. International emission trading, clean development mechanisms and joint implementation.

2000
UN Global Compact (UNGC). Signatories will share the values and principles of responsible business.

2001
Millennium Development Goals (MDGs). All UN member states to achieve eight goals by 2015.

2015
UN Sustainable Development Goals (SDGs). Seventeen goals to replace MDGs. Aim to end poverty, protect the planet, and ensure peace and prosperity by 2030.

2015
Paris Agreement (UNFCCC). Legally binding treaty to limit global warming well below 2°C, ideally below 1.5°C, compared to pre-industrial levels.

2022
The Kunming-Montreal Global Biodiversity Framework. Historic global framework to safeguard nature and halt/reverse biodiversity loss by 2050.

Image 1.3. Timeline overview of sustainable development. Source: Author

1987 - The Brundtland Report, "Our Common Future." The World Commission on Environment and Development published it and defined sustainable development as one "that meets the needs of the present without compromising the ability of future generations to meet their own needs"—the most used definition of sustainability to date. It also recognised the importance of ecosystem productivity and the global population growth that could not continue indefinitely.[18]

1988 - Intergovernmental Panel on Climate Change (IPCC). Established and endorsed by the UN General Assembly in 1988, the IPCC has played a key role as a building block for other initiatives since it published its first report in 1990. Drawing from the state of knowledge of the science of climate change, it played a role in creating the UNFCCC (United Nations Framework Convention on Climate Change) and providing material for governments to draw from in the run-up to and post-Kyoto Protocol and agreement, focusing on limiting warming to 2°C. As well as providing scientific input for the Paris Agreement, IPCC is still publishing its findings and reports, providing valuable input for the global sustainability dialogue.[19]

The 1990s - Corporate Social Responsibility (CSR). CSR has been evolving since the early 1950s. While there is no universal definition, it is generally understood as the responsibility of business professionals to adopt policies, make decisions, and take actions that align with the objectives, values, and standards desired by society.[20] Sustainability and ESG are gradually replacing CSR, illustrated by businesses' increased focus on ESG to better account for company risks and opportunities. CSR is generally seen as more of a concept for ethical business management with a lack of quantifiability, a criticism the ESG framework has answered.[21]

1992 - UN Conference on Environment and Development (UNCED). Also known as the Earth Summit, it was held to implement the Brundtland Re-

---

[18] Jarvie ME. Brundtland Report. Published 20 May 2016. Britannica. britannica.com/topic/Brundtland-Report

[19] History of the IPCC. IPCC. Accessed 15 December 2023. ipcc.ch/about/history

[20] Bowen HR. Social Responsibilities of the Businessman. University of Iowa Press; 2013.

[21] ESG vs CSR, what is the difference? Worldfavor. blog.worldfavor.com/esg-vs-csr-what-is-the-difference

port's directives.[22] Agenda 21 was one of its significant achievements, calling for immediate action on sustainable development.[23]

1992 - UN Framework Convention on Climate Change (UNFCCC). Signed at the Earth Summit in Rio, this convention aimed to stabilise greenhouse gas (GHG) concentration to prevent "dangerous" human interference with the climate system by stabilising GHG concentration. OECD (Organisation for Economic Co-operation and Development) member countries and economies in transition were expected to contribute the most to reducing emissions.[24]

1992 - The Convention on Biological Diversity (UNCBD). Inaugurated at the Rio Earth Summit, acknowledged biological diversity as a priceless global asset for current and future generations. Serving as a cornerstone in sustainable development, it boasts 196 signatory countries. It has convened fifteen Conference of Parties (COP) meetings, with the most recent in 2022 establishing the Kunming-Montreal Protocol.[25]

1997 - Kyoto Protocol (UNFCCC). It set legally binding emission reduction targets in two periods, first by 5 percent and then by 18 percent, below 1990 levels. The Kyoto Protocol included three additional market-based mechanisms: international emissions trading, clean development mechanisms, and joint implementation.[26] Large GHG emitters like China and India were excluded, which remains the source of one of its biggest criticisms, and its non-ratification by the United States (US) remains its largest failure.[27]

2000 - Millennium Development Goals (MDGs). These eight goals were meant to be achieved by 2015 to overcome challenges faced in the twenty-first century. Some progress was made, including a notable decrease in deaths

[22] Jarvie ME. Brundtland Report. Britannica. Published 20 May 2016. britannica.com/topic/Brundtland-Report
[23] United Nations Conference on Environment and Development, Rio de Janeiro, Brazil, 3-14 June 1992. United Nations. un.org/en/conferences/environment/rio1992
[24] What is the United Nations Framework Convention on Climate Change? UNFCCC. unfccc.int/process-and-meetings/the-convention/what-is-the-united-nations-framework-convention-on-climate-change
[25] What is the UN Biodiversity Conference? LSE. Published 4 October 2022. lse.ac.uk/granthaminstitute/explainers/what-is-the-un-biodiversity-conference
[26] What is the Kyoto Protocol? UNFCCC. unfccc.int/kyoto_protocol
[27] Maizland L. Global Climate Agreements: Successes and Failures. Council on Foreign Relations. cfr.org/backgrounder/paris-global-climate-change-agreements

of children and new HIV infections declining significantly.[28] However, the goals were criticised for oversimplification and overlooking key issues such as inequality and climate change, and the participation of developing countries was excluded.[29]

2000 - UN Global Compact (UNGC). More than 16,000 companies in 158 countries signed this compact to describe shared values and principles of responsible business. It is voluntary and non-binding, but participating companies must report annually on their progress.[30] It has faced competition from other, more dominant standards and initiatives under the ESG framework and is generally seen as too high-level.

The Ten Principles of the UN Global Compact (simplified)	
Human Rights	1. Respect international human rights.
	2. Avoid involvement in human rights abuses.
Labour	3. Recognise the right to unionise and collective bargaining.
	4. Abolish forced and compulsory labour.
	5. Eliminate child labour.
	6. Avoid discrimination in employment and occupation.
Environment	7. Take a precautionary approach to environmental issues.
	8. Take initiatives for environmental responsibility.
	9. Encourage eco-friendly technology development.
Anti-Corruption	10. Fight all forms of corruption, including bribery and extortion.

2015 - UN Sustainable Development Goals (SDGs). These seventeen goals, replacing the eight MDGs, aim to end poverty, protect the planet, and ensure that everybody enjoys peace and prosperity by 2030. All UN Member States adopted the SDGs as a universal call to action, applying to everyone globally. Although the SDGs are non-binding, countries are expected to take ownership and create a framework for achieving them. Widely held criticism of

[28] Millenium Development Goals (MDGs). WHO. Published 19 February 2018. who.int/news-room/fact-sheets/detail/millennium-development-goals-(mdgs)

[29] Fehling M, Nelson BD, Venkatapuram S. Limitations of the Millennium Development Goals: a literature review. Glob Public Health. 2013;8(10):1109-1122. doi:10.1080/17441692.2013.845676

[30] Frequently Asked Questions. UN Global Compact. unglobalcompact.org/about/faq

the SDGs has been that they are too lofty and intangible, hard to adapt to businesses, and designed mainly for governments and municipalities[31, 32] and that governments have been overly reliant on economic growth, for example, to lift people out of poverty.[33]

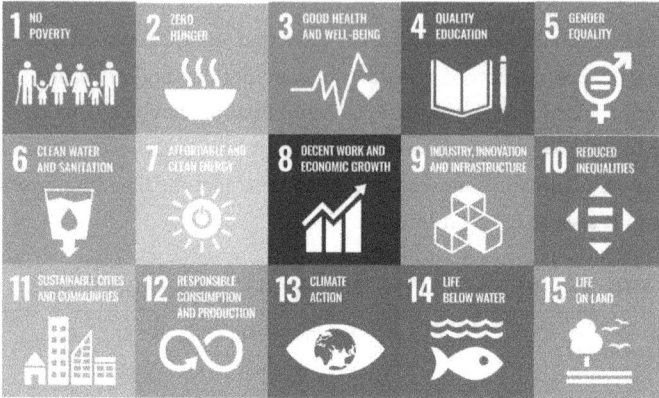

Image 1.4. The UN SDGs. Source: UN[34]

2015 - Paris Agreement (UNFCCC). It contains a binding treaty to limit global warming to well below 2°C and ideally less than 1.5°C, compared to pre-industrial levels.[35] Today, 195 countries are parties to the Paris Agreement, but Iran, Libya, and Yemen have not ratified the agreement.[36] The US publicly withdrew from the Paris Agreement under the Trump administration in 2017 but re-joined in 2021 under the Biden administration. However, one criticism of the Paris Agreement is that it is not ambitious enough.

The Paris Agreement requests each country to outline and communicate their post-2020 climate actions, known as their NDCs (nationally determined

---

[31] Sustainable Development Goals. UNDP. undp.org/sustainable-development-goals

[32] Transforming our world: the 2030 Agenda for Sustainable Development. United Nations. sdgs.un-.org/2030agenda

[33] Ending Poverty by 2030 now a fading dream. United Nations. Published 7 July 2020. ohchr.org/en/press-releases/2020/07/ending-poverty-2030-now-fading-dream-says-un-expert

[34] The content of this publication has not been approved by the United Nations and does not reflect the views of the United Nations or its officials or Member States. This statement applies to the use of other instances where the SDG logos appear in this book; all logos were downloaded from the same source. UN SDGs. UN. Accessed 12 February 2024. un.org/sustainabledevelopment

[35] The Paris Agreement. UNFCCC. unfccc.int/process-and-meetings/the-paris-agreement/the-paris-agreement

[36] Paris Agreement. United Nations Treaty Collection. treaties.un.org/Pages/ViewDetails.aspx?src=TREATY&mtdsg_no=XXVII-7-d&chapter=27&clang=_en

contributions). As of 2022, the current NDCs of 195 countries will cause the world's average global temperature to rise to 2.5°C before 2100. Based on the existing plan, they will also cause a 10.6 percent rise in GHG emissions by 2030 relative to 2010 emission levels.[37] The challenges ahead include scaling up emission-reducing efforts properly and rapidly.

2022 - Kunming-Montreal Global Biodiversity Framework (GBF) adopted. The framework has four goals and twenty-three action-oriented global targets by 2030 and aims to address biodiversity loss, restore ecosystems, and protect indigenous rights. The plan includes concrete measures to halt and reverse nature loss, including protecting 30 percent of the planet and degraded ecosystems by 2030. It also contains proposals to increase finance to developing countries.[38]

The Nine Planetary Boundaries

The planetary boundaries framework is a way of understanding the nine critical Earth systems and how human activities impact them. Pushing past these boundaries may lead to irreversible and potentially catastrophic environmental changes. The planetary boundaries framework was first introduced in 2009 and has since evolved as studies and research have increasingly assessed the various boundaries. In 2023, a group of scientists quantified all nine processes, showing that six out of the nine have already been transgressed beyond a safe operating space.[39] [40] Today, climate change and biodiversity are the two most critical systems and receive the most significant global attention.

Moving closer or further away from a planetary boundary is neither linear nor gradual. Thus, if a specific boundary is crossed, the change is not just nonlinear but also fast and widespread, causing a cascade of events. Earth's systems are complex and interconnected; not all variable relationships are fully known. This could mean the negative consequences of pushing the plan-

---

[37] Climate Plans Remain Insufficient: More Ambitious Action Needed Now. UNFCCC. Published 26 October 2022. unfccc.int/news/climate-plans-remain-insufficient-more-ambitious-action-needed-now
[38] Kunming-Montreal Global Biodiversity Framework. UNEP. 19 December 2022. unep.org/resources/kunming-montreal-global-biodiversity-framework
[39] Richardson K, Steffen W, Lucht W, et al. Earth beyond six of nine planetary boundaries. Science Advances. 2023;9(37):eadh2458. doi:10.1126/sciadv.adh2458
[40] The nine planetary boundaries. Stockholm Resilience Centre. stockholmresilience.org/research/planetary-boundaries/the-nine-planetary-boundaries.html

et's boundaries may be more extreme than forecasted. This is the case with the current impacts of warming, which are more severe than many climate models forecast.[41]

Planetary Boundary No. 1: Climate Change

Climate change occurs due to increased greenhouse gases (GHGs) being released into the air from various human activities, leading to rising global temperatures. GHGs trap heat from the sun, and as their levels in the atmosphere increase, they trap more heat. The world has experienced a faster increase in temperature in the past fifty years than in any other fifty-year period over the last two millennia.[42]

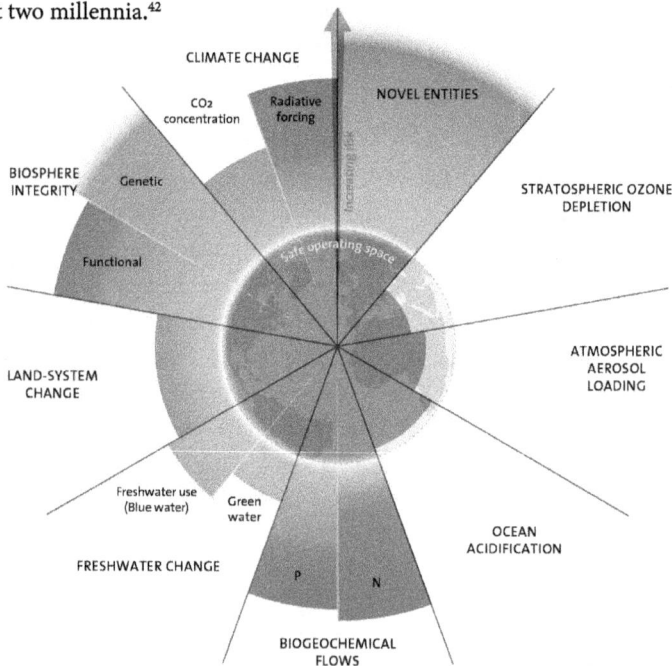

Image 1.5. Thet planetary boundaries. Source: Azote for Stockholm Resilience Centre[43]

[41] Spratt D. Faster than forecast, climate impacts trigger tipping points in the Earth system. Bulletin of the Atomic Scientists. Published 19 April 2023. thebulletin.org/2023/04/faster-than-forecast-climate-impacts-trigger-tipping-points-in-the-earth-system

[42] IPCC. AR6 Synthesis Report: Climate Change 2023: Summary for policymakers. IPCC; 2023. report. ipcc.ch/ar6syr/pdf/IPCC_AR6_SYR_SPM.pdf

[43] Azote for Stockholm Resilience Centre, based on analysis in Richardson et al 2023. Accessed 12 February 2024. stockholmresilience.org/research/planetary-boundaries.html

According to the 2023 Intergovernmental Panel on Climate Change (IPCC) report, human activities such as energy use, land use, consumption, and production have caused an increase of approximately 1.1°C in global temperatures since 1850-1900, resulting in climate change, including long-term temperature rise, and changes in precipitation and wind patterns.[44]

Climate change is not solely about rising temperatures. It also encompasses a range of life-threatening events that devastate human and planetary life, causing sharp declines in biodiversity, premature deaths, and climate refugees through migrations of whole communities, not to mention the monetary costs to individuals, governments, and businesses. For example, droughts have increased by roughly 30 percent since 2000. In the summer of 2022, significant droughts in the US, China, and across Europe caused water shortages, disrupting hydropower and shipping and impacting the global supply chain.[45]

Climate change and its effects are not future problems—they are already happening, according to the 2023 IPCC report. Despite mitigation efforts, we need more action and risk-takers in addition to policies and financial resources to meet climate goals worldwide.

Climate change is causing extreme weather worldwide, hurting both people and nature. It has a global impact, yet its impacts vary, with certain countries and regions facing heightened vulnerability and being differently equipped to protect themselves, emphasising the need for nuanced and region-specific considerations. For example, in 2019, Mozambique, Bahamas, and Zimbabwe were the most affected countries where weather events caused pollution, USD billions in losses, and many deaths.[46] Over three billion people live in areas that are vulnerable to the effects of climate change, according to the IPCC.[47]

Furthermore, the IPCC reported that in 2019, an estimated 79 percent of

---

[44] IPCC. AR6 Synthesis Report: Climate Change 2023: Summary for policymakers. IPCC; 2023. report. ipcc.ch/ar6syr/pdf/IPCC_AR6_SYR_SPM.pdf
[45] Thomson E. Droughts are creating new supply chain problems. This is what you need to know. World Economic Forum. Published 25 November 2022. weforum.org/agenda/2022/11/drought-trade-rivers-supply-chain
[46] Eckstein D, Künzel V, Schafer L. Global Climate Risk Index 2021. Germanwatch. germanwatch.org/sites/default/files/Global%20Climate%20Risk%20Index%202021_2.pdf
[47] IPCC. AR6 Synthesis Report: Climate Change 2023: Summary for policymakers. IPCC; 2023. report. ipcc.ch/ar6syr/pdf/IPCC_AR6_SYR_SPM.pdf

global GHG emissions came from the sectors of energy, industry, transport, and buildings, and 22 percent from agriculture, forestry, and other land use.[48] The International Energy Agency (IEA) has observed that energy-related emissions may be plateauing after a 1 percent increase in 2022, compared to the 6 percent increase in 2021, certainly a trend to follow. However, a 7 percent reduction per year is needed to reduce emissions significantly.[49]

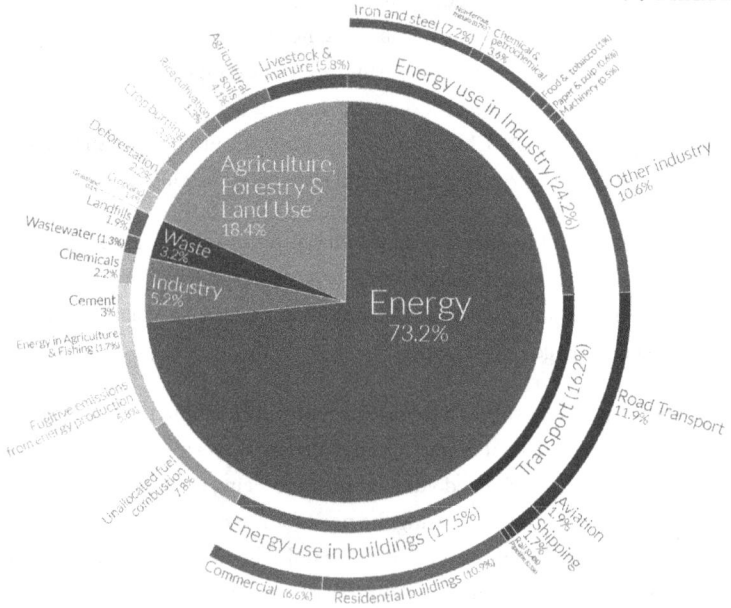

Image 1.6. The distribution and sources of GHG emissions. Source: Our World in Data[50]

[48] IPCC. AR6 Synthesis Report: Climate Change 2023: Summary for policymakers. IPCC; 2023. report. ipcc.ch/ar6syr/pdf/IPCC_AR6_SYR_SPM.pdf

[49] Harvey F. CO2 emissions may be starting to plateau, says global energy watchdog. The Guardian. Published 2 March 2023. theguardian.com/environment/2023/mar/02/co2-emissions-may-be-starting-to-plateau-global-energy-watchdog-iea

[50] Hannah Ritchie, Pablo Rosado and Max Roser (2020) - "Emissions by sector: where do greenhouse gases come from?" Published online at OurWorldInData.org. Retrieved from: 'ourworldindata.org/emissions-by-sector' [Online Resource]. Accessed 12 February 2024.

Limiting warming to 1.5°C and 2°C involves rapid, deep and in most cases immediate greenhouse gas emission reductions

Net zero CO_2 and net zero GHG emissions can be achieved through strong reductions across all sectors

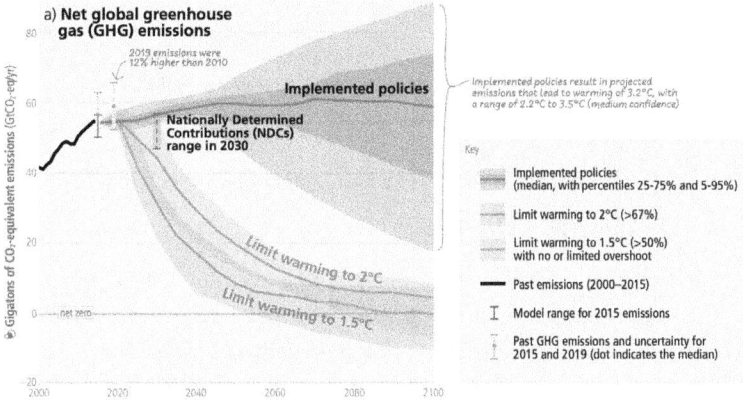

Image 1.7. If we are to limit average global warming to 1.5 degrees or less, we need to reassess policies and take more drastic actions. Source: IPCC[51]

Selected Greenhouse Gases			
Compound	Atmospheric Lifetime (years)	Main Human Activities	GWP (100 years)
Carbon dioxide (CO_2)	Variable (substantial amounts for hundreds of years)	Fossil fuels, cement production, land-use change	1
Methane (CH_4)	12	Fossil fuels, rice paddies, waste dumps, livestock	28

[51] Figure SPM.5: Panel (a) IPCC, 2023: Summary for Policymakers. In: Climate Change 2023: Synthesis Report. Contribution of Working Groups I, II and III to the Sixth Assessment Report of the Intergovernmental Panel on Climate Change [Core Writing Team, H. Lee and J. Romero (eds.)]. IPCC, Geneva, Switzerland, pp. 1-34, doi: 10.59327/IPCC/AR6-9789291691647.001.
Use of IPCC data is at the User's sole risk. Under no circumstances shall the IPCC, WMO or UNEP be liable for any loss, damage, liability or expense incurred or suffered that is claimed to have resulted from the use of any IPCC data, without limitation, any fault, error, omission, interruption or delay with respect thereto. Nothing herein shall constitute or be considered to be a limitation upon or a waiver of the privileges and immunities of WMO or UNEP, which are specifically reserved.

Nitrous oxide (N_2O)	121	Fertilisers, industrial combustion processes	265
Sulphur hexafluoride (SFs)	3,200	Electric insulation	23,500

GHG emissions involve more than CO_2; gases with higher global warming potential (GWP) warm the earth more than CO_2 over the same period. Methane, for example, has a higher GWP than CO_2 but remains in the atmosphere for less time.[52]

ADDITIONAL DETAILS: THE OIL AND GAS INDUSTRY AND CLIMATE CHANGE

It's been held that oil companies knew, as early as the 1970s, about the negative impact of burning fossil fuels on climate change. Still, they kept quiet to protect their profits, brand, and reputation. Some even cast doubt on climate change science, misled the public, and prevented or delayed regulations aimed at reducing greenhouse gas emissions. Some of their headlines included "Lies we tell our children," "Apocalypse no," and "Doomsday is cancelled. Again."[53]

Oil and gas have played a significant role in the world's progress. They have powered industrialisation, transportation, and technological advancements. Their extraction, refining, and utilisation have driven economic growth and improved living standards. It will be essential to retain the knowledge and experience of the many millions of people employed in this industry if we are to achieve a sustainable future. We will continue to rely on oil and gas to fuel our industries and transportation, but the hope remains that investments will contribute to a successful energy transition.

---

[52] Understanding Global Warming Potentials. US EPA. Published 12 January 2016. epa.gov/ghgemissions/understanding-global-warming-potentials
[53] Supran G, Oreskes N. The forgotten oil ads that told us climate change was nothing. The Guardian. Published 18 November 2021. theguardian.com/environment/2021/nov/18/the-forgotten-oil-ads-that-told-us-climate-change-was-nothing

Oil and gas have played a significant role in the world's progress. They have powered industrialisation, transportation, and technological advancements. Their extraction, refining, and utilisation have driven economic growth and improved living standards. It will be essential to retain the knowledge and experience of the many millions of people employed in this industry if we are to achieve a sustainable future. We will continue to rely on oil and gas to fuel our industries and transportation, but the hope remains that investments will contribute to a successful energy transition.

Adaptation and mitigation are two main ways to respond to climate change. **Adaptation** means preparing for the impacts of climate change, such as building sea walls, crop diversification, or implementing early warning systems. **Mitigation** of climate change is the action of reducing the severity, seriousness, or painfulness of climate change by limiting GHG emissions, switching to renewable energy, and other approaches, including afforestation and carbon capture. Although **geoengineering** is not widely discussed in this book, it refers to deliberate large-scale interventions in Earth's natural system, such as carbon capture and storage (CCS), to counteract or mitigate the effects of climate change.[54]

The cost of climate change is uncertain but could cost USD 178 trillion in economic losses over the next fifty years.[55] To put that in perspective, China's 2021 GDP was about USD 17 trillion. Additionally, it has been predicted that up to USD 20 trillion in assets could be eliminated by climate change if not addressed.[56] This economic loss means declines in productivity, job creation, standards of living, and well-being.

This cost estimation does not encompass the broader consequences of rendering vast areas uninhabitable, leading to a significant human death toll. According to the WHO, the period between 2030 and 2050 is anticipated to

[54] What is geoengineering? University of Oxford. geoengineering.ox.ac.uk/what-is-geoengineering/what-is-geoengineering
[55] Deloitte research reveals inaction on climate change could cost the world's economy US$178 trillion by 2070. Deloitte. 23 May 2022. deloitte.com/global/en/about/press-room/deloitte-research-reveals-inaction-on-climate-change-could-cost-the-world-economy-us-dollar-178-trillion-by-2070.html
[56] Partington R. Mark Carney tells global banks they cannot ignore climate change dangers. The Guardian. Published 14 April 2019. theguardian.com/environment/2019/apr/17/mark-carney-tells-global-banks-they-cannot-ignore-climate-change-dangers

witness an additional annual death toll of approximately 250,000 due to climate change impacts. These impacts include fatalities resulting from undernutrition and diarrhoea linked to crop failures and limited access to clean water, along with casualties attributed to heat stress and malaria outbreaks triggered by coastal flooding.[57]

If we transition to net-zero global emissions, it could bring a USD 43 trillion gain through innovation, job creation, and low-carbon approaches.[58] However, even with Paris Agreement countries' emissions trajectories, it is estimated we will experience an average temperature increase of 2.5°C by 2100, and if we include long-term net-zero targets, we may limit it to 2.0°C.[59] Thus, it can be seen that staying within the 1.5°C safe boundary is unlikely with current climate pledges. Accordingly, the evidence suggests that we have already exceeded the safe boundary for climate change.

ADDITIONAL DETAILS: GLACIER MELTING AND THE "THIRD POLE"

Glaciers are melting quickly due to increasing temperatures, which also causes irreversible damage to biodiversity. In the Arctic region, there are 5 million people at risk.[60] Globally, melting glaciers threaten more than 15 million people, with over half of them living in India, Pakistan, Peru, and China.[61] Millions more will be impacted through secondary effects, such as the disruption to the water cycle caused by the loss of glaciers. The Himalayas, known as the Third Pole, are at risk of melting glaciers, impacting water cycles, monsoons, and river runoff to Southeast and Central

[57] Climate change and health. WHO. 21 October 2021. who.int/news-room/fact-sheets/detail/climate-change-and-health
[58] The turning point - A Global Summary. Deloitte. Published 23 May 2022. deloitte.com/global/en/issues/climate/global-turning-point.html
[59] Temperatures. Climate Action Tracker. Published November 2022. climateactiontracker.org/global/temperatures
[60] Kaplan S. Climate change has destabilised the Earth's poles, putting the rest of the planet in peril. The Washington Post. Published 14 December 2021. washingtonpost.com/climate-environment/2021/12/14/climate-change-arctic-antarctic-poles
[61] Taylor C et al. Glacial lake outburst floods threaten millions globally. Nat Commun. 2023;14(1):487. doi:10.1038/s41467-023-36033-x

Asia, and a Third Pole process has been launched to bring nations together to address the impact of glacier melting in the region and to learn from the efforts in the North and South Pole areas. The hope is that this process will unite Asian countries that live near the Himalayas.[62]

Planetary Boundary No. 2: Novel Entities (Man-Made Pollution)

Newly created toxic pollutants, like plastics, nuclear waste, nuclear weapons, and chemicals, are called "novel entities." These harm the environment, causing a decline in bird populations and defective development of marine mammals, and also directly and indirectly adversely affect human health through direct exposure, bioaccumulation, and other poorly understood health risks. Some of these pollutants, like PFAS chemicals (per- and poly-fluoroalkyl substances), can last for hundreds of years and spread throughout the world, contaminating food and water.[63]

Even if we stop making these pollutants now, the damage they've already caused will last a long time. Recent evidence shows that we have already released too many of these pollutants, and based on scientific evidence from 2022, we have exceeded what is considered the safe boundary space. Moreover, the previously emitted entities will continue to present risks to the environment and living beings.[64]

Planetary Boundary No. 3: Stratospheric Ozone Depletion

The ozone layer in the atmosphere stops harmful ultraviolet (UV) rays from the sun. In the 1980s, scientists discovered that humans were making chemicals called chlorofluorocarbons (CFCs) that broke down the ozone layer, leading to health and environmental problems. There were frequent headlines about an ozone hole forming over the Antarctic. Thanks to the Montreal Pro-

---

[62] The Arctic Circle-UAE: Third Pole Process. Arctic Circle. arcticcircle.org/third-pole-process
[63] Salvidge R, Hosea L. Revealed: scale of 'forever chemical' pollution across UK and Europe. The Guardian. Published 23 February 2023. theguardian.com/environment/2023/feb/23/revealed-scale-of-forever-chemical-pollution-across-uk-and-europe
[64] Persson L et al. Outside the Safe Operating Space of the Planetary Boundary for Novel Entities. Environ Sci Technol. 2022;56(3):1510-1521. doi:10.1021/acs.est.1c04158

tocol, the ozone layer is healing. By 2030, the Northern Hemisphere's ozone layer is expected to be fully healed, and by 2060, the ozone layer of both polar areas will be, too.[65] This is good news because scientists believe we have not yet exceeded the safe limit for ozone depletion.

Planetary Boundary No. 4: Atmospheric Aerosol Loading

Air pollution is a big problem for human health worldwide. About 92 percent of the world's population lives in areas where air pollution levels exceed safety standards set by the WHO,[66] causing premature deaths and health problems.[67] Aerosols are particles that pollute the air and come from natural sources like sea salt, dust, volcanic ash, or human-made sources like factories and cars. Aerosols can change the climate by cooling Earth's surface and affecting clouds and rain.[68]

They also pose a threat to human health; a study in 2018 on China found that if the common atmospheric aerosol pollutant, PM2.5, were reduced, healthcare costs could decrease by over USD 9.2 billion.[69] We are estimated to operate within the defined safe boundaries for aerosol pollution.

Planetary Boundary No. 5: Ocean Acidification

Ocean acidification significantly threatens marine ecosystems and food security. Human activities such as burning fossil fuels, deforestation, and cement production cause the ocean to absorb more CO_2, making it more acidic. The oceans and seas absorb approximately 93 percent of heat captured by GHGs, and one-fourth of CO2 emissions are ultimately dissolved in the oceans.[70]

[65] WMO. Executive Summary: Scientific Assessment of Ozone Depletion: 2018. World Meteorological Organization, Global Ozone Research and Monitoring Project. Geneva, Switzerland; 2018. csl.noaa.gov/assessments/ozone/2018/executivesummary
[66] Barwick PJ et al. The Healthcare Cost of Air Pollution: Evidence from the World's Largest Payment Network. National Bureau of Economic Research; 2018:w24688. doi:10.3386/w24688
[67] Contini D et al. Contribution of Aerosol Sources to Health Impacts. Atmosphere. 2021;12(6):730. doi:10.3390/atmos12060730
[68] Aerosols and Climate. University of Leeds. environment.leeds.ac.uk/atmospheric-chemistry-aerosols/doc/aerosols-climate/page/5
[69] Barwick PJ, Li S, Rao D, Zahur NB. The Healthcare Cost of Air Pollution: Evidence from the World's Largest Payment Network. National Bureau of Economic Research. Published June 2018. doi:10.3386/w24688
[70] Rhein M et al. Observations: Ocean. In Stocker, TF et al, ed. Climate Change 2013: The Physical Science Basis. Contribution of Working Group I to the Fifth Assessment Report of the Intergovernmental Panel on Climate Change. Cambridge University Press, Cambridge, United Kingdom and New York, NY, USA; 2013.

The resulting acidification of the ocean waters is harming marine ecosystems and impacting the food chain. In addition, this adversely impacts various marine species by dissolving their shells and making it more difficult for them to form skeletons. Consequently, such species become more vulnerable to predators and have difficulty finding food. It further threatens human food security. A 2018 study projected that ocean acidification's impact on coral reefs, which support jobs, tourism, fisheries, and the seafood industry, could lead to economic losses exceeding USD 300 billion per year.[71]

While the safe boundary for ocean acidification has not yet been exceeded, the emissions that cause acidification are still rising, generating immediate concern for this planetary boundary.

Planetary Boundary No. 6: Biochemical Flows

Overuse and irresponsible application of nitrogen and phosphorus fertilisers have disrupted the natural cycles of these substances and harmed ecosystems and biodiversity in our waters. Fertilisers add nutrients to the soil, but only a small amount is absorbed by plants. The rest pollutes water, air, and other resources. Fertiliser runoff leads to large algae blooms that can cause marine and aquatic systems to cross ecological thresholds. This has economic impacts, such as reduced fish catches in the Gulf of Mexico's dead zone.[72]

It is also important to consider food security. Going from too much fertiliser to none at all may harm agriculture yield. Sri Lanka banned the use of synthetic fertilisers and pesticide imports, posed as a strategic move to promote organic farming. However, as agricultural experts had warned, this rapid measure resulted in a disaster. Sri Lanka went from being self-sufficient with rice production to having to import rice for USD 450 million.[73] According to recent evidence, the safe boundary for biogeochemical flows has already been exceeded.

[71] The real cost of ocean acidification. University of Tasmania. Published 25 July 2018. utas.edu.au/about/news-and-stories/articles/2018/681-the-real-cost-of-ocean-acidification
[72] Gulf of Mexico Dead Zone. The Nature Conservancy. nature.org/en-us/about-us/where-we-work/priority-landscapes/gulf-of-mexico/stories-in-the-gulf-of-mexico/gulf-of-mexico-dead-zone/
[73] Torrella K. Sri Lanka's organic farming disaster, explained. Vox. Published 15 July 2022. vox.com/future-perfect/2022/7/15/23218969/sri-lanka-organic-fertilizer-pesticide-agriculture-farming

Planetary Boundary No. 7: Freshwater Change

Freshwater is a limited resource, comprising only 3 percent of the water on Earth. Two-thirds of the world's population could experience water shortages by 2025.[74] The planet's climate influences the freshwater cycle through evaporation, condensation, and precipitation, allowing life on Earth to thrive. Human activities are largely responsible for freshwater shortages.

Groundwater depletion due to agriculture and population growth are the two leading causes of water scarcity. Agriculture uses 70 percent of all water and 95 percent in lower-income countries.[75] Groundwater is the primary source of freshwater, but many sources are being depleted faster than they are replenished.[76]

Climate change is making this worse, as exemplified by Day Zero in Cape Town when extreme drought nearly left millions of inhabitants without any running water.[77] Evidence also suggests that the soil moisture balance and climate have changed. Parts of the Amazon rainforest are drying out due to deforestation. Soil moisture is changing worldwide, resulting in soils that are either too wet or too dry, disrupting forests and farmlands. Recent studies and evidence showcase that we have exceeded the safe boundary for freshwater change.[78]

Planetary Boundary No. 8: Land System Changes

Land system change is alterations in how land is used driven by various factors, including human activities such as deforestation, urbanisation, infrastructure development, and more. Humans have used forests, wetlands, grasslands, and plains for centuries for agriculture and other purposes. Land-use change is regarded as a primary cause of the loss of biodiversity, which has been increasing at an unprecedented rate. Land-use change also affects the

---

[74] Water Scarcity. World Wildlife Fund. worldwildlife.org/threats/water-scarcity
[75] Water Scarcity—One of the greatest challenges of our time. FAO. Published 20 March 2019. fao.org/fao-stories/article/en/c/1185405/
[76] Thomas BF, Famiglietti JS. Identifying Climate-Induced Groundwater Depletion in GRACE Observations. Sci Rep. 2019;9(1):4124. doi:10.1038/s41598-019-40155-y
[77] Heggie J. Day Zero: Where next? National Geographic. nationalgeographic.com/science/article/partner-content-south-africa-danger-of-running-out-of-water
[78] Wang-Erlandsson L et al. A planetary boundary for green water. Nat Rev Earth Environ. 2022;3(6):380-392. doi:10.1038/s43017-022-00287-8

water cycle and biogeochemical cycles, and it can increase GHG emissions.[79] For example, drained wetlands turned into farmland release GHGs.

EU law requires countries to balance out greenhouse gas emissions from land-use changes by removing an equal or greater amount of CO2 from the atmosphere between 2021-2030.[80] Even though land-use changes may seem local, their effects add up globally—one farmer in isolation doesn't harm much, but all of them combined will have an impact. Due to excessive land use, we have now exceeded the safe boundary for land system change.

Planetary Boundary No. 9: Biosphere Integrity (Biodiversity)

Biological diversity, more commonly known as biodiversity, is the variety of life on Earth, spanning from genes and bacteria to entire ecosystems such as forests and coral reefs.[81] Biodiversity loss harms the ecosystems we rely on for food, medicine, and economic well-being. Biodiversity encompasses all life forms on Earth, including different species and ecosystems. Loss of biodiversity disrupts the balance of ecosystems, making them less resilient to environmental changes. Biodiversity is a critical issue alongside climate change, and protecting it is imperative for human and environmental health.

Global biodiversity loss is becoming increasingly alarming, and nature being a "blind spot" in economics has caused us to reach a point where we can no longer afford for accounting systems or decision-makers to ignore it.[82] The Millennium Ecosystem Assessment, published in 2005, revealed that human and economic activities have reduced biodiversity faster in the previous fifty years than at any time in human history. Furthermore, this trend shows no signs of declining.[83] This shows that biodiversity loss is not a recent problem

---

[79] Introduction to Land Use. UNFCCC. unfccc.int/topics/introduction-to-land-use
[80] Regulation (EU) 2018/841 of the European Parliament and of the Council on the inclusion of greenhouse gas emissions and removals from land use, land use change and forestry... Adopted 30 May 2018. data.europa.eu/eli/reg/2018/841/oj
[81] Biodiversity- our strongest natural defence against climate change. United Nations. Accessed 20 December 2023. un.org/en/climatechange/science/climate-issues/biodiversity
[82] Dasgupta P. The Economics of Biodiversity: The Dasgupta Review. Published February 2021. assets. publishing.service.gov.uk/media/602e92b2e90e07660f807b47/The_Economics_of_Biodiversity_The_Dasgupta_Review_Full_Report.pdf
[83] Millennium Ecosystem Assessment. Ecosystems and Human Well-Being: Biodiversity Synthesis. World Resources Institute, Washington, DC; 2005. millenniumassessment.org/documents/document.354.aspx.pdf

and has only become more severe since the assessment.

Approximately 1 million animal and plant species were found to be threatened with extinction, many within decades, in research from 2019. That accounts for 25 percent of animals and plants threatened with extinction because of human activities.[84] Human activities causing these threats include pollution, overfishing of stocks, deforestation and other land-use changes, the introduction of invasive species, and the release of GHG emissions.[85]

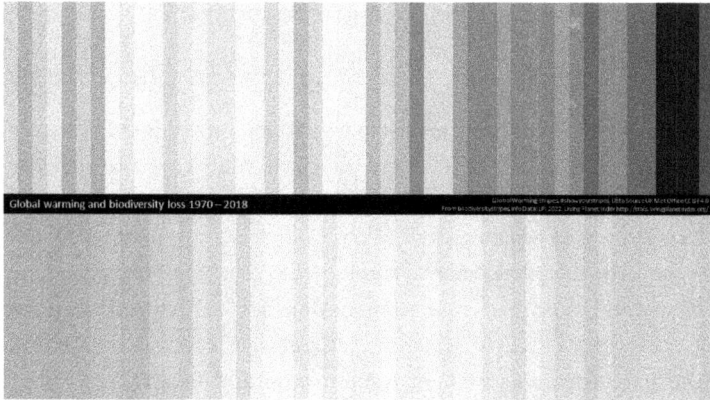

Image 1.8. The top figure represents global warming, showing how average temperature has increased over the years, and the bottom figure represents global biodiversity loss and shows how biodiversity has declined from 1970 to 2018. Source: UK Met Office and Living Planet Index[86]

The degradation of biodiversity inflicts significant social and economic damage, threatening industries like fishing, forestry, and tourism, as well as cultural values and traditional practices of many communities. More than half of the world's GDP is at risk from the sixth great extinction,[87] distinctively human-driven, unlike the previous five caused by natural events like volcanoes, meteors, and climate shifts—one famously eradicating the dinosaurs.

---

[84] Media Release: Nature's Dangerous Decline 'Unprecedented'; Species Extinction Rates 'Accelerating'. IPBES. Published 5 May 2019. ipbes.net/node/35234
[85] What is biodiversity and why is it under threat? World Wildlife Fund. worldwildlife.org/pages/what-is-biodiversity
[86] LPI 2022. Living Planet Index database. 2022. livingplanetindex.org. and #biodiversitystripes. Derby University. Accessed 12 February 2024. biodiversitystripes.info
[87] Kluger J. The Sixth Great Extinction is Underway—and Guess Which Big-Brained Species is to Blame. Time. Published 25 July 2014. time.com/3035872/sixth-great-extinction

Various factors, such as climate change and pollution, cause biodiversity loss and disrupt biosphere integrity. Natural habitats must be preserved and restored, sustainable resource use must be promoted, and climate change must be mitigated to protect biodiversity and Earth's biosphere. Decision-making processes must also consider the value of biodiversity. Nepal, for example, increased its forest cover from 26 percent to 45 percent after experiencing landslides and flooding due to significant forest loss.[88] Between 1970 and 2018, there was a 69 percent decline in animal populations.[89] Recent studies show that the biosphere integrity has exceeded safe boundaries.

We owe a debt to our planet as we have over-consumed its resources and are continuing to do so at an increasing pace. With this awareness in mind, let's transition to examining how the harmful design of our economy contributes to this pressing issue.

ADDITIONAL DETAILS: BIODIVERSITY LOSS IN THE AMAZON

Human activities like cattle farming, logging, and infrastructure have caused the Amazon rainforest to lose 3,800 square miles of forest cover (1.8 million football fields) from 2018-2019. This threatens biodiversity, leading to disease outbreaks, loss of livelihoods, deteriorating soil fertility, and species extinction.[90] The Amazon is referred to as the lungs of the world, regulating the global climate and providing necessary oxygen.[91] On top of biodiversity loss, researchers have found that its southeast part, where the most deforestation occurs due to logging and agriculture, is releasing more carbon dioxide equivalents (CO_2e) than it absorbs, thus

[88] Cassidy E. How Nepal Regenerated Its Forests. Earth Observatory. Published 9 February 2023. earthobservatory.nasa.gov/images/150937/how-nepal-regenerated-its-forests
[89] 69% average decline in wildlife populations since 1970, says new WWF report. WWF. Published thirteen October 2022. worldwildlife.org/press-releases/69-average-decline-in-wildlife-populations-since-1970-says-new-wwf-report
[90] Thomson A. Biodiversity and the Amazon Rainforest. Greenpeace. Published 22 May 2020. greenpeace.org/usa/biodiversity-and-the-amazon-rainforest/
[91] Pruitt-Young S. Parts of the Amazon Rainforest Are Now Releasing More Carbon Than They Absorb. NPR. Published 15 July 2021. npr.org/2021/07/15/1016469317/parts-of-the-amazon-rainforest-are-now-releasing-more-carbon-than-they-absorb

contributing to climate change.[92]

Linear and Consumption Economy

The market-based global economy works based on supply and demand, where products in high demand but short supply cost more. The opposite is true for products with few buyers and excess supply, which cost less. Externalities in sustainability refer to the indirect costs of economic activities, such as pollution, health impacts, and social inequality, which are not factored into market prices.[93] Negative externalities are considered a market failure and one of the reasons why governments involve themselves in economic matters.[94] To address this, regulations, carbon pricing, reporting, labelling, and certifications are intended to promote more sustainable practices.

ADDITIONAL DETAILS: THE TRAGEDY OF THE COMMONS

The 'Tragedy of the Commons,' coined in 1968, describes how a shared resource, such as a public park or a fishery, is overused and eventually depleted due to individuals acting in their self-interest.[95] The individual is neglecting the well-being of society in the pursuit of personal gain, which will lead to the depletion of the shared resource. Examples include overfishing, pollution, and deforestation. Possible solutions to counterbalance this and promote longer-term thinking include government regulations and the development of collective agreements.[96]

---

[92] Gatti LV et al. Amazonia as a carbon source linked to deforestation and climate change. Nature. 2021;595(7867):388-393. doi:10.1038/s41586-021-03629-6
[93] van den Bergh JCJM. Externality or sustainability economics? Ecological Economics. 2010;69(11):2047-2052. doi:10.1016/j.ecolecon.2010.02.009
[94] Helbling T. Externalities: Prices do not capture all costs. IMF. imf.org/en/Publications/fandd/issues/Series/Back-to-Basics/Externalities
[95] Robinson D. What is 'Tragedy of the Commons'? Earth.Org. Published 5 September 2021. earth.org/what-is-tragedy-of-the-commons
[96] Tragedy of the Commons: What It Means in Economics. Investopedia. Published 12 March 2022. investopedia.com/terms/t/tragedy-of-the-commons.asp

Today's economy is structured to promote continuous growth and increased consumption, marking a significant acceleration in economic expansion, as measured by GDP, since the Industrial Revolution in the mid-eighteenth century, a stark contrast to the slower growth rates experienced before that period.[97] This increases economic growth, corporate profits, and jobs and causes overconsumption, pollution, and social inequality. Advertising, marketing, and other techniques create a culture of consumerism, regardless of actual needs.

The current economy is also essentially linear. We take resources, use them (maybe only a handful of times), and discard them as waste, causing negative issues such as resource depletion, pollution, and climate change. This harms low-income communities and contributes to inequality. Also, the culture of excess and materialism of a consumption-based lifestyle benefits the wealthy but hurts those who cannot afford it.

Doughnut Economics, a framework for sustainable development to reframe economic problems and set new goals,[98] and the circular economy, a model of production and consumption, are alternate ways to think about our economy. Doughnut Economics considers social needs and planetary limits, while the circular economy minimises resource use and waste by designing products for reuse, leading to less waste, cost savings, and new business opportunities. Doughnut Economics broadly focuses on sustainable development, while the circular economy manages resources within economic systems. Both have been presented as solutions to our linear economy and aim for a better design of our economic system and a sustainable future.

The world's population has grown exponentially since the nineteenth century, reaching 1 billion in the early 1800s and now at 8 billion. It is expected to reach around 9 billion by 2050 and 10 billion by 2100 before ultimately levelling off and declining. Africa and Asia primarily drive the increase, while birth rates in other parts of the world are falling below replacement rates, posing

[97] Ventura J. Chapter 22 - A Global View of Economic Growth. In: Aghion P, Durlauf SN, eds. Handbook of Economic Growth. Vol 1. Elsevier; 2005:1419-1497. doi:10.1016/S1574-0684(05)01022-1
[98] What on Earth is the Doughnut?... Kate Raworth. kateraworth.com/doughnut

new challenges.[99] Ageing populations in countries like Japan and Italy also impact pension systems and healthcare. The projected decrease in the population in parts of the world by 2100 will also bring a different set of challenges, such as potential economic stagnation and a shrinking workforce.[100]

On the one hand, the increased population strains resources and contributes to environmental degradation. On the other hand, a larger population increases economic growth and innovation. Addressing factors such as education, family planning, and sustainable development is important when considering population growth that avoids adverse effects on the environment or society. If our current consumption and production patterns persist, the planet may struggle to accommodate us, even with moderate population growth.

Consumers are becoming more aware of how their purchases affect the environment and society, leading to a shift towards a circular economy. This trend is prevalent among younger generations, now a significant part of the market. Many consumers are willing to pay more for sustainable products, and this trend has been growing for the past five years.[101] Companies that do not adjust to this shift in consumer behaviour risk losing market share and damaging their reputation.

Since the early 2010s, many have argued that we have been in the fourth industrial revolution, Industry 4.0 as it's called. It includes advanced technologies such as artificial intelligence (AI), robotics, and the Internet of Things. The Green Industrial Revolution may evolve as a pivotal extension of Industry 4.0, with the EU, the US, and China, leading the charge in clean technology innovation and sustainable raw material extraction. This shift suggests that environmental sustainability is becoming an integral part of the latest industrial era, potentially redefining the core of Industry 4.0 itself.[102]

---

[99] Roser M, Rodés-Guirao L. Future Population Growth. Our World In Data. Published 2014. ourworldindata.org/future-population-growth
[100] Population in more than 20 countries to halve by 2100: Study. Al Jazeera. Published 15 July 2020. aljazeera.com/news/2020/7/15/population-in-more-than-20-countries-to-halve-by-2100-study
[101] Recent Study Reveals More Than a Third of Global Consumers Are Willing to Pay More... Business Wire. Published 14 October 2021. businesswire.com/news/home/20211014005090/en
[102] Blenkinsop P. EU announces plans to lead green industrial revolution. Reuters. Published 16 March 2023. reuters.com/business/sustainable-business/eu-unveil-plans-leadership-green-industrial-revolution-2023-03-16

Inequality

Inequality is the unequal distribution of resources and opportunities, resulting in unequal outcomes among individuals or groups. Economic inequality includes income or wealth disparity, while social inequality includes lack of access to basic needs such as education or healthcare. Political inequality refers to discrimination or a lack of representation. Income and wealth inequalities within countries have increased since the 1980s, and current global inequality levels are similar to what they were at the height of Western imperialism (historical expansion of Western powers, including European nations and the US, exerting political, economic, and cultural control over other territories).

ADDITIONAL DETAILS: GLOBAL NORTH VS. GLOBAL SOUTH

Global North and Global South refer to countries' socioeconomic, political, and historical characteristics rather than geography. This terminology replaces the developed/developing country distinction. The Global North includes Europe, the US, Australia, New Zealand, Japan, and South Korea, while the Global South includes China, India, Brazil, Nigeria, Iran, Venezuela, Indonesia, and more. However, the exact list of countries included in the Global South may vary depending on the context and definition used.

The tension between the two arises due to the unequal distribution of resources and economic power, which some argue stems from colonialism.[103] The Global North has and is benefiting from the resources and labour of the Global South, with an estimated annual extraction of around USD two trillion.[104]

Global wealth is highly concentrated, with the bottom half owning just 2 per-

---

[103] North And South, The (Global). Encyclopedia.com. encyclopedia.com/social-sciences/applied-and-social-sciences-magazines/north-and-south-global
[104] Donald R. Why The Global South Can't Go Green. Planet: Critical. Published 6 February 2023. planetcritical.com/p/why-the-global-south-cant-go-green

cent and the top 10 percent holding 76 percent of the global wealth, while the ultra-rich 1 percent gathered 66 percent of new wealth since 2020.[105] [106] This inequality extends to emissions, where twelve billionaires' carbon footprint matches 2.1 million US households, and the richest one percent emit twice as much as the poorest 3.1 billion people, highlighting the stark disparities in wealth and environmental impact.[107] [108] Inequality remains a significant issue despite economic progress, with power and influence closely linked to wealth.

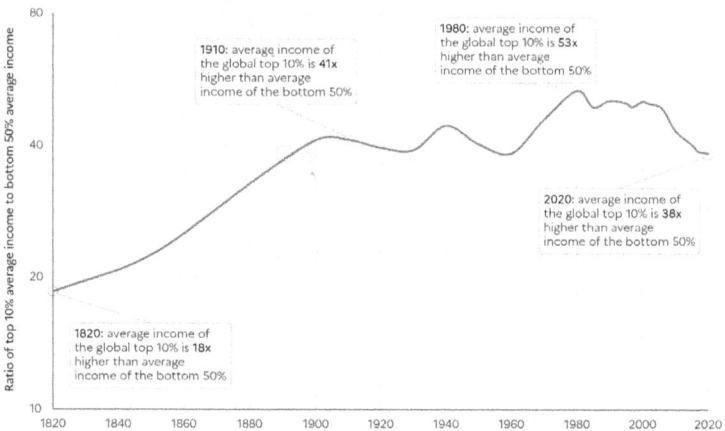

Figure 5 Global income inequality: T10/B50 ratio, 1820-2020

Image 1.9. The global inequality ratio compares the average income of the top 10% to that of the bottom 50% from 1820 to 2020. Source: Chancel L et al. [109]

Taxes are one tool to redistribute wealth, and increasing taxes on global millionaires and billionaires can help governments invest in health, education, and sustainability.[110] Some argue that if the wealthy are taxed less, they

[105] Chancel L et al. World Inequality Report 2022. World Inequality Lab; 2021. wir2022.wid.world
[106] Richest 1% bag nearly twice as much wealth as the rest of the world put together... Oxfam International. Published 1 February 2023. oxfam.org/en/press-releases/richest-1-bag-nearly-twice-much-wealth-rest-world-put-together-over-past-two-years
[107] Laville S. Twelve billionaires' climate emissions outpollute 2.1m homes, analysis finds. The Guardian. Published 20 November 2023. theguardian.com/environment/2023/nov/20/twelve-billionaires-climate-emissions-jeff-bezos-bill-gates-elon-musk-carbon-divide
[108] Carbon emissions of richest 1 percent more than double the emissions of the poorest half of humanity. Oxfam. Published 21 September 2020. oxfam.org/en/press-releases/carbon-emissions-richest-1-percent-more-double-emissions-poorest-half-humanity
[109] Executive summary. World Inequality Report 2022. World Inequality Lab. 2022. Accessed 12 February 2024. wir2022.wid.world/executive-summary
[110] Chancel L et al. World Inequality Report 2022. World Inequality Lab; 2021. wir2022.wid.world

will spend more money and boost the economy and overall wealth, but this isn't necessarily true. The latest evidence is that cutting taxes on the rich does not increase GDP but instead leads to enhanced inequality between the top 1 percent and the rest of the world.[111]

Despite inequalities in modern society, poverty has decreased in absolute numbers, with most people living above the extreme poverty line. India accomplished a historical change by reducing the number of people living in poverty by 415 million over fifteen years.[112] In the last four decades, China has managed to lift approximately 800 million people from under the international poverty line, which is defined as income of USD 1.5 per day.[113] Despite progress, efforts to eradicate extreme poverty faced a significant setback in 2022 for the first time in decades, driven by Covid-19, surging inflation, and the war in Ukraine. These factors are leading to a potential increase of 75-95 million people living in extreme poverty.[114]

Income inequality hinders sustainable development since those who are worse off may have no choice but to carry out unsustainable environmental practices to survive.[115] The wealthiest nations consume significantly more while moving their emissions abroad through reliance on manufacturing in poorer countries. All countries may need more resources to implement expensive green energy transformation projects to contribute to the energy transition.

[111] Hope D, Limberg J. The Economic Consequences of Major Tax Cuts for the Rich. Working paper 55. Published December 2022. eprints.lse.ac.uk/107919/1/Hope_economic_consequences_of_major_tax_cuts_published.pdf
The case for taxing the rich more. Financial Times. 21 March 2021. ft.com/content/dae03346-581b-4edb-838b-21c90bdb0fc3
[112] Lifting 100 million out of poverty by 2025 still possible, despite recession threat. UN. Published 17 October 2022. news.un.org/en/story/2022/10/1129592
[113] Lifting 800 Million People Out of Poverty—New Report Looks at Lessons from China's Experience. The World Bank. Published 2022. worldbank.org/en/news/press-release/2022/04/01/lifting-800-million-people-out-of-poverty-new-report-looks-at-lessons-from-china-s-experience
[114] United Nations. The Sustainable Development Goals Report 2022. United Nations; 2022. unstats.un.org/sdgs/report/2022
[115] Neumayer E. Sustainability and Inequality in Human Development. SSRN Electron J. Published 5 August 2011. doi:10.2139/ssrn.1905536

World population living in extreme poverty, World, 1820 to 2015

Extreme poverty is defined as living on less than 1.90 international-$ per day.
International-$ are adjusted for price differences between countries and for price changes over time (inflation).

Our World
in Data

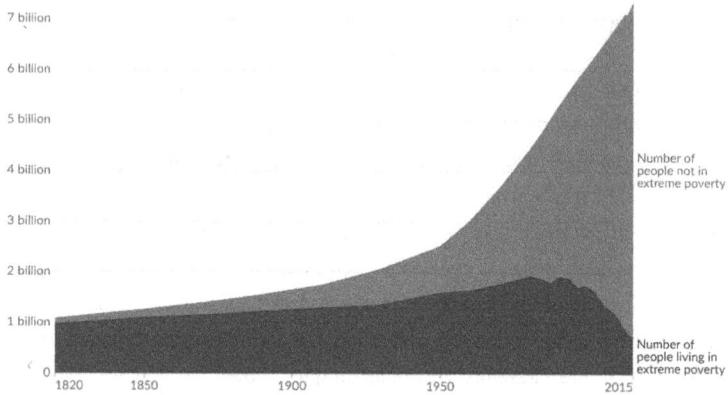

7 billion

6 billion

5 billion

4 billion — Number of people not in extreme poverty

3 billion

2 billion

1 billion

0

Number of people living in extreme poverty

1820   1850   1900   1950   2015

Image 1.10. People living under the poverty line are decreasing as the population grows.
Source: Our World in Data[116]

Climate change will affect the world unequally. Countries historically responsible for a large share of GHG emissions are also better able to tackle its impacts. Most of them are least vulnerable to climate change overall, including the US, China, Russia, Germany, and France. Countries that have contributed least to climate change through GHG emissions are likely to feel climate change affects the most, such as islands and African countries. This climate change inequality is expected to increase even further by 2030.[117]

Pakistan is an example of a country significantly suffering from climate-related disasters, such as heavy rain and flooding, while being one of the countries contributing the least to global GHG emissions.[118] Displacement due to climate change is estimated to create around 1.2 billion climate refugees by

[116] Extreme Poverty in absolute numbers - Ravallion (2016) updated with World Bank (2019)—processed by Our World in Data. Accessed 12 February 2024. ourworldindata.org/grapher/world-population-in-extreme-poverty-absolute
[117] Althor G, Watson JEM, Fuller RA. Global mismatch between greenhouse gas emissions and the burden of climate change. Sci Rep. 2016;6(1):20281. doi:10.1038/srep20281
[118] Farrer M. Pakistan floods: plea for help amid fears monsoon could put a third of country underwater. The Guardian. Published 29 August 2022. theguardian.com/world/2022/aug/29/pakistan-floods-plea-for-help-amid-fears-monsoon-could-put-a-third-of-country-underwater

2050.[119] The most at-risk groups are indigenous people, children, women, people with disabilities, and those in the least developed countries.[120]

Waste and waste hazards are also unequally distributed. The waste generated in the Global North is commonly traded to the Global South, where waste management often consists of illegal dumping and burning. Traded waste from the Global North to the South includes clothes,[121] plastics, e-waste, and decommissioned ships.[122]

Actions, such as China ceasing its plastic imports in 2018, caused a significant imbalance in the waste disposal of Europe and the US, leading to the rerouting of their waste to Indonesia, Turkey, and India.[123] In 1982, the US state of North Carolina disposed of chemical waste in a small African American community in Warren County. This case spurred the concept of environmental racism.[124] A just transition to a sustainable economy means doing so fairly and equitably. Addressing inequality becomes pivotal for realising a truly equitable, sustainable and just transformation.

[119] Ida T. Climate refugees—the world's forgotten victims. World Economic Forum. Published 18 June 2021. weforum.org/agenda/2021/06/climate-refugees-the-world-s-forgotten-victims/
[120] "Intolerable tide" of people displaced by climate change: UN expert. OHCHR. Published 23 June 2022. ohchr.org/en/press-releases/2022/06/intolerable-tide-people-displaced-climate-change-un-expert
[121] James L. Mountains of clothes washed up on Ghana beach show cost of fast fashion. The Independent. Published 27 July 2022. independent.co.uk/climate-change/news/fast-fashion-ghana-clothes-waste-b2132399.html
[122] Cotta B. What goes around, comes around? Access and allocation problems in Global North–South waste trade. Int Environ Agreem Polit Law Econ. 2020; 20(2):255-269. doi:10.1007/s10784-020-09479-3
[123] Katz C. Piling Up: How China's Ban on Importing Waste Has Stalled Global Recycling. Yale Environment360. Published 7 March 2019. e360.yale.edu/features/piling-up-how-chinas-ban-on-importing-waste-has-stalled-global-recycling
[124] Ramirez-Andreotta M. Chapter 31 - Environmental Justice. In: Brusseau ML, Pepper IL, Gerba CP, eds. Environmental and Pollution Science (Third Edition). Academic Press; 2019:573-583. doi:10.1016/B978-0-12-814719-1.00031-8

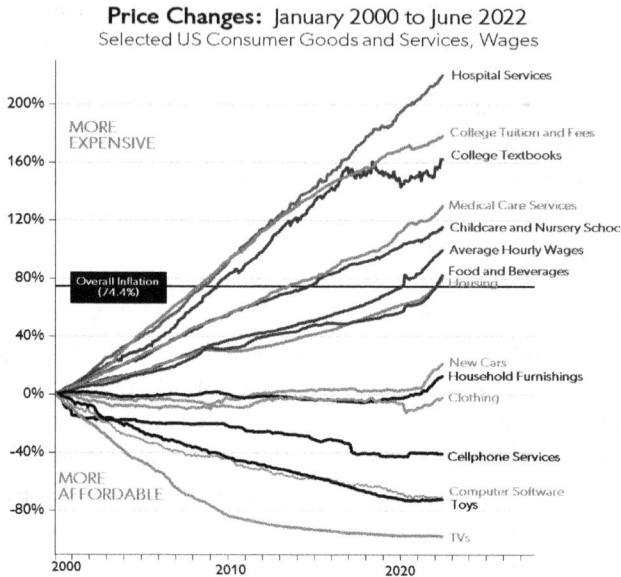

Image 1.11. Affordability of consumer goods and services in the US—hospital services are skyrocketing, but TVs cost a fraction of what they did before. Source: AEI and Bureau of Labour Statistics[125]

The Need for a Just Transition

A just transition addresses climate policy's social and economic effects by leaving no one behind and allowing everyone to participate in a sustainable economy. The term emerged from labour and environmental justice groups in the 1990s, developed further in the 2000s, and received mention in the preamble of the Paris Agreement.[126]

Companies prioritising just transitions can help to enhance human capital, elevate social value, improve their reputation, strengthen community relations, and gain a competitive edge. Just transitions also reduce systemic risk and

[125] Mark J. Perry, Senior Fellow Emeritus. Chart of the Day…or Century? American Enterprise Institute. Published 23 July 2022. aei.org/carpe-diem/chart-of-the-day-or-century
[126] CSIS, CIF. A framework for just transitions. Just Transition Initiative. Published online 2021. just-transitioninitiative.org/wp-content/uploads/2021/01/Framework-for-Just-Transitions_Download.pdf

align with a low-carbon, sustainable future.[127] A just transition ensures these workers will access jobs in the transition to a sustainable economy and not lose their livelihoods.

Countries and communities that rely heavily on environmentally harmful industries and products, such as fossil fuel, are also the most affected during a transition away from high-carbon technologies and industries. A just transition addresses these communities and ensures they are included in future livelihood options and rights.

For instance, shutting down a coal mine without providing alternative employment can have widespread socioeconomic impacts, particularly affecting women who often depend on breadwinners' income. They require special attention in the just transition process.[128] Coal miners receive low pay and have specialised skills for that industry that may become obsolete. This also impacts indirect jobs, which disappear when a large employer either significantly alters or ceases operations in an area.[129]

A just transition not only identifies consumers as important stakeholders but also actively works to address the challenges they face with energy efficiency and decarbonisation. It is essential to recognise their needs and remove barriers, creating a supportive environment that promotes sustainable decisions.[130] This approach is particularly important as price hikes or carbon taxes from climate policies can disproportionately affect those living paycheque to paycheque, who are more vulnerable to cost increases.

To support a just transition in alignment with the Paris Agreement, initiatives like the UN Development Programme (UNDP) and the EU's Just Transition Mechanism are providing critical support through financing for infrastruc-

[127] World Economic Forum, Deloitte. The Chairperson's Guide to a Just Transition. World Economic Forum. Published 22 September 2022. weforum.org/whitepapers/the-chairperson-s-guide-to-a-just-transition

[128] Lahiri-Dutt K et al. Just Transition for All: A Feminist Approach for the Coal Sector. World Bank. Published 8 December 2022. worldbank.org/en/topic/extractiveindustries/publication/just-transition-for-all-a-feminist-approach-for-the-coal-sector

[129] Supporting Coal Regions in Transition. World Bank. worldbank.org/en/topic/extractiveindustries/brief/supporting-coal-regions-in-transition

[130] Putting consumers in the heart of the energy transition. KPMG. Accessed 8 February 2024. kpmg.com/xx/en/home/insights/2022/08/putting-consumers-at-the-heart-of-the-energy-transition.html

ture, research, and re-skilling programs.[131] Moreover, the World Economic Forum (WEF) has outlined a strategy for corporations, emphasising the importance of training board members, revising board structures, and disclosing risks related to a just transition.[132]

Ensuring that policies directly account for their impact on citizens and foster their involvement in policy development is crucial, a need vividly underscored by the Yellow Vest protests in France in 2018, triggered by fuel price increases. The protests' defining motto, "the end of the world vs. the end of the month," highlights the critical balance between pursuing environmental goals and addressing immediate economic needs, emphasising the vital role of social equity in the formulation of climate policies.[133]

The human dimensions of the just transition

Image 1.12. The human dimensions of the just transition. Source: UN PRI, Image: Author

Building trust among stakeholders, including businesses, governments, and communities, is necessary to achieve a just transition in pursuing a sustainable future. In 2023, traffic cameras were installed by Transport for London to find and charge old and higher-emitting cars. Despite giving out grants to help people affected,[134] many felt this limited the freedom of movement for

[131] The Just Transition Mechanism. European Commission. commission.europa.eu/strategy-and-policy/priorities-2019-2024/european-green-deal/finance-and-green-deal/just-transition-mechanism_en
[132] World Economic Forum, Deloitte. The Chairperson's Guide to a Just Transition. World Economic Forum. Published 22 September 2022. weforum.org/whitepapers/the-chairperson-s-guide-to-a-just-transition
[133] Martin M, Islar M. The 'end of the world' vs. the 'end of the month': understanding social resistance... Sustain Sci. 2021;16(2):601-614. doi:10.1007/s11625-020-00877-9
[134] ULEZ car and motorcycle scrappage scheme. TFL. Published 21 August 2023. tfl.gov.uk/modes/driving/ultra-low-emission-zone/scrappage-schemes/car-and-motorcycle#on-this-page-2

those least able to afford it. As a result, a group called Blade Runners started taking down the cameras and destroying them.[135] This showcases distrust and resistance to government overreach and an unjust transition.

Lack of Trust

Trust is essential for implementing changes for a sustainable future as it fosters collaboration and cooperation among stakeholders, encourages collective efforts, and is key to governing and implementing effective and meaningful change. Trust is the firm belief in the ability of an individual or an organisation to do what they say they will do. This is an indispensable element of social relationships and a foundation for cooperation. It is critical to personal relationships and for society on a large scale. Governance is the tool to build and maintain trust. Without trust, individuals are more resistant to changes from governing bodies and authorities. This applies to companies, governments, and institutions alike.[136]

Trust is also required for companies to generate value. Without trust, companies lose backing and funding, causing a drop in share value. One stark example is Credit Suisse in 2023 after reported poor risk management, spying, the collapse of investment funds, rotating groups of executives, and more.[137] [138] Trust is important not only for investors but also for other stakeholders. Looking at the US, and this may differ between countries and regions, trust in business, government, civil society, and media is generally low and reportedly continues to fall.

Distrust is growing in response to widespread misinformation[139] and towards

[135] Lydall R. Ulez 'Blade Runner' vigilante: I've destroyed 150 cameras and won't stop until expansion is scrapped. Standard. Published 4 October 2023. standard.co.uk/news/transport/ulez-blade-runner-vigilante-cameras-destroyed-sadiq-khan-b1111265.html
[136] Trust in Government. OECD. oecd.org/governance/trust-in-government/
[137] Makortoff K. Furious Credit Suisse investors say bank's board should be 'put behind bars'. The Guardian. Published 4 April 2023. theguardian.com/business/2023/apr/04/credit-suisse-chair-truly-sorry-over-downfall-of-167-year-old-bank-ubs
[138] Reiff N. What Happened at Credit Suisse, and Why Did It Collapse? Investopedia. Published 28 March 2023. investopedia.com/what-happened-at-credit-suisse-and-why-did-it-collapse-7369825
[139] O'Leary J, Whittaker M. Why trust is key to leading companies unlocking value. World Economic Forum. Published 8 November 2022. weforum.org/agenda/2022/08/why-trust-is-key-to-leading-companies-unlocking-value

news media where people seek to access reliable information.[140] In addition to the media, trust towards NGOs (non-governmental organisations), governments, and businesses has declined. More than half of corporate executives think their company has engaged in greenwashing, which damages consumer trust. Of these three institutions, however, businesses are still trusted the most.[141]

Nearly half of American consumers prefer trusted companies, associating trust with balancing profits with purpose, treating employees well, managing cybersecurity, and acknowledging mistakes.[142] Rebuilding trust, though challenging, can be done; it involves mapping stakeholder perceptions, focusing on actions that enhance transparency and operational integrity and reporting on progress.[143] A Chinese study highlighted that honesty and proactive problem-solving, supported by government oversight like eco-labels, can effectively restore consumer trust after greenwashing incidents. The first step in building trust is eliminating consumer scepticism by taking legitimate actions.[144]

Trust is important not only between individuals and groups but also in international relations. It affects issues like security, trade, and environmental protection. Countries that trust each other are more likely to cooperate. Building trust involves communication, transparency, and diplomatic outreach and is necessary for cooperation between countries to transition towards a more sustainable future.

Geopolitics: Relationships of Nations

Geopolitics is a broad concept applied to various events, agreements, conflicts, or all communication between countries. Strained relationships

[140] OECD. Building Trust to Reinforce Democracy: Main Findings from the 2021 OECD Survey on Drivers of Trust in Public Institutions. OECD; 2022. doi:10.1787/b407f99c-en
[141] Edelman. Edelman Trust Barometer 2022. Edelman; 2022. edelman.com/trust/2022-trust-barometer
[142] Trust in US Business Survey. PwC. pwc.com/us/en/library/trust-in-business-survey.html
[143] O'Leary J, Whittaker M. Why trust is key to leading companies unlocking value. World Economic Forum. Published 8 November 2022. weforum.org/agenda/2022/08/why-trust-is-key-to-leading-companies-unlocking-value
[144] Wang D, Walker T, Barabanov S. A psychological approach to regaining consumer trust after greenwashing: the case of Chinese green consumers. J Consum Mark. 2020;37(6):593-603. doi:10.1108/JCM-06-2019-3257

between countries lead to increased risk to the global economy, environment, and society. Economic sanctions, trade barriers, and political tensions disrupt global supply chains and negatively impact economic growth. On the other hand, geopolitical principles such as diplomacy and mutual understanding alleviate sustainability risks by promoting cooperation and reducing tensions between nations. International cooperation is required to address sustainability challenges, such as climate mitigation, as they cross borders.

Powerful countries can influence international agreements and prevent progress towards a sustainable future.[145] The economy also plays a role: countries with natural resources necessary to the global economy can be powerful actors in the international arena. Natural resources can be an explicit part of a country's foreign policy, such as oil and gas from leading exporters, Russia and Saudi Arabia.[146] These countries rely heavily on maintaining reasonable prices for their national economy and social welfare. This prompts debatable incentives for the uptake of renewable energy sources as they depend on selling their non-renewables.

Eurasia Group's Top Political Risk Report[147]	
2023	2024
1. Rogue Russia: Russia could pose a severe security threat to Europe, the US, and globally.	1. US vs. itself: Political dysfunction in the US deepens, eroding its global stature and internal unity.
2. Maximum Xi: Xi Jinping emerged from China's 20th Party Congress in 2022 with a grip on power unrivalled since Mao Zedong.	2. Middle East on the brink: Renewed tensions and attacks unsettle the long-standing fragile peace in the Middle East.
3. Weapons of mass disruption: New technologies empower autocrats to undermine democracy domestically and abroad.	3. Partitioned Ukraine: Russia's territorial control in Ukraine solidifies, posing geopolitical dilemmas.

---

[145] Newell P. Globalization and the Environment: Capitalism, Ecology and Power. John Wiley & Sons; 2012.
[146] Overland I. Future Petroleum Geopolitics: Consequences of Climate Policy and Unconventional Oil and Gas. In: Handbook of Clean Energy Systems. John Wiley & Sons, Ltd; 2015:1-29. doi:10.1002/9781118991978.hces203
[147] Top risks 2023 / 2024. Eurasia Group. Published 3 January 2023 / 8 January 2024. eurasiagroup.net/issues/top-risks-2023 / eurasiagroup.net/issues/top-risks-2024

4. Inflation shockwaves: Rising interest rates and global recession will raise the risk of emerging-market crises.	4. Ungoverned AI: Lack of effective AI governance raises concerns as powerful technologies spread unchecked.
5. Iran in a corner: The chance of regime collapse is low but higher than in the past forty years.	5. Axis of Rouge: Russia, North Korea, and Iran bolster ties, challenging international norms and stability.
6. Energy crunch: Higher oil prices will increase friction between OPEC+ and the US.	6. No China recovery: China's economic stagnation persists, undermining global economic prospects and the risk of social instability.
7. Arrested global development: Women and girls will suffer the most, losing hard-earned rights, opportunities, and security.	7. The fight for critical minerals: The global scramble for essential minerals triggers protectionism, price volatility, and supply chain shifts.
8. Divided States of America: There is a continuing risk of political violence in the US.	8. No room for error: Persistent inflation and high-interest rates limit economic manoeuvring, raising global instability risks.
9. TikTok boom: Gen Z has the ability and the motivation to organise online to re-shape corporate and public policy, posing challenges to multinational companies and disrupting politics.	9. El Nino is back: El Nino's return brings severe weather, disrupting agriculture, water supplies, and global stability.
10. Water stress: This will become a significant and ongoing global challenge despite governments treating it as a temporary issue.	10. Risky business: US cultural conflicts increasingly influence corporate governance and stakeholder actions.

The tension between the EU and Russia about access to natural gas is geopolitical. The EU has historically relied on Russia for gas, but tensions between the EU, Russia, and Ukraine have raised concerns about this reliance. The Russian invasion of Ukraine in 2022 significantly impacted the global energy debate and has made military conflict an even greater geopolitical issue. This invasion has forced every country to rethink its energy security and policies completely and, in most cases, increase investment in energy infrastructure—potentially accelerating the energy transition by five to ten years.[148]

---

[148] War and subsidies have turbocharged the green transition. The Economist. Published 13 February 2023. economist.com/finance-and-economics/2023/02/13/war-and-subsidies-have-turbocharged-the-green-transition

Launched in 2013, China's Belt and Road Initiative (BRI) aims to boost its global influence and connectivity across Asia, Europe, and Africa by investing in infrastructure and transportation. This initiative opens new markets and resources for China and promises improved infrastructure and trade benefits for participating countries. While the BRI holds potential for sustainability through green investments, enhanced connectivity, and poverty reduction, concerns arise over its potential negative impacts, including high-carbon infrastructure, environmental damage, a lack of transparency, and potential social conflicts in communities physically linked to the BRI.[149]

There is an ongoing discussion about global leadership—or lack thereof. The US has long been considered a global leader. Still, the power balance has shifted, causing change over the last several decades due to issues such as political polarisation, the potential re-election of Trump, and unsustainable sovereign debt levels. There are several major power blocs globally, each with unique characteristics and influence. They are not fixed; their relative influence and strength will change over time. The power blocs include the following and their allies: the US, EU, Russia, India, the Middle East, and China. It can be argued that technology companies and their algorithms are a power bloc or blocs. They may or may not align with the governments where they reside, but it might open up a whole new world order if they were to do so. The race for global leadership is open!

ADDITIONAL DETAILS: FAILED STATES

A failed state is a nation-state that has lost its ability to govern effectively, resulting in a breakdown of law and order, economic collapse, social instability, chaos, and loss of legitimacy in the eyes of its citizens. They cause widespread human suffering and threaten regional and global security, harming natural resources and ecosystems and posing significant obstacles to sustainable development locally and globally. Examples of failed states include Somalia,

---

[149] World Bank. Belt and Road Economics: Opportunities and Risks of Transport Corridors. World Bank; 2019. doi: 10.1596/978-1-4648-1392-4

Yemen, Syria, Afghanistan, and the Central African Republic.[150]

ADDITIONAL DETAILS: THE MULTILATERAL SYSTEM

It includes the World Bank, the International Monetary Fund, the UN, the World Health Organization, and the World Trade Organisation. The numerous issues they are intended to solve include poverty, economic development, climate change, and global health with financial and technical assistance and fostering collaboration and cooperation between countries. The system's most significant challenges include political polarisation (rising nationalism and protectionism), limited resources, the need to adapt to new and emerging challenges, lack of inclusiveness (a few countries dominate the system), and ineffective decision-making.

Risks and Opportunities

Armed with an understanding of the big challenges we face, we recognise how multifaceted and interconnected they are. We need to respond at an unprecedented pace and scale with no real guidance. Let's now focus on the categorisation of these risks in risk language. Facing challenges, like physical and transitional risks, can lead to positive changes. Managing risks isn't just about defending ourselves; it's how to find opportunities for positive changes. Developing sustainable products and services is an example of new growth opportunities companies can unlock by navigating these risks wisely.

However, amidst these opportunities lies the danger of lock-in risk, which stems from committing to practices that hinder our transition to sustainability. This risk becomes apparent through decisions that constrain our ability to adapt, such as heavy investments in carbon-intensive assets or technologies perpetuating carbon emissions. Recognising lock-in risk in our journey to a sustainable future emphasises the importance of making informed, flexible choices that support a shift towards greener alternatives.

---

[150] The Fund for Peace. Fragile states index annual report 2022. Fragile States Index; 2022. fragilestatesindex.org/2022/07/13/fragile-states-index-2022-annual-report

Despite the definition of risk categories that follow, assigning only one of them to an event can often be hard. It usually requires a more nuanced approach emphasising the need for a holistic understanding, making it a complex challenge for the world's risk professionals.

Physical risks result from tangible and observable changes in the conditions underpinning ecosystems. Physical risks include changes in the climate (e.g., floods and fires) or to land quality via earthquakes and other geologic modifications. Such changes lead to severe pollution, nature loss, reduced raw material availability, and disruptions in supply chains. This, in turn, affects certain groups in society, such as low-income communities, marginalised populations, and vulnerable individuals.

Physical risks are divided into two categories. Acute risks are sudden and severe events, e.g., floods, wildfires, droughts, hurricanes, and other extreme events that occur over a short period, often with immediate consequences. They are exacerbated and frequently increased by climate change. Chronic risks develop slowly and gradually over time, often with delayed consequences, including climate change, air pollution, long-term exposure to toxic chemicals, rising average temperatures, precipitation patterns, and rising sea levels.

Transition risks refer to the potential economic, financial, and societal impacts on companies and industries due to the shift to a low-carbon economy or a sustainable future, i.e., regulations or policies happening faster or slower than companies anticipate. Impacts can be either positive or negative and of an economic, environmental, or social nature. For example, increased supply and demand for electric vehicles and production of renewable energy leads to new economic opportunities while the EU is banning the sale of new fossil fuel cars by 2035.[151] Transition risks are divided into lock-in, policy, legal, technology, reputational, and market risks.

Policy and legal risks refer to the potential negative impacts on a company or industry due to changing laws and regulations related to climate change or societal changes. Examples of policy changes include gender quotas, crackdowns

[151] 'Fit for 55': Council adopts regulation on CO2 emissions for new cars and vans. European Council. Published 28 March 2023. consilium.europa.eu/en/press/press-releases/2023/03/28/fit-for-55-council-adopts-regulation-on-co2-emissions-for-new-cars-and-vans

on corruption, lawsuits, stricter emissions regulations, and carbon pricing policies. Negative examples include regulatory uncertainty, inconsistent enforcement, compliance costs, and lack of incentives. For instance, a 2022 study found that climate-related lawsuits have increased globally more than twofold since 2015.[152]

Technology risks may arise as companies and assets need to keep up with advances in more climate-friendly technology. Thus, a study conducted on vehicle sales in Europe in 2021 points out that electric vehicles should soon become cheaper than traditional internal combustion engines.[153]

Reputational risks may arise as consumers, clients, workers, suppliers, and vendors pressure the private sector to become more climate-friendly, drastically reduce emissions, or uphold human rights in their supply chain. A company's image may be negatively impacted if associated with high emissions, child labour, or corruption.

Market risks include shifting demand to ethically made and cleaner products, which will ripple down the entire value chain. Furthermore, these shifts may impact demand for commodities (e.g., lithium and copper for batteries and EVs) and cause stranded assets, such as water-intensive agriculture, single-use plastic production facilities, unsustainable fisheries, etc., diminishing the market value of many companies.

Transition and lock-in risks may result in stranded assets, where investments lose economic viability and fail to yield returns. This financial erosion can stem from skyrocketing operating costs, consumers opting for superior alternatives or new governmental regulations that limit operations.

Systemic risk refers to the threat of a significant disruption within an entire industry, financial system, or economy, often sparked by the failure of a single

---

[152] Setzer J, Higham C. Global trends in climate change litigation: 2022 snapshot. Grantham Research Institute on Climate Change and the Environment. Published 30 June 2022. lse.ac.uk/granthaminstitute/publication/global-trends-in-climate-change-litigation-2022
[153] McKerracher C. Hyperdrive Daily: The EV Price Gap Narrows. Bloomberg. Published 25 May 2021. bloomberg.com/news/newsletters/2021-05-25/hyperdrive-daily-the-ev-price-gap-narrows

entity or market component.[154] Examples include the collapse of a major bank leading to widespread financial instability, as seen in the 2008 financial crisis, or the failure of Lehman Brothers, which had far-reaching effects on global markets and economies. Unlike systematic risk, which pertains to overall market risks affecting all investments due to economic, political, or natural events, systemic risk is specific to a single entity or sector but can potentially trigger broader economic turmoil. Managing systemic risk involves regulatory measures, such as those introduced by the Dodd-Frank Act, aimed at preventing the collapse of critical financial institutions and ensuring economic stability.[155] [156]

[154] Systemic Risk. CFI. Accessed 8 February 2024. corporatefinanceinstitute.com/resources/career-map/sell-side/risk-management/what-is-systemic-risk
[155] Chen J. What Is Systemic Risk? Definition in Banking, Causes and Examples. Investopedia. Published 21 September 2023. investopedia.com/terms/s/systemic-risk.asp
[156] Nguyen J. Systemic Risk vs. Systematic Risk: What's the Difference? Investopedia. February 2024. investopedia.com/ask/answers/09/systemic-systematic-risk.asp

World Economic Forum Global Risk Reports

The table showcases WEF survey findings from experts and leaders, revealing evolving risk perceptions over time. As methodologies have advanced, please consult the full reports for nuanced comparisons. While initially categorised by type, these risks can also be classified as physical, transition, or systemic, underscoring their interconnectivity and potential effects on global stability and progress.

2008	2012	2016	2020	2022	2024
Blow-up in asset prices	Severe income disparity	Large-scale involuntary migration	Extreme weather	Climate action failure	Misinformation and disinformation
Middle East instability	Chronic fiscal imbalances	Extreme weather events	Climate action failure	Extreme weather	Extreme weather events
Failed and failing states	Rising greenhouse gas emissions	Failure of climate change mitigation and adaptation	Natural disasters	Biodiversity loss	Societal polarisation
Oil price shock	Cyberattacks	Interstate conflict	Biodiversity loss	Social cohesion erosion	Cyber insecurity
Chronic diseases	Water supply crisis	Natural catastrophes	Human made environmental disasters	Livelihood crises	Interstate armed conflict
		Failure of national governance	Data fraud or theft	Infectious diseases	Lack of economic opportunity
		Unemployment or underemployment	Cyberattacks	Human environment damage	Inflation
		Data fraud or theft	Water crises	Natural resources crises	Involuntary migration
		Water crises	Global governance failure	Debt crises	Economic downturn
		Illicit trade	Asset bubbles	Geoeconomic confrontation	Pollution

Endnote

Achieving a sustainable, net-zero future and a successful global energy transition hinges on the unified participation of all superpowers, including the US, China, India, the EU, and potentially Russia. The absence of any one of these key players could significantly hinder progress. With China as a pivotal force in sustainability yet facing its own complex challenges and India as an emerging critical player, global collaboration becomes essential. The world's efforts to combat climate change and meet the Paris Agreement targets depend on each nation's commitment and cooperative action, underscoring the vital role of global unity in addressing environmental challenges.

In this chapter, we learned about the fundamental global challenges we face and the nine planetary boundaries within which we can continue to develop and thrive. Moreover, we discussed how international agreements regarding sustainability have come about and the influence of inequality on climate change and vice versa. We further discussed how the balance of global political power affects everything we do and how to think of risks and opportunities. We must work together to solve these challenges simultaneously, which is an inherently complex and multifaceted task.

In the next chapter, we will dig deeper into understanding the role of business in minimising negative impacts and increasing positive ones. This will, in turn, help us further understand what role companies play in our society and how they can unlock opportunities by strategically managing risks.

CHAPTER TWO

Corporate Sustainability: From ESG 1.0 to 2.0

This chapter digs deeper into understanding the role of business in minimising negative impacts and increasing positive ones. We will start with the Environmental, Social, and Governance framework (or ESG as it is commonly called).

ESG arose in response to the global challenges described in the previous chapter. It encourages companies to adopt sustainable practices that benefit the environment and society while enhancing long-term financial performance. ESG is constantly evolving to address issues like climate change, social inequality, and corporate governance. Stakeholders look for credible information on ESG performance.

Like anything that leads to change, the ESG framework has had its fair share of valid criticism, which has pushed the sustainability industry to upgrade it from ESG 1.0 to a newer, better ESG 2.0.[157] This update includes improved frameworks, standards, and better business practices, including requirements for third-party assurance.

What will come after 2.0, we don't know. Perhaps we will see a version upgrade to 2.1 with further improvements, new features, and bug fixes. Perhaps we'll leap to 3.0 with a total revamp of the framework, which I believe will be a proper simplification and full standardisation. An alternate reality could be

---

[157] Tavares R. High-profile critics are unwittingly driving the emergence of ESG 2.0. Fortune. Published 28 September 2022. fortune.com/2022/09/28/high-profile-critics-unwittingly-driving-the-emergence-esg-2-rodrigo-tavares

that we might move from 2.0 to perhaps 2.4 and then to 0.0—that the ESG acronym as a whole will be dropped. Time will tell.

Regardless of size or scale, every type of company can discover sustainability strategies and insights relevant to their operations. From global conglomerates to small and medium-sized enterprises (SMEs)—typically defined as businesses with fewer than 250 employees—and the local neighbourhood corner shops. However, each must tailor the approaches adopted to ensure they are applicable and effective in meeting their unique needs and objectives.

Phases of ESG

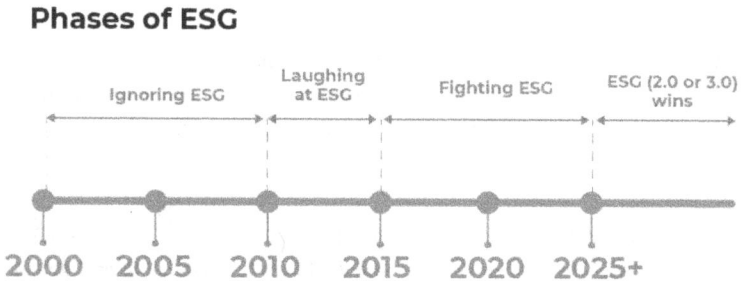

Image 2.1. Phases of ESG.[158] Source: Author

Introduction and Development of ESG

ESG is a concept that refers to the three central factors used in measuring the sustainability impact of an investment in a company or business. The idea behind ESG is that a company's performance in these areas will significantly affect the long-term financial risk profile and outcomes. The financial industry's initiative to turn the ESG process into a product has caused confusion. Therefore, it is necessary to distinguish between the actual process of ESG and ESG financial products.[159]

Here, we discuss the process, and in the Sustainable Finance chapter, we dis-

---

[158] Adapted from Beslik S. Week 39: We see things the way we are. ESG on a Sunday. Published 2 October 2022. esgonasunday.substack.com/p/week-39-we-see-things-the-way-we

[159] Serafeim G. ESG From Process to Product. Harvard Business School. Published 18 May 2023. doi:10.2139/ssrn.4460631

cuss the product. There are many ways to reference ESG, such as frameworks, standards, indicators, metrics, reports, etc. Irrelevant to the suffix, ESG is a larger framework covering many topics, such as carbon emissions, labour practices, board composition, and taxes. Investors and companies increasingly use ESG to evaluate and promote sustainable, responsible business practices. The ESG concept has been successfully branded and marketed and has united organisations towards shared goals despite the need to update to ESG 2.0 or corporate sustainability.

ESG first emerged in a 2004 report, Who Cares Wins: Connecting Financial Markets to a Changing World, issued by the UN in collaboration with eighteen financial institutes from nine different countries. It described stronger, more resilient financial markets with contributions to sustainable development and stakeholder engagement, resulting in improved trust in financial institutions.[160] Even though the term ESG did not appear until 2004, the concept has been practised much longer in different forms. Since the 1960s, investors have excluded specific industries from their investment portfolio, such as tobacco production, due to its harmful components.[161]

The 2004 report responded to a survey showing that 70 percent of CEOs believed investors were becoming more interested in "corporate citizenship issues." It is also mentioned that ESG performance is required for companies to perform well. By integrating these indicators into their operations, companies could improve their competitiveness, increase shareholder value, and better manage risks and regulations while contributing to sustainable development.[162] Following this, in 2005, the world's largest institutional investors created the Principles for Responsible Investment (PRI) to incorporate ESG principles into investment decision-making.

Most individual topics within the ESG framework, which we will explore in the following chapters, are familiar to us. However, it has evolved to include more topics like employment generation and taxes. ESG has significant finan-

[160] Who Cares Wins: Connecting Financial Markets to a Changing World. The Global Compact. unepfi. org/fileadmin/events/2004/stocks/who_cares_wins_global_compact_2004.pdf
[161] The Evolution of ESG Investing. MSCI. msci.com/esg-101-what-is-esg/evolution-of-esg-investing
[162] Who Cares Wins: Connecting Financial Markets to a Changing World. The Global Compact. unepfi. org/fileadmin/events/2004/stocks/who_cares_wins_global_compact_2004.pdf

cial implications, and the focus on "non-financial" aspects of ESG is no longer enough. By identifying material indicators (discussed later), we can measure progress, set targets, and develop incentive systems to encourage managers to achieve them.

Benefits and Costs of Integrating ESG

A well-conducted ESG integration is consistent with company strategies, and it advances business models.[163] A company without ESG considerations may still operate, but it is less likely to survive in the long run. Eventually, it may lose its "social licence to operate," which refers to losing the trust of local communities and consumers by not adapting to changing norms. This is in addition to losing its official licence by failing to meet regulations or anticipating future shifts towards sustainability.

Implementing ESG appropriately and focusing on what is material can create value and a competitive advantage. Research has pointed to strong links between ESG and cash flow. ESG value creation is realised through five main channels: revenue increase through premiums or volume increase, cost savings, reduced impact from emerging regulation, higher labour productivity, and optimising investments and assets. These are further described later.[164]

While there are costs associated with ESG implementation, the potential gains far outweigh these expenses. The strategic integration of ESG not only enhances corporate reputation, attracting sustainability-conscious investors and customers, but it also mitigates risks, fosters innovation, and ensures long-term resilience.

It's essential to remember that while ESG integration brings numerous advantages, it cannot substitute for solid business fundamentals such as revenue management, cost control, and risk assessment, which will be further discussed in the integration chapter. Nevertheless, the tangible benefits of

---

[163] Pérez L et al. Does ESG really matter—and why? McKinsey. Published 10 August 2022. mckinsey.com/capabilities/sustainability/our-insights/does-esg-really-matter-and-why

[164] Henisz W, Koller T, Nuttall R. Five ways ESG creates value. McKinsey. Published 14 November 2019. mckinsey.com/capabilities/strategy-and-corporate-finance/our-insights/five-ways-that-esg-creates-value

ESG integration affirm its value, underscoring the necessity of harmonising these principles with strong financial and operational foundations to achieve sustainable success.

Top-Line or Revenue Growth

New business models focusing on sustainability and ESG unlock revenue and market opportunities by focusing on the circular economy and sustainable investing, for example. By tapping into growing consumer demand for these products and services, companies will increase their competitiveness and attract new customers and investors, creating long-term value. A strong ESG proposition allows companies to grow or expand with increased access, approvals, or licences. A 2023 study indicates that industries, especially in energy, retail, and high-tech, are embracing ESG not just for compliance but as a significant growth opportunity.[165]

Most Gen Z shoppers are willing to pay up to 10 percent more for sustainable brands and are more likely to buy based on personal, social, and environmental values.[166] This may change as supply and demand dynamics develop, and perhaps unsustainable products will be priced appropriately to factor in their negative contribution to sustainability.

Cost Reduction

One of the primary ways to achieve cost savings is by improving resource efficiency in water, energy, waste generation, and other inputs necessary for production. These improvements may boost operating profits by up to 60 percent.[167] Apart from ESG, removing inefficiencies in a business—hence reducing cost—is one of the primary responsibilities of business managers. The company 3M has reportedly saved USD 1.7 billion since the 1975 launch of its "pollution prevention pays" (3Ps) program, reformulating products,

[165] Korkmaz B, Nuttall R, Pérez L, Sneessens J, ESG momentum: Seven reported traits that set organizations apart. McKinsey. 26 May 2023. mckinsey.com/capabilities/strategy-and-corporate-finance/our-insights/esg-momentum-seven-reported-traits-that-set-organizations-apart

[166] Gomes S, Lopes JM, Nogueira S. Willingness to pay more for green products: A critical challenge for Gen Z. Journal of Cleaner Production, Volume 390. 1 March 2023. sciencedirect.com/science/article/pii/S0959652623002500

[167] Koller T, Nuttall R. How the E in ESG creates business value. McKinsey. 20 June 2020. mckinsey.com/capabilities/sustainability/our-insights/sustainability-blog/how-the-e-in-esg-creates-business-value

improving manufacturing processes, redesigning equipment, and recycling and reusing waste from production.[168]

Reduced Regulatory and Legal Interventions

Companies that perform well on ESG have more flexibility in their strategies because they face less pressure from regulators. In addition, strong ESG performance leads to government support, helping companies address the risks of emerging regulations and policies. However, the extent of this link may differ depending on the industry. On average, around one-third of corporate profits are at risk due to state intervention, but this varies by sector. For instance, the risk is lower for healthcare and pharmaceuticals but higher for banking.

Employee Productivity

Robust ESG policies and ESG performance have repeatedly led to increased talent attraction and employee retention. Not only does ESG attract and retain talent, but it also increases employee satisfaction and motivation, which has been found to contribute to higher shareholder returns.[169] A 2021 study, using a sample of companies between 1984 and 2020, found that an equal-weighted portfolio of companies that treated employees the best earned excess returns of 2 percent to 2.7 percent annually.[170] Conversely, weak company purpose lowers employee productivity through slowdowns and strikes.

Investment and Asset Optimisation

A strong ESG strategy enhances investment returns by making capital allocation more efficient. Companies use the capital to invest in more sustainable equipment or facilities. By considering ESG indicators, companies can avoid investing in assets that may become obsolete due to environmental risks.

This enables investors to make better decisions and reduce the risk of losses.

---

[168] Henisz WJ. The Costs and Benefits of Calculating the Net Present Value of Corporate Diplomacy. Field Actions Science Reports. 2016;Special Issue 14. journals.openedition.org/factsreports/4109
[169] Edmans A. Does the stock market fully value intangibles? Employee satisfaction and equity prices. J Financ Econ. 2011;101(3):621-640. doi:10.1016/j.jfineco.2011.03.021
[170] Boustanifar H, Kang YD. Employee Satisfaction and Long-run Stock Returns, 1984-2020. SSRN. Published 30 September 2021. doi:10.2139/ssrn.3933687

For example, they can avoid investing in energy-intensive machinery or non-green-certified buildings whose value could be reduced in the future or even turn into stranded assets due to technological changes, markets, environmental policies, or climate impacts due to unanticipated or premature write-downs, devaluations, or conversion to liabilities.[171]

Costs of ESG

Achieving the benefits of ESG comes with costs. However, not engaging in ESG also costs. Despite the long-term benefits, adapting to sustainable practices can be expensive. Benefits may not be immediate, making it difficult for management to justify the expense to stakeholders as a part of their fiduciary duty.

Additionally, there is a need for a better understanding of the potential benefits of sustainability, creating a perceived trade-off between short-term costs and long-term benefits. Management may have trouble prioritising sustainability initiatives over other business objectives. Based on a survey conducted in the US, some of the major spending categories included the following:[172]

1. **Compliance:** Costs of adhering to environmental and social regulations, such as emissions reduction targets or labour standards.

2. **Third-party providers:** Need to hire external advisors, contact data providers, and obtain ESG ratings to establish ESG integration.

3. **Reporting and disclosure:** Investing in systems and processes to gather, analyse, and report on ESG indicators for greater transparency.

4. **Operations:** Investing in new technologies, processes, or training to improve environmental or social performance.

5. **Reputation:** Poor ESG performance harms a company's reputation, reducing brand loyalty and market share.

6. **Risks:** Inadequate ESG risk management results in financial and reputa-

---

[171] Stranded Assets Programme. Smith School of Enterprise and the Environment. smithschool.ox.ac.uk/research/stranded-assets
[172] Costs and Benefits of Climate Related Disclosure Activities... ERM. 17 May 2022. sustainability.com/globalassets/sustainability.com/thinking/pdfs/2022/costs-and-benefits-of-climate-related-disclosure-activities-by-corporate-issuers-and-institutional-investors-17-may-22.pdf

tional risks, such as lawsuits, fines, or investment loss.

Failure to implement ESG with genuine commitment and adaptability can lead to detrimental consequences. Companies may face legal ramifications, incur fines, witness a talent drain as skilled employees seek more responsible employers, and experience customer attrition as clients migrate to more ethical competitors. Additionally, the lack of ESG adherence may hinder access to capital, damage stakeholder trust, and result in reputational harm, creating a cascade of negative impacts on the company's overall sustainability.

Financial Statements and Triple Bottom Line Impacts

"The triple bottom line wasn't designed to be just an accounting tool. It was supposed to provoke deeper thinking about capitalism and its future."[173] Introduced in 1994, it was an innovative approach to measuring business success beyond financial profit. The top line is the revenue, and everything between the top and bottom line represents the cost or other items that impact profits.

	Balance Sheet	Profit and Loss	Cash Flow
Component	Assets Liabilities	Revenues (the top line) Expenses	Operating, investing, and financing activities
Traditional bottom lines	Net assets or equity	Net profit or net loss	Net cash flow
ESG implication	Climate events can lower the value of buildings. Governance and social issues like loss of trust or labour disputes can decrease the value of intangible assets such as goodwill.	Fines for pollution and higher wages or legal fees from labour disputes can impact revenues and operating expenses. Low-carbon products can improve revenue.	ESG initiatives can have positive and negative impacts on operating expenses, capital expenditures, access to capital, customer preferences, insurance costs, and overall business adaptability and innovation.

[173] Elkington J. 25 Years Ago I Coined the Phrase "Triple Bottom Line." Here's Why It's Time to Rethink It. Harvard Business Review. Published 25 June 2018. hbr.org/2018/06/25-years-ago-i-coined-the-phrase-triple-bottom-line-heres-why-im-giving-up-on-it

Triple bottom line Planet (Environment) People (Social) Profits (Prosperity)	The triple bottom line is a forward-thinking approach that aims to measure the financial, social, and environmental performance of a company. This thinking can help organisations navigate away from investments likely to become stranded assets in a rapidly evolving market. Traditional accounting rules provide very strong guidance on how a company must record its financial profit, but no such structure exists, nor are companies required to do so for the planet and people, yet. Therefore, companies may need to get creative. The triple bottom line may also be difficult to measure, costly to implement, and cause competing strategies across triple bottom line components.[174]

Prosperity: The Fourth Pillar of ESG

ESG included three categories or pillars, representing a tricycle. Prosperity was then added as the fourth pillar. This saw ESG mature from a tricycle to a car—hopefully an electric one! Prosperity covers economic issues such as job creation, wealth generation, innovation, and taxes.

Prosperity is a prerequisite for building a strong, inclusive, transformative economy. The prosperity concept was not part of the ESG framework until WEF introduced it in 2020 in its paper "Measuring Stakeholder Capitalism." Therefore, it may not be surprising that prosperity has not been addressed in companies' sustainability reports and policies. It seems that the acknowledgement of the prosperity pillar is growing, and it will be here to stay as an addition to ESG, although it is unlikely it will be renamed ESG-P.

The UN 2030 Agenda for Sustainable Development has its own definition of prosperity, which ensures that people enjoy fulfilling lives while promoting economic, social, and technological progress in harmony with nature.[175] Companies that address prosperity issues in their sustainability strategies better capture their direct economic contribution.

---

[174] Kenton W. Triple Bottom Line. Investopedia. Published 30 April 2023. investopedia.com/terms/t/triple-bottom-line.asp
[175] Resolution adopted by the General Assembly on 1 September 2015. A/RES/69/315. General Assembly, United Nations. Published 15 September 2015. archive.unescwa.org/sites/www.unescwa.org/files/un_resolutions/a_res_69_315_e.pdf

Materiality: Single, Double, and Dynamic

Before delving into each of the ESG and P pillars, it is necessary to understand the concept of materiality. To understand how to apply materiality, one needs to understand a company's business model and, in essence, its products and services. By understanding their supply chains, raw materials, sales channels, and customers, it starts to become more visible what negative and positive sustainability impacts are and apply appropriate metrics and goals.

Materiality is one of the fundamental concepts in corporate sustainability and should steer any sustainability application and determine its success or failure.

Materiality, in the context of corporate sustainability and financial markets, is the relevance of a sustainability factor to an organisation's financial performance. Material factors have a significant impact, both positive and negative, on various aspects of a company's success.[176] Therefore, companies must recognise which factors are material when making decisions. The primary stakeholders looking at financial materiality are investors.[177]

For a professional services firm—an IT consultant, marketing agency, or management consulting firm—it is unlikely that water issues are material. Water issues can, however, be material to a manufacturer of food processing systems or clothing, which relies heavily on the water in its supply chain. For the same professional services firm, skilling its workforce for the future and protecting its employees' physical and mental health are both material.

Materiality also becomes layered within industries. Imagine three real estate companies: One owns and manages specialised real estate for health care, the second owns and manages residential apartments, and the third owns and manages shopping malls. All have in common the ingredients of a building, concrete, wood, construction, and demolition of buildings, but they have different customers and activities in their buildings. Their materiality profile should, therefore, be different.

---

[176] Sustainable Investing: Materiality. Robeco. Published 2 June 2022. robeco.com/en/key-strengths/sustainable-investing/glossary/materiality.html
[177] The Challenge of Double Materiality: Sustainability Reporting at a Crossroad. Deloitte China. deloitte.com/cn/en/pages/hot-topics/topics/climate-and-sustainability/dcca/thought-leadership/the-challenge-of-double-materiality.html

A good exercise in this regard is to read two sustainability reports from companies in separate industries, for example, an insurance company and an energy company. If the structure and focus in their reports are the same, i.e., they both focus equally on the same ESG indicators or issues, something is wrong with either one or both and their understanding of what is material.

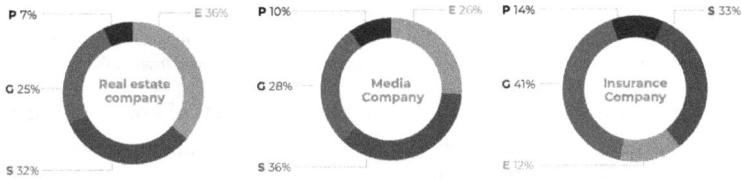

P 7%	E 36%	P 10%	E 26%	P 14%	S 33%
G 25%	Real estate company	G 28%	Media Company	G 41%	Insurance Company
S 32%		S 36%		E 12%	

Image 2.2. Materiality profiles are different between industries. Source: Author

Double materiality refers to the bidirectional impact of the outside world on a company and vice versa. This is important in ESG because sustainable practices and social impact can have a material impact on a company's performance and competitiveness. Therefore, it is necessary to consider financial and impact materiality when determining what to report.[178] Various academic studies support this concept, which is increasingly integrated into investment decision-making and corporate strategy.

To perform a double materiality assessment, a company must independently evaluate the significance of each sustainability topic from both impact and financial perspectives, considering a topic material if it holds significance in either or both areas. This process involves assessing how the company's activities cause or contribute to significant impacts on society and the environment (impact materiality) and how sustainability topics externally affect or could affect the company's finances (financial materiality) to guide appropriate sustainability disclosures.[179]

---

[178] Sustainable finance. European Commission. Published 26 July 2022. ec.europa.eu/newsroom/fisma/items/754701/en
[179] [Draft] European Sustainability Reporting Guidelines 1 Double materiality conceptual guidelines for standard-setting. ERAG. Published January 2022.efrag.org/Assets/Download?assetUrl=/sites/webpublishing/SiteAssets/Appendix%202.6%20-%20WP%20on%20draft%20ESRG%201.pdf

Double materiality

Image 2.3. Double materiality means that companies have impacts on the environment and society, and the environment and society have impacts on companies. Image: Author

Dynamic materiality recognises that the material aspects of a business can shift over time, requiring continuous assessment and adaptation to stay aligned with emerging risks and opportunities and their impact on value creation and finances of the company.[180] This approach helps ensure that the organisation addresses the most pressing ESG concerns and that its approach to sustainability is responsive to changes in the business environment and stakeholder expectations. Materiality requires ongoing monitoring and stakeholder engagement and should be reviewed regularly. This ensures that the organisation is heading in the right direction to create long-term value for itself and its stakeholders.

Hyper-materiality is a concept not discussed previously, and, in fact, I've found no traces of its discussion anywhere, so this might be my only "invention" in the book. It represents a strategic approach where company executives navigate beyond noise and clutter—such as regulations and stakeholder demands—and move away from ESG metrics, initiatives, and activities that don't add value. Instead, and this is not for the faint-hearted, they concentrate intensely on their business's core financial and operational fundamentals and the impact their products and services can have—the signal. This focus sharpens their impact on the company's financial success and their role in contributing to a sustainable future. This concept will need to be explored further by myself and others.

---

[180] Calace D. Double and Dynamic: Understanding the Changing Perspectives on Materiality. SASB. Published 2 September 2020. sasb.org/blog/double-and-dynamic-understanding-the-changing-perspectives-on-materiality

Endnote

This chapter has shown us that approaching ESG requires a phased and tailored approach that ensures the process is manageable. A simple self-assessment and reporting on material ESG indicators may be sufficient for smaller companies, but a comprehensive approach will be necessary for larger companies. Companies of all sizes must prioritise the most material ESG indicators and focus on progress in those areas. We have also introduced an important addition to the ESG model—prosperity, which cannot be divorced from companies' sustainability efforts.

Now that we understand the concept of ESG and the lens through which to consider it and its materiality, starting in the next chapter and continuing in the following four chapters, we will dig into each of the letters in the acronym, with the addition of P for Prosperity, to understand their particular subsections, risks and opportunities, and best practices. We will further discuss what to look for when measuring ESG performance.

CHAPTER THREE

Environmental: Protecting Our Planet

Over the next four chapters, we will delve into the four pillars of ESG. These are Environmental, Social, Governance, and Prosperity. This chapter will explore climate change, biodiversity, and ecosystems. Additionally, our discussion will extend to pollution of the air, water, and soil and the utilisation of the ocean and freshwater resources, ending with waste and resource use and the circular economy.

Looking back a few decades, companies mostly strove to comply with regulations when managing environmental risks. Over the last two decades, it has expanded to include a proactive and strategic approach to identifying and managing environmental risks to unlock opportunities for value creation. "Company X to become carbon neutral by 2030" or "Company Y to achieve net zero by 2040" are headlines or statements from companies we have seen. Such companies have received praise, but these headlines have also been the basis of much discussion, including credibility, greenwashing, and overall ambition levels.

Image 3.1. UN SDGs material to the Environmental pillar. Source: UN, see footnote 34

Climate Change

Increasingly, stakeholders expect companies to take responsibility for their emissions contributing to climate change. Companies that rely heavily on high volumes of fossil fuels will have their work cut out for them in the coming years, some more than others. Fossil fuels are a significant source of GHG emissions and represent around 80 percent of the global energy supply but have been estimated to decrease to 73 percent by 2030.[181] Other primary emission sources include general energy production, industrial production, and agriculture. Such sectors will, therefore, play an essential role in mitigating climate change through reduced emissions.

GHG Emissions: Scopes 1, 2, 3...and 4

Companies measure their contribution to climate change by quantifying their emissions. Emission factors come from various sources, such as government agencies, nonprofit organisations, and academic institutions. Measuring emissions is commonly done via three emission scopes to help organisations prioritise their emission reduction efforts and enable transparency and comparability in reporting emissions. The Greenhouse Gas Protocol (GHG Protocol), established in 1998, is the most widely adopted GHG accounting

---

[181] World Energy Outlook 2023. IEA. Published October 2023. iea.org/reports/world-energy-outlook-2023

standard.[182] [183]

The GHG Protocol consists of two parts: one providing clear guidelines on quantifying and reporting GHG emissions for companies, and the other for individual projects.[184] Emissions must be segregated into scopes, further detailed in the following table, because emissions occur from various sources within organisations' control (Scope 1 and Scope 2) and outside their control (Scope 3), which they may still influence through their business decisions.

There are five steps to identify and calculate GHG emissions: identify sources, select a calculation approach, collect data and choose emission factors, apply calculation tools, and roll up data to the corporate level. Establishing emission factors consists of first identifying the relevant scope and purpose, determining the emissions type, uncovering sources, checking data reliability, and calculating emissions by multiplying the emission factors by the amount of activity. The GHG protocol's reporting principles are:

- Completeness: Report on all sources of emissions within the inventory boundary.

- Consistency: Use consistent methods to track performance and document changes.

- Relevance: Ensure the inventory accurately reflects the company's emissions and helps decision-making.

- Accuracy: Accurately measure emissions without over- or underestimating.

- Transparency: Disclose all relevant information, including assumptions and references.

---

[182] Standards. Greenhouse Gas Protocol. ghgprotocol.org/standards

[183] Other GHG accounting guidelines or protocols exist, including Greenhouse Gas Inventory Guidance: Direct Emissions from Stationary Combustion Sources published by the U.S. Environmental Protection Agency (EPA), India GHG Inventory Program, ISO 14064-1, Petroleum Industry Guidelines for reporting GHG emissions and others

[184] The GHG Protocol: A corporate reporting and accounting standard (revised edition). WBCSD. Published 20 March 2004. wbcsd.org/eh3wc

Greenhouse Gas Protocol: Scope 1, 2, and 3 Emissions[185]

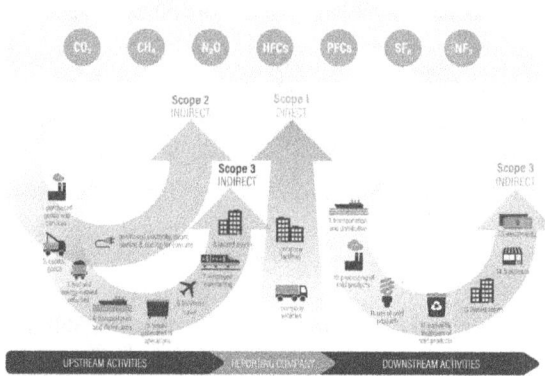

Image 3.2. Scope 1 for emissions from the organisation's assets, e.g., vehicles, buildings, and machinery. Scope 2 for emissions from purchased energy sources. Scope 3 for indirect emissions across the organisation's value chain. Scope 3 is divided into 15 categories, including upstream and downstream emissions. Source: GHG Protocol.[186]

ADDITIONAL DETAILS: SCOPE 4

Scope 4 is an emerging topic not yet covered by the GHG Protocol, initially developed without a clear definition. Despite Scopes 1 to 3 being designed to account for all emissions, Scope 4 has nonetheless emerged. Its future development and how it will be defined remain to be seen. It reflects emissions outside of a company's operation, essentially accounting for emissions that a company takes action to avoid. Current examples include using teleconferencing services for meetings instead of commuting and highlighting the positive impacts of green bonds and other sustainable finance instruments.

---

[185] Corporate Value Chain (Scope 3) Standard. Greenhouse Gas Protocol. ghgprotocol.org/standards/scope-3-standard
[186] Technical Guidance for Calculating Scope 3 Emissions (version 1.0), page 6. GHG Protocol. Accessed 9 February 2024. ghgprotocol.org/sites/default/files/2023-03/Scope3_Calculation_Guidance_0%5B1%5D.pdf

Financial institutions contribute to climate change through their portfolio as a part of Scope 3, such as financed, facilitated, and insurance-associated emissions. The Partnership for Carbon Accounting Financials (PCAF), founded in 2015, is an industry partnership of financial institutions. The main drivers for PCAF were the need to mobilise capital flows towards a low-carbon economy and disclosure providing a clear understanding of how investments align with the Paris climate goals.[187]

It supports transparency and accountability in carbon accounting for the financial sector, including measuring emissions for each asset class, having its specific formula to calculate emissions,[188] and ensuring data quality. PCAF also has guidance for listed equity and corporate bonds, business loans, private equity, commercial real estate, commercial lines, and more.

EMISSION FROM AN ASSET PORTFOLIO[189]

Financed emissions $= \sum_c$ **Attribution factor**$_c \times$ **Company emissions**$_c$

To work out the emissions that come from money invested in a company, you use this simple math: Financed emissions = Sum of (Attribution factor x Company emissions). Here, "c" stands for either the company that borrowed the money or the one you invested in. The attribution factor is just the company's share of the investment. So, for different types of companies, like those that are private or those that are publicly traded and listed on a stock exchange, the way you figure out this share will change. Calculations then differ between private and listed companies and can be impacted by the type of financial instrument involved.

---

[187] About PCAF. PCAF. carbonaccountingfinancials.com/en/about
[188] Financed Emissions - The Global GHG Accounting and Reporting Standard. PCAF. Published December 2022. carbonaccountingfinancials.com/standard
[189] Financed Emissions. PCAF. Published 2022. carbonaccountingfinancials.com/files/downloads/PCAF-Global-GHG-Standard.pdf

Mitigation Strategies: Decarbonisation and Energy Transition

Mitigation of climate change is the action of reducing the severity, seriousness, or painfulness of climate change by limiting GHG emissions, switching to renewable energy, and other approaches, including afforestation and carbon capture.

Decarbonisation describes various methods, including reducing or removing carbon emissions, mainly CO2 and CH4. This includes increasing energy efficiency, transitioning to renewable energy sources, implementing carbon pricing schemes, contributing to reforestation or soil health projects, implementing energy-efficient building codes, and promoting public transportation.

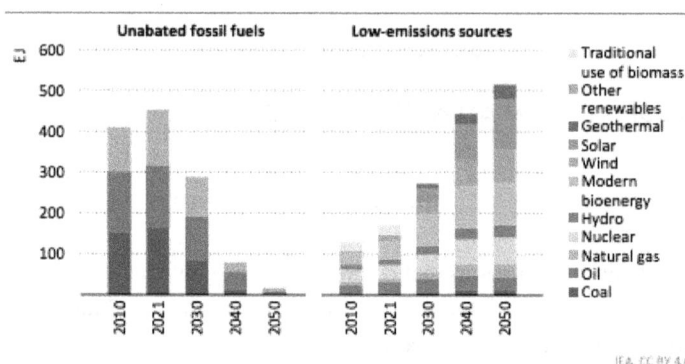

Image 3.3. Total energy supply comparing unabated fossil supply to low-emissions sources for a net-zero scenario Source: IEA World Energy Outlook 2022[190]

Decarbonisation strategies extend to investments in renewable energy projects, such as wind or solar power, and geoengineering approaches, including Carbon Capture and Storage (CCS) and its broader application, Carbon Capture, Utilisation, and Storage (CCUS) technologies. The latter aims to capture and store CO_2 and explores its use in various industrial processes. Therefore, decarbonisation is one of the key strategies for mitigating climate change. In 2022, companies globally invested over USD 1.1 trillion in low-carbon energy

---

[190] IEA 2022, World Energy Outlook 2022. iea.blob.core.windows.net/assets/830fe099-5530-48f2-a7c1-11f35d510983/WorldEnergyOutlook2022.pdf .Licence: CC BY 4.0.

technology to reduce CO2 emissions.[191] However, investments by the 2,000 largest companies need to double by 2030, or else 93 percent of them won't reach their decarbonisation targets.[192]

Carbon offsets balance out GHG emissions produced by individuals or companies by paying someone else to reduce emissions as a counterbalance. Although it does not tackle the root cause of GHG emissions, it is an effort to lower the cost of emission reductions. Some projects like tree planting and kelp forests are more common as they are cheaper but hard to monitor and verify. Projects using high-tech methods, like carbon sequestration, are more easily monitored but significantly more expensive.[193] While standards like the Gold Standard, founded by the WWF and other NGOs and positive development, aim to ensure the credibility of these projects,[194] scepticism remains, and research suggests that 90 percent of carbon offsets do not represent actual emission reductions.[195] Thus, while contributing to emission reduction efforts, the primary focus should be directly reducing emissions to meet 2050 goals.

ADDITIONAL DETAILS: CARBON TRADING, TAXES, AND INTERNAL CARBON PRICING

Market-based systems incentivise companies to reduce greenhouse gas emissions through economic mechanisms. For example, carbon trading is when companies hold permits for the amount of emissions they produce and can sell excess allowances to those

---

[191] Global Low-Carbon Energy Technology Investment Surges Past $1 Trillion for the First Time. BloombergNEF. Published 26 January 2023. about.bnef.com/blog/global-low-carbon-energy-technology-investment-surges-past-1-trillion-for-the-first-time
[192] Nearly All Companies Will Miss Net Zero Goals Without At Least Doubling Rate… Accenture. Published 1 November 2022. newsroom.accenture.com/news/nearly-all-companies-will-miss-net-zero-goals-without-at-least-doubling-rate-of-carbon-emissions-reductions-by-2030-accenture-report-finds.htm
[193] Emission Gap Report 2023: Broken Record—Temperatures hit new highs, yet the world fails to cut emissions (again). UN EP. Published 20 November 2023. wedocs.unep.org/bitstream/handle/20.500.11822/43922/EGR2023.pdf
[194] Carbon Markets. Gold Standard. Accessed 7 February 2024. goldstandard.org/impact-quantification/carbon-markets
[195] Greenfield P. Revealed: more than 90% of rainforest carbon offsets by biggest certifier are worthless, analysis shows. The Guardian. Published 18 January 2023. theguardian.com/environment/2023/jan/18/revealed-forest-carbon-offsets-biggest-provider-worthless-verra-aoe

who emit more.[196] This encourages companies to reduce emissions below their regulatory requirements. Examples include emissions trading systems like California's Cap-and-Trade Program and China and the EU's emissions trading systems (ETS).

A carbon tax is a price set on carbon by defining a tax rate on GHG emissions or the carbon content of fossil fuels. It differs from the ETS in that the emission reduction is not predefined.[197] Internal carbon pricing is a voluntary estimate made by companies on the price of their CO_2 units, sometimes called shadow price. It is a way to prepare for a low-carbon future and divert investments from carbon-intensive activities, currently in use by 2,000 companies.[198] [199] [200]

Energy transition, a subset of decarbonisation, involves shifting from fossil fuels to cleaner, renewable energy sources. Doing so improves air and water quality, creates new jobs but perhaps eliminates jobs in dying industries, and improves energy security. In 2022, around 80 percent of global primary energy came from non-renewable resources, such as coal, gas, and oil. In that same year, around 61 percent of electricity was generated from fossil fuels.[201] Fossil fuels account for over 75 percent of greenhouse gas (GHG) emissions and 90 percent of CO2 emissions,[202] making it the primary driver of climate change and global warming.[203]

Renewable energy resources include solar, wind, bioenergy, hydropower,

[196] EU Emissions Trading System (EU ETS). European Commission. climate.ec.europa.eu/eu-action/eu-emissions-trading-system-eu-ets_en
[197] Carbon Pricing. The World Bank. Accessed 14 December 2023. worldbank.org/en/programs/pricing-carbon
[198] Internal carbon pricing: What's the value of your emissions? Deloitte. Accessed 14 December 2023. deloitte.com/uk/en/focus/climate-change/internal-carbon-pricing.html
[199] CDP. Putting a price on carbon. CDP; 2021. cdp.net/en/reports/downloads/5651
[200] Carbon Pricing Dashboard. The World Bank. Accessed 19 December 2023. carbonpricingdashboard.worldbank.org
[201] Ritchie H, Roser M, Rosado P. Energy. Our World Data. Published October 2022. ourworldindata.org/fossil-fuels
[202] Renewable energy—powering a safer future. United Nations. un.org/en/climatechange/raising-ambition/renewable-energy
[203] Global Climate Agreements: Successes and Failures. Council on Foreign Relations. cfr.org/backgrounder/paris-global-climate-change-agreements

and more. It is more sustainable than fossil fuels because it will never be used up and generates up to three times more jobs than the fossil fuel industry.[204] Renewable energy capacity is expected to increase faster in the next few years than previously, with capacity going from 1,282 GW from 2016 to 2021 to 2,383 GW between 2022 and 2027. China, the EU, the US, and India largely drive this trend. Renewables are also estimated to become the largest electricity source by 2025. Solar PV and wind are estimated to be leading regarding renewables and may generate 43 percent of electricity worldwide in 2030, according to the IEA.[205]

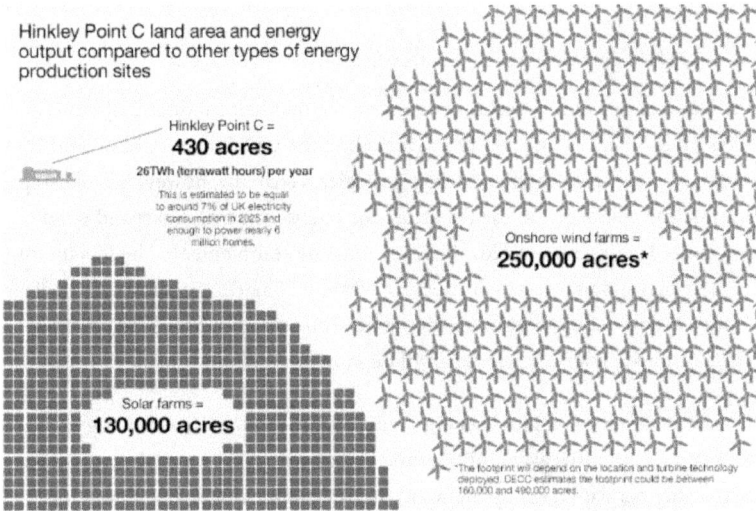

Hinkley Point C land area and energy output compared to other types of energy production sites

Hinkley Point C =
430 acres
26TWh (terrawatt hours) per year
This is estimated to be equal to around 7% of UK electricity consumption in 2025 and enough to power nearly 6 million homes.

Onshore wind farms =
250,000 acres*

Solar farms =
130,000 acres

*The footprint will depend on the location and turbine technology deployed. DECC estimates the footprint could be between 160,000 and 490,000 acres.

Image 3.4. Land use is compared between different energy sources with the same energy output. Source: UK's Department of Energy & Climate Change (DEEC)

[204] Renewable energy—powering a safer future. United Nations. un.org/en/climatechange/raising-ambition/renewable-energy
[205] IEA. Renewables 2022. IEA; 2022. iea.org/reports/renewables-2022

What are the safest and cleanest sources of energy?

Our World in Data

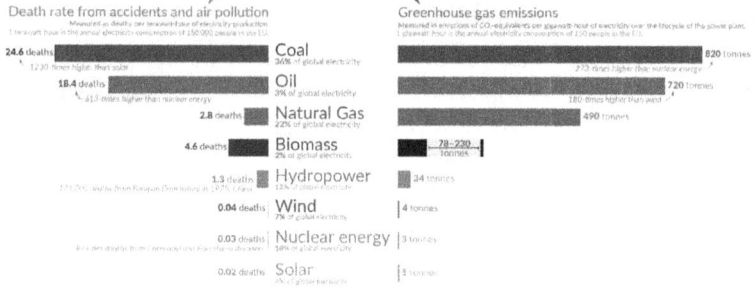

Image 3.5. Safest vs cleanest energy sources. Source: Our World in Data[206]

Nuclear energy is a low-carbon energy source that helps reduce emissions and takes up less land. Some countries, including the UK, France, China, and India, have included it in their energy strategies. Germany, however, is phasing out nuclear plants due to the debate about safety concerns. Solar and wind power are leading renewables, but they must be complemented by less intermittent energy sources such as nuclear power.[207] The IEA predicts that nuclear energy will play a big part in achieving net-zero emissions by 2050. Without nuclear power, reaching net zero will be more difficult and costly.[208]

The transition to sustainable energy will require changes in technology, society, and resource availability, while global population growth necessitates decreasing per capita energy demand by 2050. Achieving this will require innovations in energy and resource use, behavioural changes, and increased access to energy for everyone.[209]

---

[206] Hannah Ritchie (2020) - "What are the safest and cleanest sources of energy?" Published online at OurWorldInData.org. Retrieved from: 'ourworldindata.org/safest-sources-of-energy'. Accessed 12 February 2024.

[207] IEA. Nuclear Power and Secure Energy Transitions. IEA; 2022. iea.org/reports/nuclear-power-and-secure-energy-transitions

[208] IEA. Nuclear Power and Secure Energy Transitions. IEA; 2022. iea.org/reports/nuclear-power-and-secure-energy-transitions

[209] IEA. Net Zero by 2050 - A Roadmap for the Global Energy Sector. IEA; 2021. iea.blob.core.windows.net/assets/7ebafc81-74ed-412b-9c60-5cc32c8396e4/NetZeroby2050-ARoadmapfortheGlobalEnergy-Sector-SummaryforPolicyMakers_CORR.pdf

Project Drawdown's Table of Solutions

Project Drawdown is an NGO that provides a comprehensive library of science-based approaches to reducing GHG emissions and became known following the *New York Times* bestseller *Drawdown*. Here are examples reviewed by Project Drawdown that reduce heat-trapping gases. Two plausible scenarios are shown for temperature rise by 2100. Results are based on global projections, and importance varies depending on context.[210]

Solution	Numbers (in gigatonnes) of CO_2 equivalents reduced/ sequestered between 2020-2050	
	Scenario 1 - 2°C	Scenario 2 - 1.5°C
1. Reduced food waste	88.5	102.2
2. Plant-rich diets	78.3	103.1
3. Family planning and education	68.9	68.9
4. Refrigerant management	57.2	57.2
5. Tropical forest restoration	54.5	85.1
6. Onshore wind turbines	46.9	143.6
21. LED lighting	14.5	15.7
34. Indigenous peoples' forest tenure	8.7	12.5
57. Nuclear power	3.2	3.6
79. Improved Fisheries	1.0	1.5

ADDITIONAL DETAILS: TOYOTA

Car manufacturers, such as Toyota, are strategising whether to transition to electric vehicles (EVs) quickly or gradually with hybrid vehicles due to concerns such as limited charging infrastructure and uncertain lithium availability.[211] In the UK, this is already

[210] Table of solutions. Project Drawdown. drawdown.org/solutions/table-of-solutions
[211] Davis R. Toyota Rethinks EV Strategy With New CEO. The Wall Street Journal. Published 29 January 2023. wsj.com/articles/toyota-akio-toyoda-koji-sato-evs-electric-vehicles-new-ceo-11675008222

> the case, where GBP 200 billion worth of green energy projects are on hold because they cannot plug into the electricity system.

Net-Zero And Target Setting: Science-Based Targets

More than 140 countries aim to reach net-zero emissions by 2050. This includes the biggest polluters, China, the US, India, and the European Union, which cover about 88 percent of global emissions. In addition, 9,000 companies, 1,000 cities, and over 600 financial institutions have joined the "Race to Zero"[212] to limit global temperature increase well below 2°C in line with the IPCC's recommendations and the Paris Agreement. These targets require massive and unprecedented action to reduce GHG emissions globally.

Net-zero ambitions have drawn scepticism, including accusations of greenwashing, lack of clear definitions, reliance on offsetting, and technology and economic viability challenges. Fewer than one in 200 organisations' climate plans are credible,[213] and fewer than one in five are currently on track to reach net-zero goals by 2050, with more than a third claiming they cannot invest further in decarbonisation efforts.[214] Listed companies may be on track to increase global temperatures to 2.9°C, partly due to common neglect of Scope 3 emissions, the largest emission source.[215]

Transitioning to net zero is costly. According to a 2022 study, the estimated annual cost increase for governments, businesses, and individuals on capital spending on physical assets for energy and land-use systems in the net-zero transition between 2021 and 2050 is USD 3.5 trillion—equivalent to half of the world's corporate profits in 2020 and 60 percent more than what was

---

[212] For a livable climate: Net-zero commitments must be backed by credible action. UN. Accessed 19 December 2023. un.org/en/climatechange/net-zero-coalition

[213] CDP. Are Companies Developing Credible Climate Transition Plans? CDP; 2023. cdn.cdp. net/cdp-production/cms/reports/documents/000/006/785/original/Climate_transition_plan_report_2022_%2810%29.pdf

[214] Only a Fifth of Companies on Track for Net Zero, with Heavy Industry Key to Breaking Decarbonization Stalemate. Accenture. 16 November 2023. newsroom.accenture.com/news/2023/only-a-fifth-of-companies-on-track-for-net-zero-with-heavy-industry-key-to-breaking-decarbonization-stalemate-accenture-reports-find

[215] MSCI. The MSCI Net-Zero Tracker. MSCI; 2022. msci.com/documents/1296102/26195050/MSCI-Net-ZeroTracker-October.pdf

being invested in 2022.[216] The EU will have to invest about EUR 1.5 trillion a year between 2031 and 2050 to meet its mid-century target of bringing GHG emissions down to zero.[217]

As previously stated, climate change could cost USD 178 trillion in economic losses over the next fifty years. Some analysis has even gone as far as estimating a 50 percent GDP destruction somewhere between 2070 and 2090, presenting a strong argument for net zero becoming a part of fiduciary duty. This showcases that if we do not succeed in mitigating climate change, ensuring economic and social development will be an enormous challenge.[218] Mitigating climate change will help avoid climate risks and create a new low-emission economy with new business opportunities, making it worth the investment.

Some companies are increasing their emissions despite pledging to reach net zero. Amazon, for instance, has increased its emissions by 40 percent since 2019.[219] BP has backtracked on its climate pledges to reduce its emissions by 40 percent before 2030 to 20-30 percent reduction instead.[220] Some companies hide their climate goals, with 25 percent not planning to mention their science-based targets.[221] Despite some companies' lagging climate action plans, investment in low-carbon strategies is increasing.

A successful net-zero transition hinges on four critical and independent objectives: emission reduction, ensuring affordability, maintaining reliability, and bolstering industrial competitiveness.[222] This involves a decisive shift

[216] The net-zero transition: What it would cost, what it could bring. McKinsey. January, 2022. mckinsey.com/capabilities/sustainability/our-insights/the-net-zero-transition-what-it-would-cost-what-it-could-bring

[217] Hancock A. EU must invest about €1.5tn a year to meet net zero targets, says Brussels. Financial Times. 23 January 2024.ft.com/content/ababab4c-7d81-4e63-b48c-0c59b687b5f2

[218] Trust S, Joshi S, Lenton T, Oliver J. The Emperor's New Climate Scenario: Limitations and assumptions of commonly used climate-change scenarios in financial services. Institute and Faculty of Actuaries, University of Exeter. July 2023.actuaries.org.uk/media/qeydewmk/the-emperor-s-new-climate-scenarios.pdf

[219] Temple J. We must fundamentally rethink "net-zero" climate plans. Here are six ways. MIT Technology Review. Published 24 August 2022. technologyreview.com/2022/08/24/1058459/we-must-fundamentally-rethink-net-zero-climate-plans-here-are-six-ways-how

[220] Halper E, Gregg A. BP dials back climate pledge amid soaring oil profits. The Washington Post. Published 7 February 2023. washingtonpost.com/business/2023/02/07/bp-climate-emissions-oil-profits/

[221] South Pole. Net Zero and Beyond. South Pole; 2022. southpole.com/publications/net-zero-and-beyond

[222] An affordable, reliable, competitive path to net zero. McKinsey Sustainability. 30 November 2023. mckinsey.com/capabilities/sustainability/our-insights/an-affordable-reliable-competitive-path-to-net-zero

away from fossil fuels and reducing reliance on offsetting measures as primary solutions.[223] Achieving significant progress towards 2050 targets is challenging when CEOs often focus on short-term returns and politicians prioritise re-election, operating within timeframes that often overlook long-term objectives.

ADDITIONAL DETAILS: DEFINITIONS

Many terms related to emissions reduction are used interchangeably and without universal definitions, leading to confusion. Our list is an attempt to define them.

1. Carbon neutrality: When there is a balance in carbon emissions and absorption, such as if carbon offsets are used to remove the same amount of CO_2 released.[224]

2. Climate positive (or carbon negative): Defined as going further than achieving net-zero CO_2 emissions, such as by capturing more carbon than a product or activity emits to achieve net-negative carbon emissions.

3. Climate neutrality: Reducing GHG emissions as much as possible so they are equal (or less than) the emissions that get removed through the planet's natural absorption while compensating for any remaining emissions. This is how net-zero emissions balance can be achieved.[225]

4. Net-zero emissions: The balance between the amount of GHG emitted and the amount removed from the atmosphere, i.e., through offsetting measures.[226]

[223] Fagwebinar: hva betyr netto nullutslipp i finansnæringen? Finans Norge. 12 June 2023. finansnorge.no/arrangementer/tidligere-arrangementer-2023/fagwebinar-hva-betyr-netto-nullut-slipp-i-finansnaringen

[224] Bernoville T. What is the difference between carbon-neutral, net-zero and climate positive? Plan A. Published 8 June 2022. plana.earth/academy/what-is-difference-between-carbon-neutral-net-zero-cli-mate-positive

[225] A Beginner's Guide to Climate Neutrality. UNFCCC. 26 February 2021. unfccc.int/news/a-beginner-s-guide-to-climate-neutrality

[226] 5 facts about the EU's goal of climate neutrality. European Council. Accessed 15 December 2023. consilium.europa.eu/en/5-facts-eu-climate-neutrality

Organisations set targets to reduce GHG emissions, such as reducing emissions by a certain percentage by a specific year. Science-based targets (SBTs) are based on the latest science and are aligned with the Paris Agreement. SBTs increase the credibility of emission-reduction targets and have verified 1,399 net-zero commitments of 3,821 companies globally.[227]

The Science-based Target initiative (SBTi) can further validate SBTs for companies seeking additional rigour. SBTi provides a road map for companies to set SBTs and reduce their GHG emissions. They have also published industry-specific guidance to support companies in sharpening their climate goals.[228]

SBTi and its rigorous process hold credibility in the market, especially with investors, despite some concerns over governance and methodology.[229] For instance, 52 percent of executives say their science-based target commitment has boosted investor confidence in their business. Furthermore, customers are increasingly looking to become more sustainable, so it is of little surprise that 55 percent of those firms surveyed said that commitment to the SBTi gave them a competitive advantage.[230] SBTi's five key steps are:

1. **Commit:** send a letter expressing the intent to set a science-based target.

2. **Develop:** create an emission reduction target according to SBTi criteria.

3. **Submit:** present the target to SBTi for validation after forming a decarbonisation strategy.

4. **Communicate:** announce the target and inform stakeholders.

5. **Disclose:** report company-wide emissions and track progress yearly.

Climate Risks and Opportunities

Climate risks for businesses encompass a range of challenges stemming from the adverse impacts of climate change. Until October 2023, the Task Force on

---

[227] Ambitious corporate climate action. Science Based Targets. sciencebasedtargets.org
[228] Sector Guidance. Science Based Targets. sciencebasedtargets.org/sectors
[229] Azizuddin K. SBTi to hear complaint from prominent critic after multi-year delay. Responsible Investor. 23 August 2023. responsible-investor.com/sbti-to-hear-complaint-from-prominent-critic-after-multi-year-delay
[230] FAQs. Science Based Targets. sciencebasedtargets.org/faqs

Climate-Related Disclosures (TCFD) was one of the best-known climate-related risk disclosure initiatives and helped identify measurable, material climate-related risks and opportunities. It helped organisations more effectively disclose through their existing processes for investors, lenders, and insurance providers. Providing guidelines focused on financial materiality to incorporate climate-related risks into corporate governance, strategy, business models, and risk management.

Image 3.6. Core elements recommended by TCFD. Source: TCFD

The TCFD has been replaced by the International Financial Reporting Standards (IFRS), which now oversees companies' climate disclosure progress. While companies can still follow TCFD recommendations, reporting on climate risks is mandatory in several countries like New Zealand, Japan, the UK, Singapore, and Canada, with Malaysia, South Korea, China, and Brazil planning to do the same.[231][232][233] Companies must now adopt either IFRS S1 for general sustainability disclosures or IFRS S2 for climate-related disclosures, both of which align with TCFD recommendations and are part of the ISSB's Standards.[234]

TCFD's framework has recommendations on what to disclose regarding cli-

[231] ISSB and TCFD. IFRS. Accessed 6 February 2024. ifrs.org/sustainability/tcfd
[232] Germain OCM et al. US proposals for TCFD-aligned disclosure rules mark a big step towards global adoption. Lexology. Published 8 April 2022. lexology.com/library/detail.aspx?g=8ce2790d-77ca-486c-9e94-cc7460b7580a
[233] What is the TCFD? Everything you need to know. Worldfavor. blog.worldfavor.com/what-is-the-tcfd
[234] ISSB and TCFD. IFRS. Accessed 6 February 2024. ifrs.org/sustainability/tcfd

mate risk. The first disclosure element is reporting on the company's governance structure around climate risks and opportunities. The second disclosure element concerns the strategy around the impacts of risks and opportunities on the company. The third disclosure element involves the company's processes to identify, evaluate, and manage climate risks. The fourth and final disclosure element involves metrics and targets deployed to assess and manage risks and opportunities.[235]

Companies and assets will have different levels of exposure and vulnerability. For instance, sectors with substantial emissions, such as fossil fuel plants, are particularly susceptible to incurring steep carbon prices (i.e., significant transition risk exposure). At the same time, real estate in coastal regions faces considerable risk from rising sea levels (i.e., high physical risk exposure).

Climate-Related Risks, Opportunities, and Financial Impact

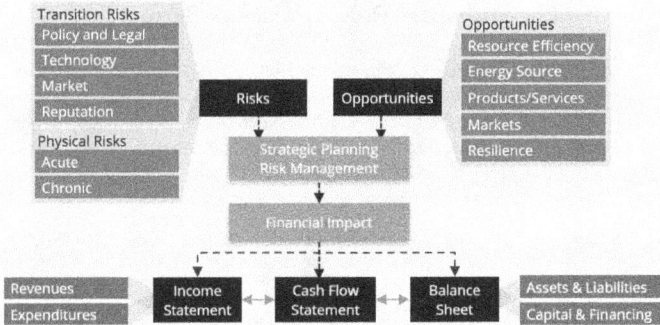

Image 3.7. Financial impact of climate-related risks. Source: TCFD

---

[235] Implementing the Recommendations of the Task Force on Climate-related Financial Disclosures. TCFD. Published 2021. assets.bbhub.io/company/sites/60/2021/07/2021-TCFD-Implementing_Guidance.pdf

ADDITIONAL DETAILS: SHELL AND CLIMATE RISK

Shell has experienced legal challenges and repercussions related to climate issues. One case was based on the claim that Shell had not sufficiently accounted for climate change risks in its bulk storage and fuel terminal infrastructure in Rhode Island and that they were consciously ignoring the risks.[236]

In another case in the Netherlands, a court ordered Shell to reduce its GHG emissions by 45 percent by 2030, following a lawsuit by activists where it was held that Shell's contributions to climate change and misleading statements on the matter violated the duty of care under Dutch law and human rights obligations.[237]

Climate-related Risks by Example Sectors[238]

The formula for understanding the climate risk a single company faces = the chance of a climate-related event occurring (like hurricanes or floods, determined by past events, ongoing patterns, and future forecasts) x how much of the company's operations, employees, and assets are located in areas likely to be affected (such as near the sea or in regions prone to drought) x how susceptible the company is to damage from these events and its ability to adapt and bounce back from their effects.

Sector	Physical Risk	Transition Risk

---

[236] Conservation Law Foundation, Inc. v. Shell Oil Products US. Sabin Center for Climate Change Law. climatecasechart.com/case/5619

[237] Brady J. In A Landmark Case, A Dutch Court Orders Shell To Cut Its Carbon Emissions Faster. NPR. Published 26 May 2021. npr.org/2021/05/26/1000475878/in-landmark-case-dutch-court-orders-shell-to-cut-its-carbon-emissions-faster

[238] Caldecott B et al. Stranded assets: environmental drivers, societal challenges, and supervisory responses. Annual Review of Environment and Resources. 2021;46(1). ora.ox.ac.uk/objects/uuid:c2f290b5-9469-4232-829f-5e4161fc2f32

Energy and utilities	**Acute:** Droughts disrupt hydropower, and nuclear plants need water for cooling. Storms and floods can damage energy infrastructure. **Chronic:** Rising temperatures increase costs due to lower productivity and the need for cooling energy systems.	**Policy:** Forced closure of coal power plants, mandated phasing out coal power plants, and cost of emissions. **Technological:** Renewables are becoming cheaper, making them more cost-effective and competitive.[239]
Materials: steel	**Acute:** The 2019 report by the Carbon Disclosure Project found extreme weather puts 50% of inland steel production at risk.[240] **Chronic:** Challenges due to rising temperatures affecting productivity and incurring costs for cooling equipment.	**Policy:** Steel causes 8% of global CO_2 emissions and faces stricter carbon emission rules (higher emission prices). **Reputation:** The industry is decarbonising due to pressure from the demand for sustainable products. **Market:** Institutional Investor Group on Climate Change, with over USD 30 trillion in assets, pushes for environmental responsibility.[241]
Real estate	**Acute:** Exposed to wildfires, floods, and more frequent storms and hurricanes. **Chronic:** Rising sea levels, especially in coastal areas. In Europe, 19% of retail spaces and 16% of offices are vulnerable.[242]	**Legal:** Required to meet higher energy efficiency standards (e.g., UK's Minimum Energy Efficiency Standard).

[239] Renewable Power Remains Cost-Competitive amid Fossil Fuel Crisis. IRENA. Published 13 June 2022. irena.org/newsroom/pressreleases/2022/Jul/Renewable-Power-Remains-Cost-Competitive-amid-Fossil-Fuel-Crisis

[240] Crocker T et al. Melting point. CDP. Published July 2019. cdn.cdp.net/cdp-production/cms/reports/documents/000/004/659/original/CDP_Steel_2019_Executive_summary.pdf

[241] Hoffmann C, Van Hoey M, Zeumer B. Decarbonization challenge for steel. McKinsey. Published 3 June 2020. mckinsey.com/industries/metals-and-mining/our-insights/decarbonization-challenge-for-steel

[242] Chatain L. Real estate climate risks: How will Europe be impacted? PreventionWeb. Published 6 September 2019. preventionweb.net/news/real-estate-climate-risks-how-will-europe-be-impacted

Climate Adaptation

Throughout history, people have adapted to their environment, but climate change has made it more urgent, with losses and damage happening more frequently and unpredictably. Climate adaptation measures are a response to changes that are likely to occur. These measures include building sea walls to protect against sea level rise, developing drought-resistant crops, and designing buildings to withstand extreme weather. People can also make behavioural changes like using less water, and farmers can change how they use their land to adapt to climate change.

Adaptation has its limits. Securing every organisation and its operations from intolerable risks is impossible, either due to the inability to access the necessary preventative actions or their absence altogether.[243] Low-income countries and their respective populations are generally more vulnerable to climate risks. The most vulnerable countries may not have sufficient resources to tackle what will come. Adaptation measures will have to be taken, such as within the Paris Agreement and the SDGs, to help reduce vulnerability and strengthen resilience.[244]

Unlike mitigation, which focuses on reducing greenhouse gas emissions, adaptation reduces climate risks and unlocks new opportunities, such as developing new technologies and creating new jobs. Companies should use climate models and geographic data to identify how their facilities and supply chains are exposed to risks like rising sea levels, extreme heat, flooding, and wildfires. These models look at different future scenarios. Climate change is already happening, and it's hard to predict how it will change.

---

[243] IPCC. Summary for policymakers. In: Pörtner et al., eds Climate Change 2022: Impacts, Adaptation, and Vulnerability. Contribution of Working Group II to the Sixth Assessment Report… IPCC; 2022. doi:10.1017/9781009325844.001
[244] What is climate change adaptation? LSE. 21 January 2021. lse.ac.uk/granthaminstitute/explainers/what-is-climate-change-adaptation

What to report	**How to report**
GHG emission Scope 1, 2, 3 (Source: GHG protocol)	• GHG emissions in tonnes of CO_2 equivalent separately for each scope and then total emissions.
GHG intensity (European Sustainability Reporting Standard or ESRS E1)	• GHG emissions in tonnes of CO_2 equivalent to net turnover or production output.
Energy consumption, mix, and intensity per net turnover (ESRS E1)	• Energy consumption in MWh to net turnover.
Potential financial impact of material physical and transition risks (ESRS E1)	• Physical and transition risks to assets and liabilities in the short, medium, and long term. • Portion of assets and liabilities covered by a climate adaptation plan. • Portion of net turnover at risk due to climate change in the short, medium, and long term.

Reporting on Climate Change (simplified indicators)

A simplified set of indicators for a more in-depth understanding. I encourage further discovery in the numerous reporting frameworks and standards mentioned in this book.

Biodiversity and Ecosystems

Around 55 percent of the global GDP depends on robust biodiversity and ecosystems. The agriculture, food and beverage, and construction sectors rely most on nature. Research shows that 85 percent of the world's largest companies depend significantly on nature, showcasing the importance of risk management and awareness of biodiversity and ecosystems.[245] Furthermore, many other sectors have hidden dependencies through their supply chains, including chemicals and materials, aviation, tourism, real estate, mining and

[245] S&P Global Sustainable1 Launches New Nature & Biodiversity Risk Dataset. S&P Global. Published 10 May 2023. press.spglobal.com/2023-05-10-S-P-Global-Sustainable1-Launches-New-Nature-Biodiversity-Risk-Dataset

metals, retail, and consumer goods.[246]

Attention to biodiversity is increasing within the global sustainability discussion, and in business terms, biodiversity and ecosystems are nature's assets and capital. Around 46 percent of companies globally report climate change risks, while 40 percent disclose biodiversity risks. Notably, the difference in reporting between climate change and biodiversity is narrowing.[247] Investors are also becoming more aware of the importance of protecting ecosystems. For example, the World Bank's 2022 issuance of a USD 473 million sustainable development bond supports sustainable management of biodiversity and ecosystems.[248]

Transitioning to a clean energy system necessitates a significant increase in mineral resources compared to traditional energy sources, with a subsequent negative impact on our Earth. Solar panels, wind turbines, electric vehicles (EVs), batteries, motors, and energy infrastructure demand more minerals. From 2022 to 2050, the energy transition may need 6.5 billion tonnes of materials, mainly steel, copper, and aluminium (95 percent), with lesser amounts, but yet essential, of critical minerals like lithium, cobalt, and graphite.[249][250]

Despite their crucial role in enabling sustainable energy technologies, the mining industry faces environmental challenges, including the controversial practice of seabed mining, which poses risks to marine biodiversity, leading to the establishment of the International Seabed Authority of which most countries in the world are members.[251] These minerals, predominantly found in areas like the Democratic Republic of the Congo, Australia, and China, are vital for the energy transition. However, their extraction must be balanced

[246] Half of World's GDP Moderately or Highly Dependent on Nature, Says New Report. World Economic Forum. Published 19 January 2020. weforum.org/press/2020/01/half-of-world-s-gdp-moderately-or-highly-dependent-on-nature-says-new-report
[247] Big shifts, small steps - Survey of Sustainability Reporting 2022. KPMG. Published October 2022. assets.kpmg/content/dam/kpmg/xx/pdf/2022/10/ssr-small-steps-big-shifts.pdf
[248] World Bank Raises NOK 5 Billion Sustainable Development Bond While Highlighting Biodiversity. World Bank. Published 15 November 2022. worldbank.org/en/news/press-release/2022/11/15/world-bank-raises-nok-5-billion-sustainable-development-bond-while-highlighting-biodiversity
[249] Material and Resource Requirements for the Energy Transition. Energy Transition s Commission. 20 July 2023. energy-transitions.org/new-report-scale-up-of-critical-materials-and-resources-required-for-energy-transition
[250] The Role of Critical Minerals in Clean Energy Transitions. IEA. March 2022. iea.org/reports/the-role-of-critical-minerals-in-clean-energy-transitions
[251] International Seabed Authority. Accessed January 2024. isa.org.jm

with environmental protection and sustainable practices to ensure a truly sustainable future.[252]

Global Goal for Nature: Nature Positive by 2030

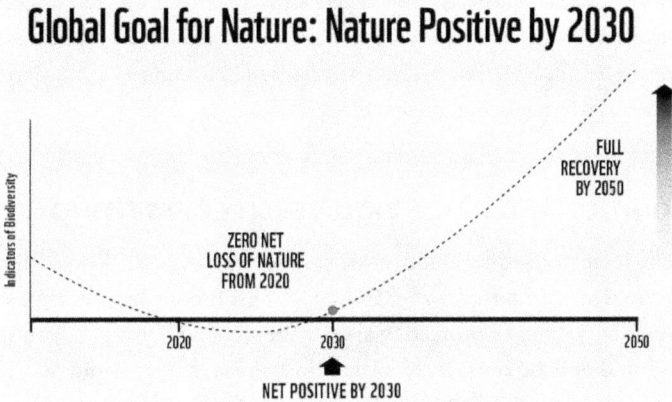

Image 3.8. Nature Positive is a global societal goal defined as 'halt and reverse nature loss by 2030 on a 2020 baseline, and achieve full recovery by 2050.' Source: Locke et al.[253]

The Kunming-Montreal Global Biodiversity Framework (GBF), adopted by 196 governments in December 2022, marks a significant step in addressing biodiversity loss, akin to the Paris Agreement's approach to climate change. The framework sets forth a Global Goal for Nature with progressive targets: to halt further nature loss by 2020, achieve a net positive impact on nature by 2030, and accomplish full biodiversity restoration by 2050. This will be reached, among other actions, by reducing impacts of agriculture and energy production, assessing and disclosing nature-related risks for large companies, and significantly increasing financial resources to bridge the nature-related funding gap.[254] These goals are extremely ambitious, considering how rapidly we deplete natural resources.

Building on the ambitious goals set by the Kunming-Montreal Global Bio-

---

[252] The Role of Critical Minerals in Clean Energy Transitions. IEA. March 2022. iea.org/reports/the-role-of-critical-minerals-in-clean-energy-transitions

[253] Locke et al. A Nature-Positive World: The Global Goal for Nature. Published April 2021. f.hubspotusercontent20.net/hubfs/4783129/Nature%20Positive%20The%20Global%20Goal%20for%20Nature%20paper.pdf

[254] Locke H et al. A nature-positive world: The global goal for nature. The Nature Conservancy. nature.org/content/dam/tnc/nature/en/documents/NaturePositive_GlobalGoalCEO.pdf

diversity Framework, accurate and up-to-date data must underpin company targets. Adopting science-based targets, like those from the Science-Based Targets Network (SBTN), for climate and nature objectives offers a robust framework. SBTN's Science-Based Targets for Nature, released in May 2023, seeks to establish a global benchmark for corporate commitment to nature conservation.[255] Its adoption has been widespread, reflecting its utility despite critiques on governance and methodology.[256] [257]

ADDITIONAL DETAILS: BIODIVERSITY OFFSETTING

Biodiversity offsetting compensates for adverse impacts which can't be avoided, minimised, or rehabilitated. This is done by restoring degraded habitat or protecting areas with projected loss. However, it should only be considered a last resort after trying to avoid or minimise harm.[258] The International Union for Conservation of Nature (IUCN) advises that organisations should use offsets only if they have carefully tried to reduce harm.[259]

Biodiversity Risks and Opportunities

To better understand the impact of nature on financial performance, businesses need improved information on the risks and opportunities associated with biodiversity. The Taskforce on Nature-Related Financial Disclosures (TNFD) was created in 2021 to address this issue. Composed of members from financial institutions, companies, and others, the TNFD published its final framework in September 2023. It provides a set of disclosure recommendations and guidance for organisations to report and act on evolving nature-related

[255] The Science-Based Targets for Nature are Here! EU Commission. 26 May 2023. green-business. ec.europa.eu/news/science-based-targets-nature-are-here-2023-05-26_en

[256] Azizuddin K. SBTi to hear complaint from prominent critic after multi-year delay. Responsible Investor. 23 August 2023. responsible-investor.com/sbti-to-hear-complaint-from-prominent-critic-after-multi-year-delay

[257] Public consultations on technical guidance for companies. Science Based Targets Network. science-basedtargetsnetwork.org/resources/sbtn-public-consultation-2022

[258] EFRAG Project Task Force on European sustainability reporting standards (PTF-ESRS). [Draft] ESRS E4 - Biodiversity and ecosystems. Published April 2022. efrag.org/Assets/Download?assetUrl=%2F-sites%2Fwebpublishing%2FSiteAssets%2FED_ESRS_E4.pdf

[259] Biodiversity offsets. IUCN. Published February 2021. iucn.org/resources/issues-brief/biodiversity-offsets

dependencies, impacts, risks, and opportunities.[260]

The initiative, promoting nature-related disclosures following the TNFD, has garnered positive responses from 320 early adopters across 46 countries. These diverse early adopters include top publicly listed companies with a combined valuation of USD 4 trillion, along with over 100 key financial players such as asset owners, managers, banks, and insurers.[261]

The TNFD recommends the identification of risks and opportunities over the short, medium, and long terms, which should be identified based on materiality.[262] As such, impacts on nature through economic activities may cause short-, medium-, and long-term effects. Thus, financial risks for these economic activities may arise in the medium or long term due to their impacts. This is a direct result of the location-specific aspect of nature-related risks, which are different in comparison to, say, climate change risks that are global.[263]

In September 2023, the Network for Greening the Financial System (NGFS) also released a conceptual framework to guide action by central banks and supervisors on nature-related financial risks. This will be a useful guide in identifying, assessing, and managing risks related to biodiversity.[264]

According to the World Wildlife Fund's Living Planet Report 2022, wildlife populations have decreased by almost 70 percent on average since 1970.[265] Industries such as energy, mining, tourism, infrastructure, and agriculture significantly impact biodiversity, making it a material risk for them.[266] From a double-materiality perspective, nature-related opportunities can positively affect businesses, biodiversity, and ecosystems by avoiding or decreasing harm

---

[260] About us. TNFD. tnfd.global/about
[261] TNFD Early Adopters announced. TNFD. Accessed 6 February 2024. tnfd.global
[262] The TNFD draft disclosure recommendations. TNFD. framework.tnfd.global/disclosure-recommendations
[263] The TNFD Nature-related Risk & Opportunity Management and Disclosure Framework. TNFD. Published March 2022. framework.tnfd.global/wp-content/uploads/2022/06/TNFD-Full-Report-Mar-2022-Beta-v0-1.pdf
[264] Nature-related Financial Risks: a Conceptual Framework to guide Action by Central Banks and Supervisors. NGFS. September 2023. ngfs.net/sites/default/files/medias/documents/ngfs_conceptual-framework-on-nature-related-risks.pdf
[265] The 2022 Living Planet Report. WWF. livingplanet.panda.org/en-US/
[266] Johari S. Biodiversity: The Roots of Our Economy. American Century Investments. Published 20 May 2022. americancentury.com/insights/biodiversity-the-roots-of-our-economy

to nature or contributing to its restoration. Some examples of nature-related opportunities are providing insurance and creating or financing nature-based solutions.[267]

Various strategies can be implemented to mitigate nature loss and restore biodiversity. These include flood and storm protection, thorough screenings, engaging with suppliers about nature-related risks, and regular supplier audits. Minimising the production, sourcing, and consumption of scarce raw materials and resources is important to ensure their sustainable use. Furthermore, promoting certifications for biodiversity-friendly production and the purchase of sustainable raw materials is essential.[268]

Climate change and biodiversity are intrinsically connected, as the former causes the latter's loss. For example, while hydropower plants generate renewable energy, they can significantly alter water flow and aquatic habitats, thereby impacting and disrupting ecosystems.[269] Regulations like the EU taxonomy require that economic activities do no significant harm (DNSH) on one environmental topic while addressing another, which is intended to ensure a balanced and holistic approach.

[267] The TNFD Nature-related Risk & Opportunity Management and Disclosure Framework. TNFD. Published March 2022. framework.tnfd.global/wp-content/uploads/2022/06/TNFD-Full-Report-Mar-2022-Beta-v0-1.pdf
[268] EFRAG Project Task Force on European sustainability reporting standards (PTF-ESRS). [Draft] ESRS E4 - Biodiversity and ecosystems. Published April 2022. efrag.org/Assets/Download?assetUrl=%2F-sites%2Fwebpublishing%2FSiteAssets%2FED_ESRS_E4.pdf
[269] Hydropower. WWF. wwf.eu/what_we_do/water/hydropower/

TNFD's Definitions of Nature-related Risks[270]		
Physical Risk	**Transition Risk**	
Acute risk Storm damage to coastal areas due to loss of natural coastal protection. **Chronic risk** Crop yield decline due to loss of pollination services.	**Policy & Legal** New rules or policies, like land protection. **Technology** Replace products/ services with less impact on natural capital or ecosystem services.	**Market** Changes in consumer and investor preferences affect supply, demand, and financing. **Reputation** Organisation's involvement in nature loss affects societal, customer, and community perceptions.
Systemic Risk		
Ecosystem collapse Tipping points of physical risks are reached, resulting in rapid and irreversible loss of biodiversity and nature services.	**Aggregated risk** Nature loss from transition and physical risks affecting multiple sectors and portfolios.	**Contagion** Financial instability in the system due to ignoring exposure to nature-related risks in one or more financial institutions.
TNFD Opportunities[271]		
Resource efficiency	**Markets**	**Financing**	**Resilience**	**Reputation**

[270] The TNFD Nature-related Risk & Opportunity Management and Disclosure Framework. TNFD. Published March 2022. framework.tnfd.global/wp-content/uploads/2022/06/TNFD-Full-Report-Mar-2022-Beta-v0-1.pdf
[271] The TNFD Nature-related Risk & Opportunity Management and Disclosure Framework. TNFD. Published March 2022. framework.tnfd.global/wp-content/uploads/2022/06/TNFD-Full-Report-Mar-2022-Beta-v0-1.pdf

Using fewer natural re-sources, such as water and energy, by transitioning to more efficient services and processes.	Creating less resource-in-tensive products and services, including green solutions and diversifying business activities.	Access to funds, bonds, or loans for biodiversi-ty-related and green projects.	Diversifying biodiversity resources, like using different plant species, and business activities, such as starting restoration projects.	Good stakeholder relationships due to the pro-active nature of risk manage-ment, leading to preferred partner status and positive reputation.

Reporting on Biodiversity (simplified indicators)	
What to report	**How to report**
Operational sites, significant impacts, and protected and restored habitats (GRI 304)	• List of owned, leased, or managed site locations. • Description of site operations in terms of type and size. • Site location relative to protected areas. • Protected area type, biodiversity value (terrestrial, freshwater, etc.), and legal status. • Significant impacts due to pollution or the introduction of invasive species, pests, pathogens, habitat conversion, and species reduction. • Species impacted, affected areas, impact period, and reversibility. • Condition of each location. • External independent verifications.
IUCN Red List species (GRI 304)	• Number of threatened species, by extinction risk, impacted by company operations.

List of transition, physical, and systemic risks relevant to the organisation (ESRS E4 and TNFD)	• Report on biodiversity risks emerging from a materiality assessment.

Pollution: Air, Water, and Soil

Companies use various chemicals and processes, apart from GHGs, that contribute to various types of pollution. Common pollutants from industrial processes include heavy metals, pesticides, microplastics, nitrogen oxide, particulate matter, volatile and synthetic organic and inorganic compounds, and more.[272]

Indoor and outdoor air pollution cause the premature deaths of approximately 6.7 million people every year.[273] Emitted pollutants linger in the atmosphere and travel long distances. Controlled forest burning in Indonesia results in pollution haze in Singapore, and controlled forest burning in South America and southern Africa results in major air pollution in the Southern Hemisphere.[274]

Around 80 percent of global wastewater returns to the natural environment largely untreated, with devastating impacts on biodiversity and ecosystems.[275] Soil pollution due to corporate activities includes releasing soil pollutants directly at the operating facility or indirectly consuming the corporation's products and services. Sectors contributing to soil pollution include metal, mining, and manufacturing industries such as agrochemicals, textiles, and leather.[276]

Companies that are irresponsible about the pollution they cause are subject to several risks, including physical health impacts on employees and the impairment of resources used for their operations. Legal risks are also

[272] EFRAG Project Task Force on European sustainability reporting standards (PTF-ESRS). [Draft] ESRS E2 - Pollution. Published April 2022. efrag.org/Assets/Download?assetUrl=%2Fsites%2Fwebpublishing%2FSiteAssets%2FED_ESRS_E2.pdf
[273] Ambient (outdoor) air pollution. WHO. 19 December 2022. who.int/news-room/fact-sheets/detail/ambient-(outdoor)-air-quality-and-health
[274] Nuwer R. Are there any pollution-free places left on Earth? BBC. Published 4 November 2014. bbc.com/future/article/20141104-is-anywhere-free-from-pollution
[275] Denchak M. Water Pollution: Everything You Need to Know. NRDC. Published 11 January 2023. nrdc.org/stories/water-pollution-everything-you-need-know
[276] FAO. Global assessment of soil pollution: Report. FAO; 2021. doi:10.4060/cb4894en

significant, as seen in the consumer agency of Peru reportedly suing Repsol in 2022 for a massive oil leak and seeking USD 4.5 billion in environmental and local community compensations.[277] Additionally, initiatives in China, Russia, the US, and the EU's zero-pollution vision for 2050 include placing a cap on air pollution, as well as ensuring that the industry uses correct methods to achieve those targets through the Best Available Techniques (BAT).[278] [279]

Sri Lanka experienced its worst maritime disaster in June 2021, when the X-Press Pearl sank with hazardous cargo, including nitric acid, oil, and the single largest release of microplastics, a record 75 billion pellets, posing a severe threat to marine life and human health and will take up to 1000 years to disintegrate.[280] [281] The incident reportedly devastated local livelihoods and food sources, leading to a USD 40 million claim, of which USD 3.6 million has been received as initial compensation.[282]

Consumers are also increasing their awareness and demanding safer, more sustainable, and less polluting products. For instance, they seek verified products such as the Nordic Swan Ecolabel over those without sustainability certifications.

MATERIALITY IN POLLUTION

The energy, industrial, and materials sectors will likely consider pollution a more important environmental issue than other sectors. These sectors include oil, gas, consumable fuels, chemicals, metals

---

[277] Iimmins B. Peru to sue Repsol for $4.5bn over oil spill. BBC. Published 24 August 2022. bbc.com/news/business-62659241
[278] Pathway to a Healthy Planet for All EU Action Plan: "Towards Zero Pollution for Air, Water and Soil." Published 12 May 2021. eur-lex.europa.eu/legal-content/EN/TXT/?uri=CELEX%3A52021D-C0400&qid
[279] OECD. Best Available Techniques (BAT) for Preventing and Controlling Industrial Pollution. Environment Directorate, OECD. Published 2018. oecd.org/chemicalsafety/risk-management/approaches-to-establishing-best-available-techniques-around-the-world.pdf
[280] Smith S. Oil, acid, plastic: Inside the shipping disaster gripping Sri Lanka. UNEP. July 2021. unep.org/news-and-stories/story/oil-acid-plastic-inside-shipping-disaster-gripping-sri-lanka
[281] X-Press Pearl: The 'toxic ship' that caused an environmental disaster. BBC. 10 June 2021. bbc.com/news/world-asia-57395693
[282] Casey S. London P&I Club makes initial $3.6mn X-Press Pearl payment. Insurance Insider. Published 13 July 2021. insuranceinsider.com/article/28scmtu4zgo90eo74gutc/london-p-i-club-makes-initial-3-6mn-x-press-pearl-payment

and mining, construction materials, textiles, apparel, luxury goods, and containers and packaging.

For all similar materiality boxes, we have used the SASB Materiality Finder (other good tools exist as well), which we can recommend for you to conduct a deeper analysis and gain an understanding of the relevance of various ESG issues to your sector.[283]

Reporting on Pollution (simplified indicators)	
What to report	**How to report**
Air pollutants (e.g., NOx, SOx, PM) (GRI 305)	• Emissions produced in a period relative to production outputs and, when applicable, the land or water impacted (in km²).
Water pollutants (e.g., oil, heavy metals, microplastics) (ESRS E2)	
Soil pollutants (e.g., pharmaceuticals, nitrogen) (ESRS E2)	

Ocean and Freshwater

Climate change heavily affects water resource availability as extreme weather increases the risk of food and water insecurity. Water quality is an environmental, economic, and major societal risk. In a report from 2020, the WEF ranked the water crisis as the fifth highest risk to society.[284] Also, the most recent IPCC report from 2023 found that half of the global population now experiences severe water scarcity for at least part of the year.[285] Water is essential to the operation of many sectors, from agriculture to textiles.

---

[283] Materiality Finder. SASB. sasb.org/standards/materiality-finder/find
[284] World Economic Forum. The Global Risks Report 2020. World Economic Forum; 2020. weforum.org/docs/WEF_Global_Risk_Report_2020.pdf
[285] IPCC. AR6 Synthesis Report: Climate Change 2023: Summary for policymakers. IPCC; 2023. report.ipcc.ch/ar6syr/pdf/IPCC_AR6_SYR_SPM.pd

The ocean provides and regulates rainwater, drinking water, weather, food, and other factors that make Earth habitable. Around 30 percent of CO_2 is absorbed by oceans, reducing global warming. Ocean-related challenges include overfishing and pollution, which are both major threats to marine life.[286] Ocean acidification (resulting from the excessive CO_2 the ocean has been absorbing) affects the functioning of marine ecosystems and biodiversity.[287]

ADDITIONAL DETAILS: WATERLOOP FACTORIES ESTABLISHED AT L'ORÉAL

L'Oréal is the world's leading cosmetic brand. It has publicly announced how important water security is for the company and the world. L'Oréal has six of the company's factories using technology that recovers and recycles wastewater for industrial processes. The technology uses inverse osmosis (filtration with membranes) and evapoconcentration (distillation). For its waterloop factory in Belgium, the wastewater recycling produced 60 million litres yearly, or around the yearly water consumption of 600 families.[288]

MATERIALITY IN OCEAN AND FRESHWATER

The food and drink industry faces risks from water scarcity, particularly in areas with little rainfall. Cotton farming, oil and gas extraction, and mining also use large amounts of water and harm water quality.[289] Fisheries and other seafood companies rely on healthy fish stocks to operate and be profitable, affecting other industries that follow the production process, such as food retailers, distributors, processed foods, and restaurants.

---

[286] Energy and resources from the ocean. World Ocean Review. Published 2021. worldoceanreview.com/en/wor-7/energy-and-resources-from-the-ocean

[287] Goal 14: Conserve and sustainably use the oceans, seas and marine resources. United Nations. un-.org/sustainabledevelopment/oceans

[288] Libramont Factory: A Fourth Waterloop Factory. L'Oréal. loreal.com/en/articles/sharing-beauty-with-all/libramont-factory-a-fourth-waterloop-factory

[289] The new CDP tool "Water Watch" ranks the most water-intensive sectors—Which are they? Water Europe. Published 22 September 2021. watereurope.eu/the-new-cdp-tool-water-watch-ranks-the-most-water-intensive-sectors-which-are-they

Water Risks and Opportunities

Water quality is a major threat to human health, food production, ecosystem functions, and economic growth. The availability of water is becoming more limited due to increased pollution of freshwater resources by the disposal of insufficiently treated wastewater, as well as pharmaceuticals, pesticides, and household chemicals.[290] A report by CDP from 2020 indicates that approximately USD 301 billion of corporate value is at risk if no major improvements in water usage emerge. It will cost around USD 55 billion to mitigate these risks by developing water-saving solutions like recycling water and creating water-efficient products.[291]

Companies should assess their water use and impacts throughout their entire value chain, including direct and indirect impacts from their products and services. Water-related risk includes the likelihood of water scarcity, water stress, flooding, drought, and infrastructure decay. It is rooted in two dimensions: the likelihood of a water-related challenge and the severity of its impact. The source of such risks is either risk due to basin conditions (derived from the basin context in which the business and its suppliers operate) or the risk due to the company (stemming from its operations, products, and services).[292]

According to the WWF, there are several risks and opportunities associated with water governance.[293] Companies face various water-related risks, such as legal and regulatory risks due to changing water regulations and reputational risks from customers and investors who prefer water-friendly companies. These risks affect the company's financial outcome by causing disruptions, reducing production, increasing the cost of goods sold, and delaying the supply chain. Water-related events such as droughts, floods, conflicts, and regulation changes all affect the company's operations. With climate change causing

---

[290] The global water quality challenge & SDGs. UNESCO. Accessed 19 December 2023. en.unesco.org/waterquality-iiwq/wq-challenge

[291] Cost of water risks to business is five times higher than the cost of taking action. CDP. Published 19 March 2021. cdp.net/en/articles/media/cost-of-water-risks-to-business-five-times-higher-than-cost-of-taking-action

[292] Understanding Water Risks In A Changing Climate—Why It Matters. ISS. 20 March 2021. insights.issgovernance.com/posts/understanding-water-risks-in-a-changing-climate-why-it-matters

[293] Freshwater risks & opportunities: An overview and call to action for the financial sector. WWF. Published November 2019. wwfeu.awsassets.panda.org/downloads/wwf_waterrisk_financialvalue_part4_keypiece_web.pdf

extremes in weather, a risk overlaps with climate change and water scarcity.

Companies that have addressed water-related risks are more resilient and likely to perform better than their competitors. Focusing on responsible water use may also attract more capital and gain market share. Investments in water pay back very quickly, not just due to the price of the water but also via energy and chemical savings and by extending the useful life of capital assets.

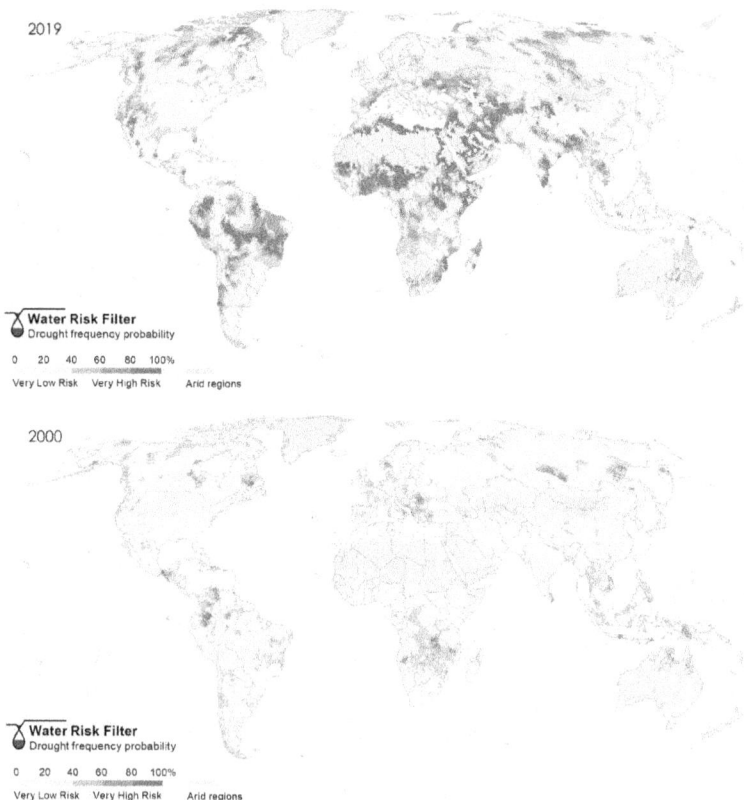

Images 3.9 and 3.10. Drought probability risk has increased from 2000 to 2019, with the red areas representing higher risk. Source: World Wildlife Fund[294]

---

[294] Morgan A. Freshwater risks & opportunities: an overview and call to action for the financial sector. WWF Germany. Published November 2019. wwfeu.awsassets.panda.org/downloads/wwf_waterrisk_financialvalue_part4_keypiece_web.pdf

Marine Resource Risks and Opportunities

Companies obtain valuable ocean resources like seafood, minerals, and raw materials. However, ocean resources are being harmed by oil and gas, overfishing, and being a dumping ground for waste and pollutants. Around 11 million tonnes of plastic waste flow into the ocean annually. If left unchecked, it could triple by 2040. A shift to a circular economy is necessary to reduce the amount of plastics entering the ocean. In 2022, a UN resolution to end plastic pollution was endorsed at the UN Environmental Assembly, and it aims to create a binding agreement to address the life cycle of plastics to improve reuse and recycling.[295]

Large amounts of raw materials remain unexplored in the oceans, but the environmental consequences of exploiting them could be devastating.[296] For example, deep-sea mining for metals needed for the energy transition could endanger marine ecosystems. While deep-sea mining increases the availability of raw materials, it also poses significant risks.[297]

[295] Historic day in the campaign to beat plastic pollution: Nations commit to develop a legally binding agreement. UNEP. Published 2 March 2022. unep.org/news-and-stories/press-release/historic-day-campaign-beat-plastic-pollution-nations-commit-develop

[296] Energy and resources from the ocean. World Ocean Review. Published 2021. worldoceanreview.com/en/wor-7/energy-and-resources-from-the-ocean

[297] Bryan K, Dempsey H. Deep-sea mining is key to making transition to clean energy, says Loke. Financial Times. Published 1 April 2023. ft.com/content/1d58455b-60f6-499d-aabe-2a7a3a108fef

Earth's surface

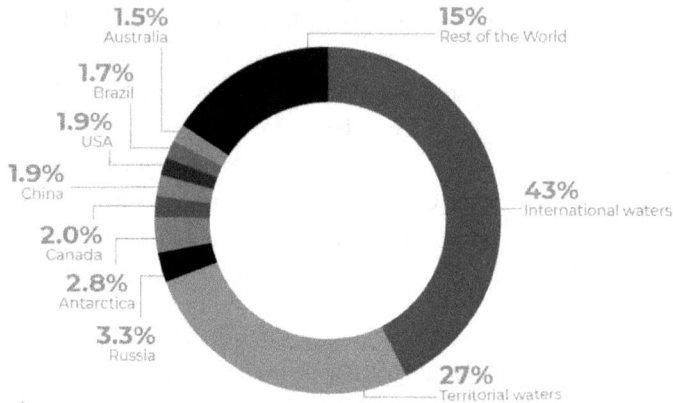

Image 3.11. Earth's surface is mostly ocean water. Source: UN Statistic Division, Protected planet, Image: Author

Overfishing threatens more than one-third of global fish stocks, which in turn affects future supply.[298] Seafood companies can obtain certifications such as from the Marine Stewardship Council (MSC), which has gained popularity due to increased demand for sustainable seafood. MSC certification requires adhering to three principles: maintaining sustainable fish stocks, reducing environmental impact, and managing fisheries effectively.[299] Certification includes minimising bycatch and showing evidence of sustainable fish stocks.[300] Over 18,000 seafood products were certified with the MSC sustainability label in 2019-2020.[301]

Many countries, including Iceland, Norway, the EU, Australia, Indonesia, and others, have introduced quota-based or other regulation types to control overfishing in their national jurisdictions. Even in places where these national efforts do not exist, community-based solutions have been very effective in

---

[298] FAO. The State of World Fisheries and Aquaculture 2022. Towards Blue Transformation. FAO; 2022. doi.org/10.4060/cc0461en
[299] How the MSC Fisheries Standard Works. MSC. msc.org/standards-and-certification/fisheries-standard/how-the-standard-works
[300] Understanding seafood consumers. MSC. msc.org/understanding-seafood-consumers
[301] Sustainable fish to eat. MSC. msc.org/what-you-can-do/eat-sustainable-seafood/fish-to-eat

controlling overexploitation, i.e., shared natural resources can be managed in a non-exploitative manner when those who benefit from the resource and are close to it manage it through a bottom-up approach.[302]

Despite many laws and regulations, the ocean is still being overexploited due to the difficulty of monitoring such a vast area (the tragedy of the commons). There is empirical evidence that shared stocks are especially at risk of over-exploitation.[303] After almost twenty years of debate, the UN agreed in 2023 to protect marine biodiversity in international waters. This treaty will provide a legal framework to protect wildlife and share resources in almost two-thirds of the ocean that lies outside national boundaries.[304]

Climate change will undoubtedly stress fish stocks, pushing fishing companies, scientists, and governments to think beyond addressing overexploitation simply through the MSC certification. This could mean transforming catch quotas to reflect large-scale disruptions to fish stocks due to climate change and transform how nations communicate, negotiate, and utilise global fish stocks,[305] a significant transition from the status quo in fishing.

ADDITIONAL DETAILS: AQUACULTURE

Aquaculture, or fish farming, has been around for hundreds of years but has developed and snowballed. It produces around 50 percent of the fish for human consumption, an important food source for many. Major producers include China, Bangladesh, Chile, Indonesia, and Norway. However, fish farming has been linked to negative environmental impacts such as water resource conflicts, biodiversity disruption due to escaped farmed fish into

[302] Elinor Ostrom. Econlib. econlib.org/library/Enc/bios/Ostrom.html
[303] McWhinnie SF. The tragedy of the commons in international fisheries: An empirical examination. J Environ Econ Manag. 2009;57(3):321-333. doi:10.1016/j.jeem.2008.07.008
[304] McVeigh K. High seas treaty: historic deal to protect international waters finally reached at UN. The Guardian. Published 5 March 2023. theguardian.com/environment/2023/mar/05/high-seas-treaty-agreement-to-protect-international-waters-finally-reached-at-un
[305] Currey R. How can fishing sustain us in a changing climate? Race to Resilience. Published 21 October 2021. climatechampions.unfccc.int/how-can-fishing-sustain-us-in-a-changing-climate

the environment, pollution, pathogens, and parasites. As with other animal feed, fish feed used for aquaculture is also largely soy-based, with soybean agriculture causing conversion of natural ecosystems and deforestation.[306] The need to mitigate these negative effects is growing.[307]

Reporting on Water and Ocean (simplified indicators)	
What to report	How to report
Total water withdrawal, consumption, discharges, recycled or reused (GRI 303 and ESRS E3)	• Volume in m³. • Total water usage and recycling.
Commodity use of marine resources (ESRS E3)	• Quantity and weight of resources, e.g., minerals and seafood by type.
Sites located in areas of high water stress (GRI 303)	• Number of sites with high or extremely high water use. • Water source and usage for each site.

Waste and Resource Use

Inefficient use of resources results in higher costs, reducing a company's profitability. Waste generation negatively affects the environment and human health, leading to regulatory compliance issues, reputational damage, and potential legal liabilities. By adopting life cycle thinking, waste management hierarchy, and circular economy principles, companies will identify opportunities to optimise resource use, reduce waste generation, and create closed-loop systems, benefiting the environment, society, and their bottom line. Subaru is a good example of a company that has achieved its zero waste to landfill goal since 2004, leading to reduced risks and costs, saving USD 1-2 million a year through the initiative.[308]

[306] Sustainable agriculture - Soy. WWF. Accessed 20 December 2023. worldwildlife.org/industries/soy
[307] Fisheries and Aquaculture. FAO. fao.org/fishery/en/aquaculture
[308] The Zero-Waste Factory. Scientific American. Published June 2017. scientificamerican.com/custom-media/scjohnson-transparent-by-design/zerowastefactory

As the global population grows, waste generation becomes a more signifi-cant challenge. To meet the needs of more people, food production needs to increase by 60 percent, yet about one-third of the food produced is wasted. Food waste has a significant environmental impact, and the carbon footprint of uneaten food would be the third largest emitter globally after the US and China.[309] [310]

We know the daily challenge of sorting waste in our kitchen bins. Although we can have some positive impacts, this challenge reaches far outside of our own kitchen and is global and systemic. Governments and municipalities can achieve much more by designing better waste management and distribu-tion systems, bringing transparency to the process and introducing stringent policies. In 2022, 0.79 kg of solid waste was generated daily per person, a total of 2.24 billion tonnes. Waste generated is expected to increase by 73 percent in 2050.[311] Globally, only around 20 percent of solid waste is recycled or com-posted.[312] However, solutions like the circular economy are available, which will require a lot of effort and investment.

Regarding plastic waste specifically, twenty companies are responsible for pro-ducing around 55 percent of the global single-use plastic packaging waste.[313] Poor waste management directly affects our ecosystems by contributing to climate change and air, soil, and water pollution.[314] Better waste management and correct handling of different types of waste—for example, source separa-tion of organic and recyclable from non-recyclable and hazardous waste—will reduce these negative impacts.

Poorly managed single-use waste has resulted in significant ecological harm

---

[309] FAO. Food Wastage Footprint: Impacts on Natural Resources: Summary Report. FAO; 2013. fao.org/3/i3347e/i3347e.pdf

[310] 5 facts about food waste and hunger. World Food Programme. Published 6 February 2020. wfp.org/stories/5-facts-about-food-waste-and-hunger

[311] Solid Waste Management. World Bank. Published 11 February 2022. worldbank.org/en/topic/urban-development/brief/solid-waste-management

[312] Kaza S et al. What a Waste 2.0: A Global Snapshot of Solid Waste Management to 2050. World Bank; 2018. hdl.handle.net/10986/30317

[313] Laville S. Twenty firms produce 55% of the world's plastic waste, report reveals. The Guardian. Published 18 May 2021. theguardian.com/environment/2021/may/18/twenty-firms-produce-55-of-worlds-plastic-waste-report-reveals

[314] Waste: a problem or a resource? European Environment Agency. Published 2 June 2014. eea.europa.eu/publications/signals-2014/articles/waste-a-problem-or-a-resource

as it is the primary source of secondary microplastics in our environment.[315] Microplastics do not break down easily and take up to thousands of years to become harmless molecules. Waste generation is closely linked with our production and consumption. Decreasing raw materials consumption through reducing, reusing, and recycling and the sharing economy are among the solutions to decrease the world's waste. They inspire alternative business models that do not rely on linear consumption.

Circular Economy

The circular economy is a model of production and consumption. It is an alternate way to think about our economy and has an end goal of minimising waste and maximising the recirculation of materials. It is essentially about designing out waste, pollution, emissions, and energy inefficiency while minimising resource loops.[316] Therefore, it is a system that aims to tackle climate change, pollution, waste generation, and nature loss all at once.[317]

The 10R model describes actions to implement the circular economy. The 10Rs are recovering, recycling, repurposing, remanufacturing, refurbishing, repairing, reusing, reducing, rethinking, and refusing products and services. Companies must focus more on durability and long-term use to participate successfully in the circular economy. This circular approach mimics nature, as nothing in nature is wasted but becomes a resource for further natural processes. A circular economy uses everything currently considered waste as resources for other products or uses.

Designing products or services with circular principles in mind, such as durability, reparability, and recyclability, reduces waste and extends its life, thus reducing environmental impact. Manufacturers can integrate these principles during the design phase, laying the foundation for the product's life cycle. All waste has potential value and can be recirculated for value creation if there is imaginative and purposeful design. Additionally, the design phase identifies

---

[315] Microplastics. National Geographic Society. education.nationalgeographic.org/resource/microplastics
[316] Geissdoerfer M et al. The Circular Economy—A new sustainability paradigm? J Clean Prod. 2017;143:757-768. doi:10.1016/j.jclepro.2016.12.048
[317] Circular economy introduction. Ellen MacArthur Foundation. ellenmacarthurfoundation.org/topics/circular-economy-introduction/overview

opportunities for product-service systems, where companies focus on selling services that use their products instead of just selling products.

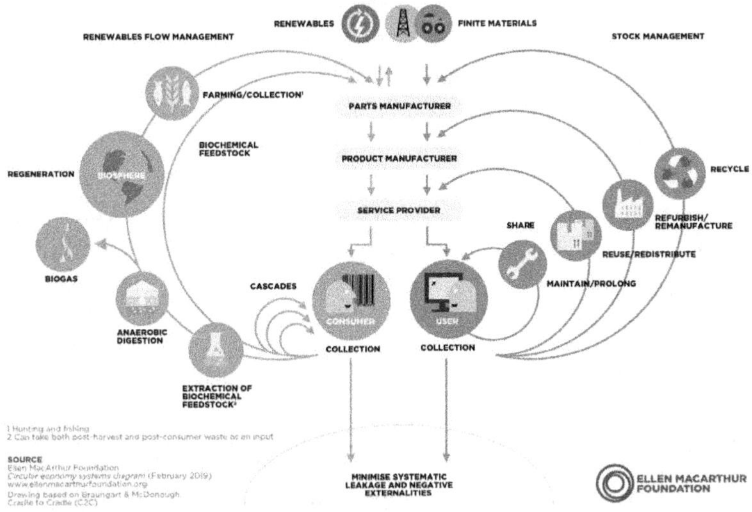

Image 3.12. The butterfly diagram represents the circular economy. Source: Ellen MacArthur Foundation[318]

The circular economy clashes with the predominant ideas of our consumption economy, which relies on manufacturing and consumption rather than making products last. With the circular economy, we need to rethink our entire supply chain. However, risking the planet's natural resources is detrimental to the continuation of an economy and its growth in the first place. Because a circular economy means more efficiency in the production, reuse, and repair of products, it has the potential to reduce GHG emissions by 70 percent and increase job availability by 4 percent, based on a study of seven countries in Europe.[319]

However, transitioning to a circular economy is not without risks. For example, the transition can lead to increased GHG emissions as it may require en-

---

[318] Copyright wording: Copyright © Ellen MacArthur Foundation, (Circular economy system diagram, 2019). ellenmacarthurfoundation.org/circular-economy-diagram
[319] Stahel WR. The circular economy. Nature. 2016;531(7595):435-438. doi:10.1038/531435a

ergy-intensive activities, such as machinery and process lines, and increased transportation and logistics to collect and redistribute materials. These downsides must be carefully managed to ensure that circular practices contribute positively. We must consider the whole life cycle of products and processes to transition successfully to circularity. With our current practices, we may need the natural resources of two planets by 2030.[320]

This underscores the critical need for a shift towards a circular economy. The rate of global circularity has steadily decreased, from 9.1 percent in 2018 to 8.6 percent in 2020 and further to 7.2 percent in 2023. This decline, driven by increased material extraction and use, means that over 90 percent of materials end up wasted, lost, or locked away in durable goods like buildings and machinery, leading to a heavy reliance on new (virgin) materials.[321]

Investors are focusing more on circular economy principles as part of their investment decisions. Consumers increasingly demand that corporations reduce their environmental impacts and become more circular, which presents reputational risks for corporations in linear systems. Furthermore, there are risks for laggard corporations due to new technologies being more circular and efficient.[322]

However, policy changes and regulations promoting a circular economy, including single-use-plastic bans, waste taxes, right-to-repair legislations, and extended producer responsibility acts, also carry transition risks. These measures may increase costs for businesses still operating in a linear production system and raise the likelihood of legal action being taken against them. Already, some companies and the public sector have faced lawsuits related to plastic pollution.[323]

Organisations have several opportunities to contribute to a circular economy.

---

[320] WWF. 2012 Living Planet Report. WWF; 2012. wwf.panda.org/discover/knowledge_hub/all_publications/living_planet_report_timeline/lpr_2012
[321] The Circularity gap report 2023. Circularity Gap Reporting Initiative. circularity-gap.world/2023
[322] Closing the loop: Responsible investment and the circular economy. PRI. Published 4 October 2022. unpri.org/sustainability-issues/environmental-social-and-governance-issues/environmental-issues/circular-economy
[323] Kaminski I. Rush of lawsuits over plastic waste expected after 'historic' deal. The Guardian. Published 9 March 2022. theguardian.com/environment/2022/mar/09/lawsuits-plastic-waste-expected-historic-deal

Companies may tap into new markets through innovation by developing new, circular products that attract sustainability-minded modern consumers. Reducing resource use such as raw materials, energy use, and water and increasing the circularity of those resources within operations may significantly reduce operating costs, which, in turn, brings positive outcomes for investors and other financial market participants.[324]

ADDITIONAL DETAILS: THE SHARING ECONOMY

Sharing resources through online platforms allows individuals to exchange products and services without owning them.[325] However, companies like Airbnb and Uber have commercialised this idea to make profits. While these companies have benefits, such as making services affordable and accessible to a broader audience, they also have downsides. For example, increasing Airbnb apartments can lead to gentrification and may push out lower-income residents.[326] Additionally, Uber may contribute to more emissions if the cars are fossil fuel-driven, as already observed in some US cities.[327]

---

[324] Closing the loop: Responsible investment and the circular economy. PRI. Published 4 October 2022. unpri.org/sustainability-issues/environmental-social-and-governance-issues/environmental-issues/circular-economy

[325] Schor J. Debating the Sharing Economy. J Self-Gov Manag Econ. 2016;4(3):7-22. proquest.com/docview/1906046874/abstract/F542ADF1B9A24979PQ/1

[326] Barron K, Kung E, Proserpio D. Research: When Airbnb Listings in a City Increase, So Do Rent Prices. Harvard Business Review. Published 19 April 2019. hbr.org/2019/04/research-when-airbnb-listings-in-a-city-increase-so-do-rent-prices

[327] Anair D et al. Ride-Hailing's Climate Risks: Steering a Growing Industry toward a Clean Transportation Future. Union of Concerned Scientists; 2020. ucsusa.org/resources/ride-hailing-climate-risks

ADDITIONAL DETAILS: ROLLS-ROYCE'S "POWER BY THE HOUR"

The product-as-a-service model involves manufacturers providing repair and remanufacturing services throughout their product's life cycle. This approach helps reduce waste and the need for raw materials. Rolls-Royce uses this model through its "power by the hour" service for its jet engines. Rolls-Royce provides engine maintenance and charges customers based on the number of hours the engines are in use. This incentivises engine performance.[328]

Reporting on Waste (simplified indicators)	
What to report	**How to report**
Total amount of waste generated (ESRS E5)	• Amount and type of waste and how it's disposed of.
Material and water circularity (WBCSD's Circular Transition Indicators V3.0)	• Amount of recycled materials used in products. • Amount of water used and discharged.
Renewable energy (WBCSD's Circular Transition Indicators V3.0)	• Proportion of renewable energy used.

Endnote

In this chapter, we looked in some detail at climate change, biodiversity and ecosystems, air, water, and soil pollution, the ocean and freshwater, and waste and resource use.

We now know why it is important for companies to focus on environmental risks and opportunities because it allows them to measure their impact,

[328] Power by the hour. Rolls-Royce. rolls-royce.com/media/our-stories/discover/2017/totalcare.aspx

improve their environmental performance, and gain a competitive advantage. We have explored strategies to minimise negative environmental impact and discussed how to adapt to a new reality. Moreover, we have seen a glimpse of assessing and disclosing climate and biodiversity risks, understood that the ocean is critical for our society, and realised that we have an alternative in the circular economy.

Global environmental discussion has been centred around climate change over the last decade. Biodiversity is the "rising star" and will receive considerably more attention over the coming decade, perhaps not at the cost of climate change, but equally.

In the next chapter, we will examine the second of the four pillars of ESG: Social.

CHAPTER FOUR

Social: Individuals and Society

In this chapter, we will examine the Social pillar of ESG, the second of the four, referring to us as individuals who are the building block of society, each of us having unique characteristics, experiences, and abilities. Our examination covers human rights, diversity, equality, and inclusion, in addition to the health and well-being of individuals, essential to a fulfilling life. We will further discuss skills for the future that prepare individuals to thrive in an ever-changing world, as well as data and privacy.

Individuals are the building blocks of society, each with unique characteristics, experiences, and abilities. Companies are becoming increasingly aware of their impact on people, including employees, customers, suppliers, and communities, known as the social aspect of sustainable development. Human rights protect everyone's freedoms and well-being, and violations can have devastating consequences. Physical and mental health and well-being are essential to a fulfilling life. Skills for the future prepare individuals to thrive in an ever-changing world.

Social capital is a network of relationships among people who live and work in a particular society. They share social norms and values that shape acceptable behaviour and enable cooperation, reducing the cost of economic exchange by building trust. As a result, social capital is often regarded as the glue that holds societies together.[329]

---

[329] Social and natural capital is the wealth all around us and we should invest in it. LSE. 27 March 2019. lse.ac.uk/granthaminstitute/news/social-and-natural-capital-is-the-wealth-all-around-us-and-we-should-invest-in-it

Increased inequality has adverse effects on social capital, such as increased civilian tension and violence that negatively impacts community trust towards governing institutions.[330] Socioeconomic inequalities exacerbate climate change, namely through excessive production and consumption and the wealthy elite blocking climate policy and undermining community trust, leading to non-cooperation.[331] It is a relevant concern for businesses due to its ability to disrupt supply chains, company culture, or policies.

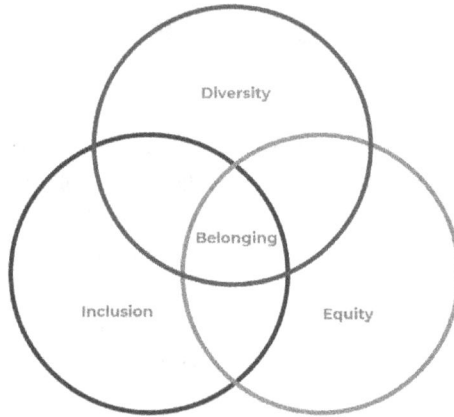

Image 4.1. The DEI and DEIB concepts combined. Source: Author

Diversity, Equality, and Inclusion (DEI) is an emerging term, and we've even seen DEIB, including belonging. DEI has been described as such: diversity is being invited to a party despite your background; equality ensures that everyone at the party has a voice; inclusion is being asked to dance, ensuring that once at the party, everyone feels welcomed and valued. The difference between DEI and DEIB is in the mindset rather than in the letters. Inclusion is action, while belonging is feeling, and that is essential because without belonging, fewer employees will want to work—or stay—at the company or community.[332] Aside from the party metaphor, we want to be understood and appreciated, not just present and participating.

[330] Neumayer E. Sustainability and Inequality in Human Development. SSRN Electron J. Published 5 August 2011. doi:10.2139/ssrn.1905536

[331] Green F, Healy N. How inequality fuels climate change: The climate case for a Green New Deal. One Earth. 2022;5(6):635-649. doi:10.1016/j.oneear.2022.05.005

[332] Adapted from and attributed to Verna Mayers: What is DEIB. workhuman. Accessed 10 February 2024. workhuman.com/blog/deib

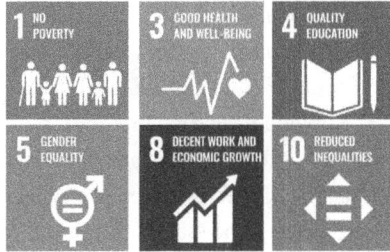

Image 4.2. UN SDGs material to the Social pillar. Source: UN, see footnote 34

Human Rights

Human rights encompass essential rights and freedoms inherent to all individuals, yet regrettably, these rights are occasionally unjustly denied or taken away from people. They include the right to life, freedom of expression and religion, the right to work and education, and protection against child and forced labour. Human rights promote a fair society and protect individuals from oppression and discrimination. Human rights risks relate to harmful labour practices, leading to lost revenue and possible loss of a company's social licence to operate as a result of reputational damage.[333]

Indigenous people are among the world's most vulnerable and marginalised, garnering the support of the international community and deploying measures to ensure their rights and self-determination. Their rights are essential to protect their unique cultural, social, political, and economic characteristics based on the principle of self-determination.[334] Recognising indigenous peoples' rights means addressing historical and ongoing injustices and inequalities. This is especially material for mining, oil, and gas industries because they often operate in more remote areas where indigenous people live. Not protecting those rights can lead to protests, monetary settlements, and other legal repercussions,[335] apart from directly hurting this group.

[333] Addressing human rights in business: Executive perspectives. KPMG. Published 22 December 2020. assets.kpmg/content/dam/kpmg/xx/pdf/2016/11/addressing-human-rights-in-business.pdf
[334] Indigenous Peoples at the United Nations. United Nations. un.org/development/desa/indigenous-peoples/about-us.html
[335] Materiality Finder. SASB. sasb.org/standards/materiality-finder/find

While many may consider slavery a thing of the past, modern slavery still exists. It is defined as forced labour and forced marriage; 22 million people have not given consent to their marriage, of whom 15 million are women and girls. From 2017 to 2021, the number of people in modern slavery has increased: reportedly, every day, 27.6 million people are in forced labour across all regions, and 3.3 million are children. Accounting for population size, forced labour is highest in the Arab States, followed by Europe and Central Asia, and 86 percent of such cases are in the private sector.[336]

Another current topic is women's access to abortion, declared a human rights issue by Amnesty and WHO.[337] The US has heatedly debated the subject, especially after the 2022 overturning of Roe v. Wade, which made abortion a federal right. The Global South faces 97 percent of unsafe abortions, resulting in health and social complications for women and communities.[338] In response to these challenges, companies such as Microsoft and JPMorgan Chase have taken steps to support women's reproductive rights, with initiatives such as covering travel expenses for employees who require an abortion.[339]

Violating human rights is unethical, no matter where it occurs. This includes a company's entire value chain. Violations such as facilitating or using children and forced or compulsory labour can have legal and reputational consequences, ultimately leading to financial repercussions regardless of the outcomes of individual legal cases.[340] In the US, child labour violations have surged by 37 percent since 2015, mainly among immigrant children in risky jobs due to workforce shortages. Some states have eased labour laws for minors, and notable companies have been implicated in these violations.[341][342]

[336] ILO. Global Estimates of Modern Slavery: Forced Labour and Forced Marriage. ILO; 2022. ilo.org/wcmsp5/groups/public/---ed_norm/---ipec/documents/publication/wcms_854733.pdf
[337] Key facts on abortion. Amnesty International. amnesty.org/en/what-we-do/sexual-and-reproductive-rights/abortion-facts
[338] Abortion. WHO. Published 25 November 2021. who.int/news-room/fact-sheets/detail/abortion
[339] Hudson C. Abortion Looms as ESG Issue for Companies After Voiding of Roe. Bloomberg Law. Published 8 July 2022. news.bloomberglaw.com/esg/abortion-looms-as-esg-issue-for-companies-after-voiding-of-roe
[340] World Economic Forum. Measuring Stakeholder Capitalism Towards Common Metrics and Consistent Reporting of Sustainable Value Creation. World Economic Forum; 2020. weforum.org/docs/WEF_IBC_Measuring_Stakeholder_Capitalism_Report_2020.pdf
[341] Cocco F et al. US child labour violations rise as businesses defy laws to fill roles. Financial Times. Published 28 February 2023. ft.com/content/656ba14d-0c41-4d65-88ac-8ba928bdc399
[342] Sainato M. 'It's just crazy': Republicans attack US child labor laws as violations rise. The Guardian. Published 11 February 2023. theguardian.com/us-news/2023/feb/11/us-child-labor-laws-violations

The 2022 Amnesty International World Report mentions an emergence in legislation limiting rights for freedom of expression and association in 64 of the 154 countries covered in the report. Civil conflicts deepened, such as in Afghanistan, where the Taliban takeover has resulted in women and girls losing significant and fundamental human rights and several thousand civil deaths.[343] Companies must factor these realities into their operations and value chain assessments, adapting to legislative changes and considering the risk of civil conflicts.

ADDITIONAL DETAILS: GLOBAL SUPPLY CHAINS AND COBALT

Cobalt is used in rechargeable batteries, but its production involves hazardous working conditions, including child labour. Over half of the world's supply comes from the Democratic Republic of Congo. The journey of cobalt starts in the DRC, continues to China, and ends up in the US, Europe, Japan, and South Korea.

Researchers visited the mines to gain insights since there was no collaboration from desk research. Although Huayou Cobalt, owner of the largest cobalt companies in Congo, claimed to have ethical policies, they were reportedly not in place. Researchers linked companies such as Apple and Microsoft to Huayou Cobalt's supply chain through publicly available information. Microsoft publicly responded: "We have not traced the cobalt used due to the complexity and resources required."[344]

Workers' right to unionise is a human right. It protects workers when dealing with unfair employers. A recent example of unionisation of workers is the job cut of 12,000 in tech company Alphabet (parent company of Google) in 2023 due to Covid-19 repercussions, spurring a walkout in Google Switzerland. Google employees responded by collectively demanding that the company

---

[343] Amnesty International. Amnesty International Report 2021/22: The State of the World's Human Rights. Amnesty International; 2022. amnesty.org/en/documents/pol10/4870/2022/en/

[344] Amnesty International. "This Is What We Die for": Human Rights Abuses in the Democratic Republic of the Congo... Amnesty International; 2016. amnesty.org/en/documents/afr62/3183/2016/en

allow voluntary work reduction, stop new hires, try to protect the jobs of people from countries with active conflict, and more. Around 1,400 Google employees signed a petition that called for improved treatment of workers during layoffs.[345]

Furthermore, in 2023, Tesla faced conflict across Scandinavia for refusing a vital collective bargaining agreement, a fundamental labour principle and a human right in the region safeguarding workers' rights to negotiate various conditions. Due to Tesla's persistent resistance, one of Denmark's major pension funds divested holdings, unable to influence the company through active ownership and deeming owning the shares inconsistent with their responsible investment policy. This standoff also led to operational disruptions across the region.[346]

Building on the foundation of human rights, we now turn to diversity to explore how embracing our varied identities enriches and strengthens our communities and workplaces.

ADDITIONAL DETAILS: TONY'S CHOCOLONELY

Tony's Chocolonely works to combat illegal labour in the cocoa industry and inspire change. They collaborate directly with cocoa farmers, particularly those with the greatest need for improvement, to establish professional cooperatives and reduce child labour. They pay a higher price for cocoa, enabling farmers to live with dignity.[347] Tony's is B Corp (meets certain standards for social and environmental performance) and Fairtrade certified (an organisation changing the way trade works through better prices, decent working conditions, and a fairer deal for farmers and workers in developing countries), with revenue growing 24 percent from EUR

[345] Solon O, Bloomberg. Google workers hit back at CEO over layoffs: 'Nowhere have workers' voices adequately been considered'. Fortune. Published 17 March 2023. fortune.com/2023/03/17/google-employees-petition-sundar-pichai-ceo-job-cuts

[346] Smith E. Musk's Scandinavian woes deepen as Tesla loses Swedish court case, Finnish union joins port blockade. CNBC. 8 December 2023. cnbc.com/2023/12/08/musks-scandinavian-woes-deepen-as-tesla-loses-swedish-court-case.html

[347] Tony's annual FAIR report 2020/2021. Tony's Chocolonely. tonyschocolonely.com/int/en/annual-fair-reports/annual-fair-report-2020-2021

88.4 to 109.6 million in 2020/2021.

UN GUIDING PRINCIPLES ON BUSINESS AND HUMAN RIGHTS[348]

They outline the duty of companies to respect human rights and remedy any adverse human rights impacts they cause or contribute to. This responsibility extends across the company's value chain, and businesses should establish policies and processes to identify, prevent, and mitigate risks of human rights violations. Companies should also ensure access to remedies and conduct due diligence to assess and address human rights risks.

Diversity

Valuing every individual's inherent worth is key to diversity, ensuring respect and fairness across age, race, gender, colour, language, ability, religion, social origin, and political opinions. This approach enriches businesses and societies by embracing varied perspectives and experiences, driving innovation and prosperity. Prioritising ethics and fairness, companies can build a more inclusive world where diversity is represented and celebrated, fostering equal opportunities for all.

A diverse workforce boosts business performance by mirroring society and catering to varied customers. Inclusivity enhances creativity, innovation, and decision-making in 87 percent of instances while also minimising legal risks.[349] It contributes to improved financial outcomes, customer and employee satisfaction, and talent retention. Moreover, diversity can make companies more appealing to investors. To achieve this, firms might need to update hiring practices and tackle biases, ensuring they reflect the broader population.

Women are still underrepresented in leadership roles. Yet women-led com-

---

[348] UN Guiding Principles on Business and Human Rights. OHCR. Published online 2011. ohchr.org/sites/default/files/Documents/Publications/GuidingPrinciplesBusinessHR_EN.pdf

[349] Larson E. Infographic: Diversity + Inclusion = Better Decision Making At Work. Cloverpop. Published 19 September 2017. cloverpop.com/blog/infographic-diversity-inclusion-better-decision-making-at-work

panies outperform those that women do not lead. According to a study from 2017 of over 11,000 publicly traded companies globally in the past several years, women-led companies had a 25 percent annual shareholder return throughout eight years, while the MSCI World Index was 11 percent.[350] Additionally, LGBT-led companies are very few, and research has further found that they are repeatedly undervalued through investor discrimination.[351]

Diversity enhances creativity and profitability by bringing together varied thought processes and experiences and drives innovation and sustainability. A diverse workforce is crucial for bold sustainability actions, such as redesigning products and reimagining supply chains by challenging norms and fostering sustainable practices. Representation from different demographics enables a deeper understanding of the company's impact on society and the environment, leading to more effective policies and strategies. This culmination of diverse perspectives ensures that companies are better equipped to navigate challenges and embrace opportunities for growth.[352]

Having explored the richness of diversity, we transition to equality, where we examine the pursuit of equitable opportunities and treatment for all individuals.

---

[350] Diversity and inclusion: Lessons from top business leaders. Nordea. Published 18 March 2021. nordea.com/en/news/diversity-and-inclusion-lessons-from-top-business-leaders

[351] Shanaev S, Skorochodova A, Vasenin M. LGBT CEOs and Stock Returns: Diagnosing Rainbow Ceilings and Cliffs. SSRN. Published 14 May 2022. doi:10.2139/ssrn.4111210

[352] The Link Between Sustainability & DEI (Diversity, Equality, Inclusion) MENA. Published 19 May 2022. linkedin.com/pulse/link-between-sustainability-dei-diversity-equity

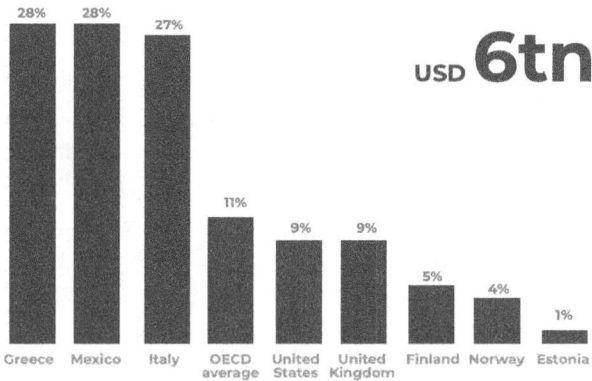

Image 4.3. USD 6 trillion in potential GDP gain in the OECD countries from raising the female employment rate to match Sweden's. Source: PwC, Image: Author

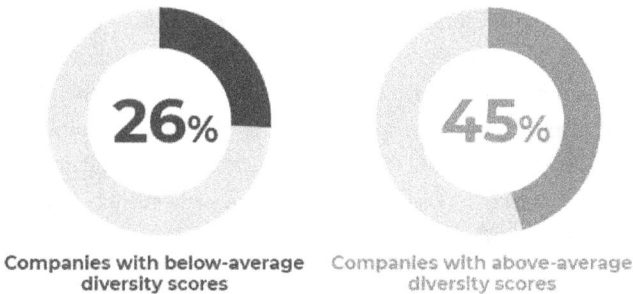

Image 4.4. Companies with more diverse leadership teams tend to report greater revenue from innovation. Source: PwC, Image: Author

Equality

Although equality is ingrained in universal human rights concepts through examples such as equal treatment without discrimination, equal pay for work of equal value, and gender equality, inequalities remain. Inequality represents the unequal distribution or access to various resources, opportunities, and privileges. Income inequality is rising globally, fuelled by economic globalisation, technological advances, and tax policies. Examples include the increasing wealth gap between the rich and poor, unequal access to healthcare and education, and unequal distribution of political power.

The rising CEO pay in S&P 500 companies starkly illustrates the growing gap in income inequality, spotlighting executive compensation as a clear indicator of economic disparities. CEOs of S&P 500 companies are getting paid more and more, with an average pay of USD 18.8 million in 2022, a 21 percent increase from 2021. This average pay represents a 324 to 1 ratio to the median-paid workers. This ratio was 20 to 1 in 1965 and 59 to 1 in 1989. Amazon's CEO-to-worker pay ratio is 6,474 to 1. Shareholders reject CEO pay packages more frequently, with a 13 percent opposition rate. Companies with CEOs paid at the higher end of the spectrum also perform worse financially. The companies with the 100 most "overpaid" CEOs lag behind the S&P 500 index, and the ten most "overpaid" CEOs perform the worst.[353]

Regulations addressing inequalities in the workplace, including equal pay between genders, have long been a topic and have now been formalised into laws. However, the existence of regulations still does not guarantee favourable outcomes. A significant pay gap indicates the presence of structural inequality within the company and can also be a deterring factor for investors. It is often women and ethnic minorities who are disproportionately paid less.[354] Gender pay gaps can harm companies as they lack fairness and equality in the workplace, leading to low morale, high turnover, and negative publicity.

Despite the prevailing belief in robust gender inequality in hiring practices in 2023, a meta-analysis spanning 44 years and encompassing 26 countries and territories suggests a noteworthy decline in discrimination against female applicants for traditionally male-dominated roles. This discrimination is no longer observable in the last decade, signalling a positive shift in hiring dynamics. In contrast, bias against male applicants for female-typed jobs has remained robust and stable. The results of this study demonstrate both welcome declines

---

[353] Weaver RL, Walton M. The 100 most overpaid CEOs 2023. Published 15 February 2023. asyousow. org/reports/the-100-most-overpaid-ceos-2023
[354] World Economic Forum. Measuring Stakeholder Capitalism Towards Common Metrics and Consistent Reporting of Sustainable Value Creation. World Economic Forum; 2020. weforum.org/docs/ WEF_IBC_Measuring_Stakeholder_Capitalism_Report_2020.pdf

in and the stubborn persistence of different forms of gender discrimination.[355]

Providing employees with a living wage and parental leave helps to address socioeconomic and gender inequalities in the wider society. In some countries, parents receive financial support from the government, such as the UK, Norway, France, Japan and Germany. Although the length of parental leave varies between these countries, from 16 weeks in France to 59 weeks in Norway.[356] In those cases, companies front the costs of losing an employee temporarily.[357] Nordic companies have started offering full salaries in already long parental leaves compared to other regions to level the playing field. Providing parental leave also enables a company to recruit and retain talent better, contribute to employees showing appreciation towards their employer, and increase motivation and productivity in their work.[358]

From the principles of equality, we move to inclusion, focusing on creating environments where everyone feels valued and an integral part of the community.

Inclusion (and Belonging)

Inclusion creates an environment of dignity where everyone is valued and respected. This means equal access to opportunities and resources regardless of heritage, identity, or other personal characteristics. Companies must foster inclusion to promote diversity, creativity, and innovation and attract and retain top talent. Belonging is the feeling of being truly understood and appreciated, not just present and participating.

Inclusion in the workplace means a feeling of belonging in a safe environment. At the other end of the spectrum, employees may experience harassment,

---

[355] Schaerer M, Plessis C, et. al. On the trajectory of discrimination: A meta-analysis and forecasting survey capturing 44 years of field experiments on gender and hiring decisions. Vol. 179. 2023. ScienceDirect. sciencedirect.com/science/article/pii/S0749597823000560
[356] Maternity Leave in Europe: Exploring Policies & Benefits by Countries EuroDev. 8 January 2024. eurodev.com/blog/maternity-leave-europe
[357] Marks G. Paid parental leave isn't just the right thing to do—it's smart business. The Guardian. Published 4 September 2022. theguardian.com/business/2022/sep/04/small-businesses-offer-paid-parental-leave-benefit
[358] Colantuoni F et al. Paternity leave benefits extend beyond personal. McKinsey. Published 5 March 2021. mckinsey.com/capabilities/people-and-organizational-performance/our-insights/a-fresh-look-at-paternity-leave-why-the-benefits-extend-beyond-the-personal

discrimination, or bullying. Harassment, discrimination, and bullying happen in the workplace and are often based on sex, religion, race, social origin, disability, sexual orientation, different views, and more. It is considered good business practice to have policies in place to deal with such incidents that could, for example, include zero tolerance, in addition to a culture of accountability and non-retaliation. The absence of such mechanisms may result in lawsuits, financial loss, and damage to a company's reputation.[359]

Regular harassment awareness programs and training for managers should be provided, demonstrating the company's commitment to creating a safe working environment.[360] Prioritising accountability—encompassing investigations and consequences for misconduct without retaliation against the reporting individual—alongside transparent incident management and follow-up processes (while safeguarding privacy) proves more impactful than training perceived as mere legal compliance, which may not always command the seriousness it deserves.

Workplace bullying can take various forms, such as continuous put-downs or career sabotage, and it can originate from colleagues, superiors, or even those in lower positions. Victims often fear retaliation for reporting such incidents. Statistics reveal varying prevalence rates across countries, with 30 percent of employees in the US experiencing workplace bullying, compared to 46 percent in India and 17 percent in Germany.[361] Notably, migrant nurses in the UK have been particularly affected, facing racial microaggressions and bullying from both patients and colleagues. This underscores the vulnerability of foreign workers to workplace harassment.[362]

Workplace culture is a starting point for addressing bullying, fostering a culture where excessive internal competition is avoided, reducing stress, and hav-

[359] World Economic Forum. Measuring Stakeholder Capitalism Towards Common Metrics and Consistent Reporting of Sustainable Value Creation. World Economic Forum; 2020. weforum.org/docs/WEF_IBC_Measuring_Stakeholder_Capitalism_Report_2020.pdf

[360] Becton JB, Gilstrap JB, Forsyth M. Preventing and correcting workplace harassment: Guidelines for employers. Bus Horiz. 2017 60(1):101-111. doi:10.1016/j.bushor.2016.09.005

[361] Praslova L, Carucci R, Stokes C. How Bullying Manifests at Work—and How to Stop It. Harvard Business Review. Published 4 November 2022. hbr.org/2022/11/how-bullying-manifests-at-work-and-how-to-stop-it

[362] Estacio EV, Saidy-Khan S. Experiences of Racial Microaggression Among Migrant Nurses in the United Kingdom. Glob Qual Nurs Res. 2014; 1. doi:10.1177/2333393614532618

ing a no-tolerance policy for racist language. Training employees in effective communication is also beneficial. Not eradicating bullying in the workplace will, over time, push out good employees and create a toxic environment where the bullies are the ones remaining.[363]

The human rights, diversity, equality, and inclusion chapters explore essential principles for fair treatment and valuing differences in society and workplaces. These frameworks naturally lead us to the importance of physical and mental health and well-being, highlighting how inclusive and equitable environments contribute to the overall health of individuals and communities.

MATERIALITY IN HUMAN RIGHTS AND DEI

Male-dominated industries, such as hardware, internet, and media, and professional services (such as consulting) may find diversity and inclusion particularly important. Textile, apparel, luxury goods, metals, and mining industries may be vulnerable to child, forced, or compulsory labour risks or incidents, as they often operate where labour laws are lacking.

---

[363] Praslova L, Carucci R, Stokes C. How Bullying Manifests at Work—and How to Stop It. Harvard Business Review. Published 4 November 2022. hbr.org/2022/11/how-bullying-manifests-at-work-and-how-to-stop-it

Reporting on Human Rights and DEI (simplified indicators)	
What to report	**How to report**
Diversity and inclusion (WEF Common metrics)	• Employee diversity by categories (age, gender, ethnicity, etc.).
Wage levels and pay equality (WEF Common metrics and GRI 405)	• Basic salary and remuneration by employee category. • Employee wages compared to living wages. • Pay gap for full-time employees between genders and diversity variables. • Ratio of CEO compensation to median employee compensation.
Freedom of association and collective bargaining (WEF Common metrics and GRI 407)	• Percentage of employees under collective bargaining agreements. • Description of risks to freedom of association and measures taken to address them in the supply chain.
Parental leave (GRI 401)	• Parental leave rights and return-to-work rates by gender.
Discrimination and harassment incidents (WEF Common metrics and GRI 406)	• Number and status of discrimination and harassment incidents, response, and impact.
Risks or incidents of child, forced, or compulsory labour (WEF Common Metrics and GRI 408)	• Risks of child and forced labour practices in operations and suppliers.

Rights of Indigenous peoples (GRI 411)	• Incidents violating Indigenous people's rights, with status and actions taken by the organisation.
	• Status of incidents and remediation plans for Indigenous rights violations.

Health and Well-Being

Organisations are generally expected to enable employees to lead healthy and safe lives. This includes physical and mental health,[364] with the latter increasingly moving into the spotlight. Lack of well-being at work is allegedly one of the reasons behind a movement called the Great Resignation, referring to the high number of people leaving their jobs spurred by the Covid-19 pandemic, with one in five employees planning on resigning in 2022.[365] Healthcare and technology industries saw the highest resignation rates in 2021.[366]

Companies can attract and retain new talent by providing resources to balance life and work and caring for their well-being and safety.[367] This includes things such as fair wages, generous benefits, and reasonable hours and workload. This reduces costs related to hiring and onboarding that can often be undervalued.[368] We should also consider the impacts on well-being and health—both physical and mental—that occur outside the company's premises, especially with the increase of remote working and its effects on local communities and customers.[369]

---

[364] World Economic Forum. Measuring Stakeholder Capitalism Towards Common Metrics and Consistent Reporting of Sustainable Value Creation. World Economic Forum; 2020. weforum.org/docs/ WEF_IBC_Measuring_Stakeholder_Capitalism_Report_2020.pdf

[365] Ellerbeck S. The Great Resignation is not over: Here's what employees say matters most at the workplace. World Economic Forum. Published 24 June 2022. weforum.org/agenda/2022/06/the-great-resignation-is-not-over/

[366] Chugh A. What is the 'Great Resignation?' An expert explains. World Economic Forum. Published 29 November 2021. weforum.org/agenda/2021/11/what-is-the-great-resignation-and-what-can-we-learn-from-it/

[367] The Deloitte Global 2022 Gen Z and Millennial Survey. Deloitte. Published 2022. deloitte.com/global/en/pages/about-deloitte/articles/genzmillennialsurvey.html

[368] Hall J. The Cost Of Turnover Can Kill Your Business And Make Things Less Fun. Forbes. Published 9 May 2019. forbes.com/sites/johnhall/2019/05/09/the-cost-of-turnover-can-kill-your-business-and-make-things-less-fun

[369] EFRAG Project Task Force on European sustainability reporting standards (PTF-ESRS). [Draft] ESRS S1 - Own workforce. Published April 2022. efrag.org/Assets/Download?assetUrl=%2Fsites%2F-webpublishing%2FSiteAssets%2FED_ESRS_S1.pdf

Not tending to employees' health and safety can negatively impact a company's productivity. For example, if employees are often on sick leave or injured. The International Labour Organisation (ILO) has specifically identified occupational diseases, such as ones caused by mercury, lead, phosphorus, asbestos, vibrations, and noise. Additionally, the International Labour Organisation (ILO) lists post-traumatic stress disorder as an occupational disease.[370] Compromising the health and safety of any stakeholder within and outside business operations can also open companies to lawsuits, high legal costs, and negative impacts on their reputation.

Physical Health and Well-Being

Work-related incidents cause about 3 percent of global deaths. Poor health and injuries from work lead to a loss of about 4 percent of the global GDP. This results in costs associated with sick pay, disability benefits, and allowances of 2-3 percent of GDP in many advanced economies—more than is spent on unemployment benefits.[371] Legal costs and direct compensation from work injuries can further impact companies that don't prioritise employee health and safety.[372]

Ensuring customers' safety is paramount. This involves examining the entire product or service life cycle to ensure compliance with safety regulations and avoid using hazardous materials that could harm customers. SHEIN, an online fashion company, was reportedly found to have high levels of toxic chemicals, including lead and phthalates, in its clothing, according to a Canadian investigation in 2021. This is a problem for customers and employees, particularly garment workers who may be exposed to these chemicals.[373]

Communities should be involved and informed about operations that

---

[370] Diagnostic and exposure criteria for occupational diseases—Guidance notes for diagnosis and prevention of the diseases... ILO. Published 2022. ilo.org/wcmsp5/groups/public/---ed_dialogue/---lab_admin/documents/publication/wcms_836362.pdf

[371] Pouliakas K, Theodossiou I. The Economics of Health and Safety at Work: An Interdisciplinary Review of the Theory and Policy. J Econ Surv. 2013; 27(1):167-208. doi:10.1111/j.1467-6419.2011.00699.x

[372] World Economic Forum. Measuring Stakeholder Capitalism Towards Common Metrics and Consistent Reporting of Sustainable Value Creation. World Economic Forum; 2020. weforum.org/docs/WEF_IBC_Measuring_Stakeholder_Capitalism_Report_2020.pdf

[373] Akhtar A. 5 toxic chemicals used in fast fashion clothing and how they can affect your immune system. Insider. Published 27 August 2022. insider.com/toxic-chemicals-in-shein-and-other-fast-fashion-clothing-2022-8

could impact them. Depending on the industry and operations, these could negatively impact the health and well-being of nearby communities. This is especially relevant for polluting industries or operations that cause environmental or social disruption and affect community culture. Economic impacts on communities also need to be considered.[374]

DuPont's industrial activities in West Virginia, specifically its discharge of perfluorooctanoic acid (PFOA) into local waterways, starkly illustrate the negative impact of industrial activities on neighbouring communities. This reportedly led to livestock deaths and serious health issues among residents, culminating in a series of lawsuits and substantial financial settlements with individuals who contracted cancer due to PFOA contamination.[375]

MATERIALITY IN PHYSICAL HEALTH AND WELL-BEING

The health and safety indicator is essential for hazardous industries like agriculture, waste management, metals, and mining because they work with chemicals, heavy machinery, and dangerous environments. These industries are prone to extreme weather, and hazardous chemicals threaten workers' physical health.

Mental Health and Well-Being

It is estimated that depression and anxiety result in losses of 12 billion workdays a year, which corresponds to global economic costs of a staggering USD 1 trillion. Thus, the WHO and the ILO (International Labour Organisation) called for action to address mental health issues among the global workforce, especially after the rise in anxiety and depression globally after Covid-19.[376]

---

[374] Global Sustainability Standards Board (GSSB). Consolidated Set of the GRI Standards. Published 2022. globalreporting.org/how-to-use-the-gri-standards/gri-standards-english-language

[375] Rich N. The Lawyer Who Became DuPont's Worst Nightmare. The New York Times. Published 6 January 2016. nytimes.com/2016/01/10/magazine/the-lawyer-who-became-duponts-worst-nightmare.html

[376] WHO and ILO call for new measures to tackle mental health issues at work. ILO. Published 28 September 2022. ilo.org/global/about-the-ilo/newsroom/news/WCMS_856821/lang--en/index.html

Further, one in four people in Australia experience burnout symptoms,[377] costing the country an estimated AUD 200 billion a year.[378]

Executives are also part of the Great Resignation trend due to declining mental health. A survey conducted in 2022 across the US, UK, Canada, and Australia found that 70 percent of executives were considering leaving their jobs for better well-being. Promoting workplace well-being is crucial for retaining both employees and executives.[379]

Managing mental health in the workplace is crucial, especially as around 45 percent of Millennials and Gen Z report feeling burned out due to work and societal pressures and are seeking out more meaningful work.[380] Managing mental health in the workplace through employee well-being indicators may be less straightforward than physical health. ISO 45003, the global occupational health and safety standard, is valuable as it offers practical guidance on identifying, preventing, and managing psychosocial risks, promoting a healthier and more supportive work environment.

---

[377] Carmichael A, Coe EH, Dewurst M. Employee mental health and burnout in Asia: A time to act. McKinsey. Published 18 August 2022. mckinsey.com/featured-insights/future-of-asia/employee-mental-health-and-burnout-in-asia-a-time-to-act

[378] Whiteford H. The Productivity Commission inquiry into mental health. Aust N Z J Psychiatry. 2022; 56(4):328-331. doi:10.1177/00048674211031159

[379] Hatfield S, Fisher J, Silverglate PH. The C-suite's role in well-being. Deloitte. Published 22 June 2022. deloitte.com/us/en/insights/topics/leadership/employee-wellness-in-the-corporate-workplace.html

[380] The Deloitte Global 2022 Gen Z and Millennial Survey. Deloitte. Published 2022. deloitte.com/global/en/pages/about-deloitte/articles/genzmillennialsurvey.html

Top reasons for choosing to work for an organisation

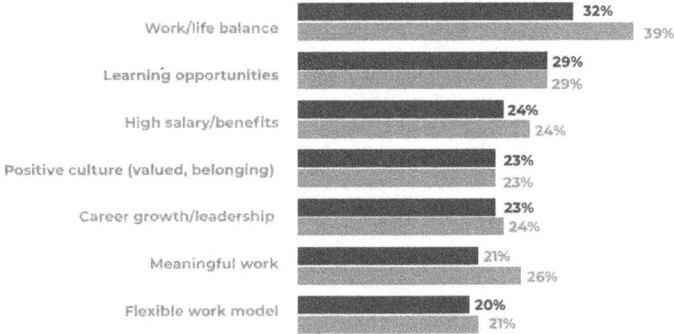

Work/life balance	32%	
	39%	
Learning opportunities	29%	
	29%	
High salary/benefits	24%	
	24%	
Positive culture (valued, belonging)	23%	
	23%	
Career growth/leadership	23%	
	24%	
Meaningful work	21%	
	26%	
Flexible work model	20%	
	21%	

Image 4.5. Gen Zs' and Millennials' concerns for the future. Top reasons respondents chose to work for their current organisation. Source: Deloitte, Image: Author

Furthermore, strategies from the WHO and the ILO include making mental health an element of occupational health and safety management, conducting a psychosocial risk assessment and implementing prevention measures. Interventions can include adjusting workloads, increasing work variety, improving the work environment, and clarifying responsibilities.[381]

It may also be necessary to eradicate certain aspects of the workplace culture to foster health and safety in general. For example, the lack of sleep and working more, accompanied by chronic workplace stress, ultimately leads to burnout. When a person is in a state of physical and mental exhaustion, it results in negative mental impact and decreased productivity.[382]

Allegedly, women experience burnout more than men, especially since the Covid-19 pandemic.[383] This may be because recent generations of women have been raised with traditional gender roles, taking on more household respon-

[381] WHO, ILO. Mental health at work: Policy brief. ILO. Published 2022. ilo.org/wcmsp5/groups/public/---ed_protect/---protrav/---safework/documents/publication/wcms_856976.pdf

[382] Burn-out an "occupational phenomenon": International Classification of Diseases. WHO. Published 28 May 2019. who.int/news/item/28-05-2019-burn-out-an-occupational-phenomenon-international-classification-of-diseases

[383] Women in the workplace 2023. McKinsey. Published 5 October 2023. mckinsey.com/featured-insights/diversity-and-inclusion/women-in-the-workplace

sibilities while being empowered to have careers. One in three women, and 60 percent of mothers with young children, spend five or more hours daily on housework and caregiving. This is equivalent to having at least another half-time job.[384] Companies have yet to recognise this imbalance, but addressing it will help retain talent and improve productivity.

Reporting on Health and Safety (simplified indicators)	
What to report	**How to report**
Health and safety and its monetary impact (WEF Common metrics)	• Number of work injuries, fatalities, and access to medical services. • Total costs of work-related incidents, including fines and damages.
Employee well-being (WEF Common metrics)	• Number of work-related fatalities and illnesses and types of illnesses recorded. • Percentage of employees participating in wellness programs and best practices for health.
Customer health and safety (GRI 416)	• Oversight of customer health and safety across product/service life cycle stages. • Number of non-compliance instances with regulations or voluntary codes.
Local communities (GRI 413 and ESRS S3)	• Stakeholder definition, communication, and impact management. • Community complaint and concern pathways for company operations.

Skills for the Future

Skilled employees are vital for a company's growth and success. Future-ready skills make employees more adaptable, innovative, and productive, which

---

[384] The state of burnout for women in the workplace. McKinsey. Published 4 January 2022. mckinsey.com/featured-insights/diversity-and-inclusion/the-state-of-burnout-for-women-in-the-workplace

helps companies succeed. Organisations must invest in developing their employees' skills to continue improving their performance and success. The global economy is rapidly changing; in Europe, a skill shortage is already adversely impacting the growth of companies.[385][386]

THE GREAT RESHUFFLE

The Great Reshuffle refers to employees' changing skills and work expectations. Executives are adapting by offering more flexible policies. 25 percent of LinkedIn members have seen their skills change for the same job since 2015, with a projected 40 percent change by 2025. This makes learning and development critical for companies, focusing on talent development, skill-based planning, and internal mobility.[387]

Investing in employees and creating a culture of continuous learning increases productivity, job satisfaction, and a better company reputation. This attracts and retains top talent and creates a competitive workforce. High turnover rates are time-consuming and costly, with companies potentially losing up to 33 percent of a worker's yearly salary per new hire.[388] Moreover, the law increasingly requires companies to educate employees on safety and labour rights. Thus, investing in employee development and education is a smart business strategy for long-term success.[389]

Companies should invest in their employees through training and education to stay up to date by identifying necessary skills for each business model,

[385] Tupper H, Ellis S. It's Time to Reimagine Employee Retention. Harv Bus Rev. Published 4 June 2022. hbr.org/2022/07/its-time-to-reimagine-employee-retention

[386] Santarsiere R. Digital skills shortage in Europe poses risks for the continent's future growth. EY. Published 18 December 2018. ey.com/en_gl/news/2018/12/digital-skills-shortage-in-europe-poses-risks-for-the-continents-future-growth

[387] 2022 Workplace Learning Report. LinkedIn. Published 2022. learning.linkedin.com/content/dam/me/learning/resources/pdfs/linkedIn-learning-workplace-learning-report-2022.pdf

[388] Hall J. The Cost Of Turnover Can Kill Your Business And Make Things Less Fun. Forbes. Published 9 May 2019. forbes.com/sites/johnhall/2019/05/09/the-cost-of-turnover-can-kill-your-business-and-make-things-less-fun

[389] World Economic Forum. Measuring Stakeholder Capitalism Towards Common Metrics and Consistent Reporting of Sustainable Value Creation. World Economic Forum; 2020. weforum.org/docs/WEF_IBC_Measuring_Stakeholder_Capitalism_Report_2020.pdf

providing learning programs addressing skill gaps, and allowing employees the time and space to attend to them.[390] However, offering education and skills training programs may not be enough as employee participation rates can be low, sometimes less than 5 percent.[391] The effectiveness of learning programs should be evaluated regularly to be successful.

Training and education have delayed and non-monetary impacts, making it challenging to measure their success accurately.[392] However, these impacts are significant in the long term and result in increased productivity and improved communication. Additionally, training and education indirectly improve workplace culture and employee well-being and decrease turnover. Internships help develop skills for the future. When paid, they are beneficial as they offer practical work experience, skills development, and the opportunity to network. Companies identify future employees and benefit from fresh perspectives and new ideas. Unpaid internships, however, contribute to the exploitation of people, as the interns often work long hours for little or no compensation and do not receive the benefits of a formal job. This perpetuates income inequality and leads to the undervaluation of entry-level positions, which labour laws are beginning to forbid more frequently.

Over 1 billion jobs worldwide are estimated to radically change due to technological advances and digitisation in the next decade.[393] At the same time, reskilling programs enable companies to adjust to and better deal with the impact of chance.[394] Therefore, human resource and learning and development leaders must be on top of the programmes provided to their employees, ensuring they reflect market needs. A workforce with future-ready skills

[390] Agrawal S et al. To emerge stronger from the Covid-19 crisis, companies should start reskilling their workforces now. McKinsey. Published 7 May 2020. mckinsey.com/capabilities/people-and-organizational-performance/our-insights/to-emerge-stronger-from-the-Covid-19-crisis-companies-should-start-reskilling-their-workforces-now

[391] McDonough T, Oldham C. Why Companies Should Pay for Employees to Further Their Education. Harv Bus Rev. Published 19 October 2020. hbr.org/sponsored/2020/10/why-companies-should-pay-for-employees-to-further-their-education

[392] Martins PS. Employee training and firm performance: Evidence from ESF grant applications. Labour Econ. 2021; 72:102056. doi:10.1016/j.labeco.2021.102056

[393] Reskilling revolution. WEF. Published 27 June 2023. weforum.org/impact/reskilling-revolution

[394] Agrawal S et al. To emerge stronger from the Covid-19 crisis, companies should start reskilling their workforces now. McKinsey. Published 7 May 2020. mckinsey.com/capabilities/people-and-organizational-performance/our-insights/to-emerge-stronger-from-the-Covid-19-crisis-companies-should-start-reskilling-their-workforces-now

benefits society overall because such individuals will drive economic growth, innovation, and social progress.

ADDITIONAL DETAILS: THE JOB IMPACT OF ARTIFICIAL INTELLIGENCE (AI)

AI technology could automate up to 25 percent of work in the US, especially data entry, bookkeeping, and basic customer service roles, potentially affecting 300 million workers worldwide. Generative AI systems could boost productivity, and it's estimated that it can lead to a 7 percent increase in global GDP over ten years.[395] In the US alone, 80 percent of its workforce could see at least 10 percent of their tasks performed by generative AI, which could potentially free them up for other tasks.[396]

"The rise of artificial intelligence (AI) promises to revolutionise society and the environment, offering unparalleled opportunities for growth and innovation. Yet, it also poses significant risks, including ethical dilemmas, intellectual property disputes, and accuracy concerns. As AI becomes more integrated into our daily lives, it challenges us to navigate its impact responsibly, ensuring that technological advancements foster sustainability and equitable development. Addressing these issues demands a balanced approach, where the benefits of AI are harnessed to enhance human capabilities and improve environmental stewardship, while actively mitigating its potential downsides."[397]

---

[395] Generative AI could raise global GDP by 7%. Goldman Sachs. Published 5 April 2023. goldmansachs.com/intelligence/pages/generative-ai-could-raise-global-gdp-by-7-percent.html

[396] Generative AI set to affect 300mn jobs across major economies. Financial Times. Published 27 March 2023. ft.com/content/7dec4483-ad34-4007-bb3a-7ac925643999

[397] This was written by ChatGPT 4.0, and is unaltered, with the prompt from the author: "Write one paragraph about the rise of artificial intelligence, how it will impact society and the environment, what risks and opportunities are involved, how it will support growth or not, ethical issues, intellectual property issues, accuracy issues, and more that you feel relevant to address. Write no more than 100 words in an active voice, using UK English."

MATERIALITY IN SKILLS

In industries like healthcare and professional services, having the right skills is essential due to staff shortages and the need for quality service. With more tasks being digitised, training is a requirement for various industries, especially software and IT, due to cybersecurity and artificial intelligence.

Reporting on Skills (simplified indicators)	
What to report	**How to report**
Training and education (WEF Common metrics and GRI 404)	• Company training programs offered. • Average hours of training and total cost per employee. • Assessment of training effectiveness based on revenue, productivity, or engagement changes.
The number of unfilled skilled positions (WEF Common metrics)	• Number of open skilled positions and percentage to be filled by unskilled hires needing training.

Data and Privacy

Data security intersects two pillars in ESG. On the one hand, the social focus is on customer privacy breaches and preventing data breaches, highlighting the importance of maintaining trust and confidentiality in customer relationships. On the other hand, the governance focus includes cybersecurity and data management.

Data refers to the personal information companies collect, such as phone numbers and addresses, and confidential records, such as medical information. Companies use data to make money, but as more data breaches happen globally, sensitive information is made public or sold to bad actors, putting companies and individuals at risk. In 2023, 120 zettabytes (1 zettabyte = 1

trillion gigabytes) of data was generated; that number is expected to increase to 180 zettabytes in 2025.[398]

Average weekly attacks per organisation by industry (2021)

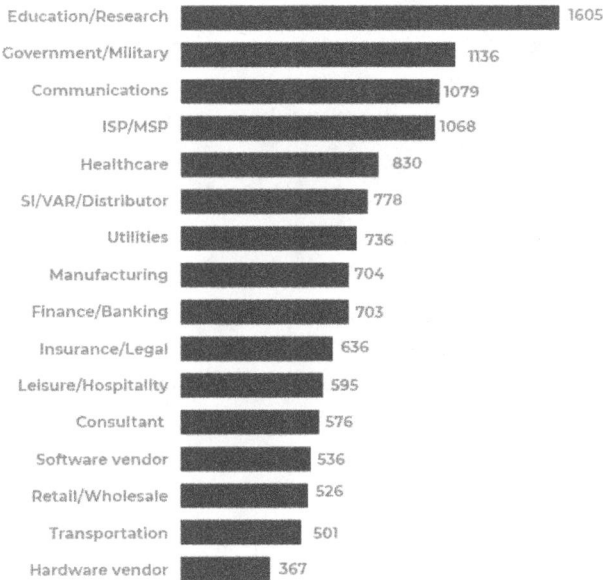

Education/Research	1605
Government/Military	1136
Communications	1079
ISP/MSP	1068
Healthcare	830
SI/VAR/Distributor	778
Utilities	736
Manufacturing	704
Finance/Banking	703
Insurance/Legal	636
Leisure/Hospitality	595
Consultant	576
Software vendor	536
Retail/Wholesale	526
Transportation	501
Hardware vendor	367

Image 4.6. Average weekly attacks per organisation per industry increasing per year. Source: Check Point, Image: Author

Investment in data security to counter data breaches has increased, yet security breaches are still commonplace. This results in large amounts of data compromised on a global scale. In the digital economy, data breaches have become one of the most prominent cybersecurity risks.[399] Regulations have been set globally, e.g., the General Data Protection Regulation (GDPR)[400]

---

[398] Taylor P. Volume of data/information created, captured, copied, and consumed worldwide... Statista. Published 8 September 2022. statista.com/statistics/871513/worldwide-data-created
[399] Ibrahim A et al. The Challenges of Leveraging Threat Intelligence to Stop Data Breaches. Front Comput Sci. 2020; 2. frontiersin.org/articles/10.3389/fcomp.2020.00036
[400] What is GDPR, the EU's new data protection law? GDPR. Published 7 November 2018. gdpr.eu/what-is-gdpr

implemented in the EU. Similar frameworks have been implemented in other countries, such as the California Customer Privacy Act (CCPA)[401] and Brazil's Lei Geral de Proteção de Dados (LGPD), as well as China's Personal Information Protection Law (PIPL).

GDPR PRINCIPLES

These include the right to be informed, the right of access, the right to rectification, erasure, restrict processing, data portability, object, and rights about automated decision making and profiling.[402]

Companies with poor data privacy policies or lacking transparency in data handling risk compromising their customer base. Customers are becoming increasingly aware of the data they share and, therefore, more careful where and with whom they communicate.[403] It is challenging to deal with data and fulfil the emerging regulations for data privacy. Addressing these challenges, such as meeting customer requests to delete data, is also technically difficult. When data comes from different geographical locations, the regulatory environment becomes more complicated.[404]

Companies that fail to comply with the GDPR may receive high fines: up to EUR 20 million or 4 percent of a company's global annual revenue from the previous year, whichever is higher.[405] Companies such as Google and Facebook have been fined for not complying with the GDPR, with over EUR 114 million in fines issued in the first twenty months of the GDPR's implementa-

---

[401] 2020 developments for data protection and the GDPR. GDPR. Published 20 February 2020. gdpr.eu/gdpr-in-2020

[402] What is GDPR, the EU's new data protection law? GDPR. Published 7 November 2018. gdpr.eu/what-is-gdpr

[403] Ringel G. Why Data Privacy Is Good For Business: Online Privacy As A Branding Imperative. Forbes. Published 7 October 2021. forbes.com/sites/forbestechcouncil/2021/10/07/why-data-privacy-is-good-for-business-online-privacy-as-a-branding-imperative

[404] Anant V et al. The consumer-data opportunity and the privacy imperative. McKinsey. Published 27 April 2020. mckinsey.com/capabilities/risk-and-resilience/our-insights/the-consumer-data-opportunity-and-the-privacy-imperative

[405] What are the GDPR Fines? GDPR. Published 11 July 2018. gdpr.eu/fines

tion.[406] Chinese companies can receive administrative fines of up to 5 percent of the previous year's annual revenue or RMB 50 million for the organisation and RMB 100,000 for the responsible person if the offence is severe.[407] Therefore, a significant financial risk exists for companies that need to handle data appropriately.

During the Covid-19 pandemic, employers monitored remote workers more to track their productivity, which raised concerns about employee privacy. A 2019 global report showed that 62 percent of participating CEOs stated that their company was using new technology to gather employee data, but less than 30 percent were confident about responsible usage.[408] The increased surveillance has led to high-stress levels for employees, negatively impacting their well-being and satisfaction with their employers. Productivity suffers when employer-employee trust is broken.[409]

Innovations are happening rapidly within cybersecurity to avoid data breaches. This includes the emergence of threat intelligence for an organisation's digital infrastructure to defend against data attacks before they occur proactively. Overall, data management has grown more complex as cyber threats become increasingly elaborate, and there is no uniform solution for organisations.[410] Failure to be transparent with customers and to strictly observe regulations present financial, reputational, and legal risks. As the volume of data being generated and used increases, so do these risks.

[406] 2020 developments for data protection and the GDPR. GDPR. Published 20 February 2020. gdpr. eu/gdpr-in-2020

[407] Navigating data breach notification requirements in Asia-Pacific. DLA Piper. Published February 2023. dlapiper.com/-/media/project/dlapiper-tenant/dlapiper/pdf/dlapiper_navigating_apac_data_breach_notification_requirements_2023.pdf

[408] More Responsible Use of Workforce Data Required to Strengthen Employee Trust... Accenture. Published 21 January 2019. newsroom.accenture.com/news/more-responsible-use-of-workforce-data-required-to-strengthen-employee-trust-and-unlock-growth-according-to-accenture-report.htm

[409] Blackman R. How to Monitor Your Employees—While Respecting Their Privacy. Harv Bus Rev. Published online May 28, 2020.hbr.org/2020/05/how-to-monitor-your-employees-while-respecting-their-privacy

[410] Ibrahim A et al. The Challenges of Leveraging Threat Intelligence to Stop Data Breaches. Front Comput Sci. 2020; 2 frontiersin.org/articles/10.3389/fcomp.2020.00036

ADDITIONAL DETAILS: BRIGHTON HOSPITAL'S DATA THEFT

In 2010, Brighton and Sussex University Hospital lost data on 10,000 people when 250 hard drives were stolen and later found on sale on eBay. The data included sensitive medical information on patients, children, and treatments. The hospital was fined GBP 325,000, the highest fine at the time.[411] The fine set an example for public and private organisations about keeping personal data secure.

MATERIALITY IN DATA AND PRIVACY

Specific industries consider data security more material than others. Financial institutions, internet media and services, professional services, healthcare delivery, software and IT, and e-commerce are sectors where data and security are essential considerations.

Reporting on Data Privacy (simplified indicators)	
What to report	How to report
Customer privacy (GRI 418)	• How the company protects customer privacy. • Reported incidents by customers or regulators.

---

[411] Brighton hospital fined record £325,000 over data theft. BBC News. Published 1 June 2012. bbc.com/news/uk-england-sussex-18293565

Endnote

In this chapter, we examined the importance of justice, fairness, and respect along with the health and well-being of individuals working in organisations. Further discussion was provided on the skills that should be developed for the future and protecting the data and privacy of individuals.

We now understand how businesses benefit from engaging with local communities and addressing social issues, including treating their employees well and ensuring their well-being. Doing so can enhance the businesses' reputations and reduce the risk of conflicts. Because individuals significantly impact society, businesses need to consider their well-being and the impact of their actions to build trust with customers and contribute to a more sustainable society. Society must also be ready for AI's changes to government, business and the individual. Developing future-ready skills offers individual, organisational, and societal benefits. It improves productivity, creates a culture of continuous learning, and gives organisations a competitive advantage.

The common attitude of "not in my backyard" or NIMBYism has perhaps disassociated people from the fact that we all belong to the same planet. Pollution in the Global South will affect the Global North and vice versa. NIMBYism further is when a person objects to the siting of something perceived as unpleasant or hazardous in the area where they live, such as waste disposal, hazardous production plants, social blocks, or even sustainable projects such as wind turbines, but have no objections to similar developments elsewhere.

This chapter enabled us to see that at the societal level, individuals with future-ready skills can contribute to economic growth, innovation, and social progress while addressing complex challenges like climate change and inequality. Therefore, skill-building for the future is key to sustainable development.

In the next chapter, we will examine the third of the four pillars of ESG: Governance.

CHAPTER FIVE

Governance: Purpose-Driven Business

This chapter examines the third of the four pillars of ESG: governance. Our examination will cover corporate governance, governing purpose, governing body, ESG-linked remuneration and incentives, stakeholder engagement and analysis, ethical behaviour, cybersecurity, and oversight of risks and opportunities.

The 2008 financial crisis resulted mainly from a failure of corporate governance in many financial institutions, including banks, governments, supervisory authorities, and key service providers. Their structures needed to be simplified, and their risk management practices needed to be revised, leading to a need for more transparency, accountability, and ethical behaviour. Before the financial crisis, executives and board members were incentivised to take excessive risks to increase short-term profits, ultimately causing the system to fail and incurring widespread economic damage.

This financial crisis revealed the need for better corporate governance standards to prevent similar failures in the future. Stricter regulations and new institutions were established to oversee corporate behaviour, and the concept of corporate governance has expanded to include a broader range of considerations. Today, investors, regulators, and society expect companies to have robust governance mechanisms critical to a commitment to sustainable practices.

Image 5.1. UN SDGs material to the Governance pillar. Source: UN, see footnote 34

Corporate Governance

Corporate governance describes how organisations will contribute to value creation in the short and long term. This value creation can be realised by ensuring effective oversight, accountability, and transparency of a company's operations, decisions, and strategies. Good governance creates an environment of trust and attracts long-term investments and financial stability, thereby mitigating risks and fostering ethical decision-making.[412] A top-down approach where the board of directors has active oversight over measuring and reporting combined with clear management roles is the most effective way to integrate ESG.

Good corporate governance balances all stakeholders' diverse needs and interests, striking a fair and equitable balance. It refers to the rules, practices, and processes which direct a company to enhance corporate performance and consider stakeholder interests as much as possible. It includes the roles and responsibilities of the board of directors, management, shareholders, and other stakeholders such as customers, suppliers, governments, and communities.

On the other hand, bad corporate governance practices render companies and their stakeholders more vulnerable to risks and less equipped to unlock opportunities. This results in environmental and social commitment breaches and is a risk driver. It is a core cause of many adverse outcomes such as corruption, money laundering, increased inequality, high levels of waste, or even death.[413]

---

[412] OECD. G20/OECD Principles of Corporate Governance 2015. OECD Publishing; 2015. doi:10.1787/9789264236882-en
[413] Defining the 'G' in ESG. World Economic Forum. Published June 2022. weforum.org/docs/WEF_Defining_the_G_in_ESG_2022.pdf

Country-level governance is indispensable for people engaged in international business. It sets the legal and regulatory framework that impacts their ability to do business effectively and sustainably. Good governance promotes the rule of law, protects property rights, and reduces corruption and political risk. Thus, strong governance is essential for attracting investment, promoting trade, and facilitating cross-border business activities. A country with poor governance can experience economic instability by deterring investment and hindering business opportunities.

ADDITIONAL DETAILS: ACCOUNTING AND OIL SPILLS

Enron went from winning the Fortune award "America's Most Innovative Company" six years in a row in the 1990s to filing for bankruptcy in 2001. As has been reported, Enron committed fraud and had fake holdings, resulting in a loss of USD 74 billion and the introduction of new regulations such as the Sarbanes-Oxley Act in the US.[414] The energy company BP also experienced a governance issue following the Deepwater Horizon oil spill in the Gulf of Mexico in 2010. BP's former vice president was found guilty of withholding information on the amount of oil spilt.[415]

Governing Purpose

A business should aim to make a profit from solving problems, not by causing them.[416] As such, a company uncovers its core purpose by answering a simple question: "What would the world lose if your company disappeared?"[417] A company should be committed to all of its stakeholders, such as employees,

---

[414] Segal T. Enron Scandal: The Fall of a Wall Street Darling. Investopedia. Published 26 November 2021. investopedia.com/updates/enron-scandal-summary
[415] Muskal M. BP pleads guilty to manslaughter in 2010 Gulf oil spill. Los Angeles Times. Published 29 January 2013. latimes.com/world/la-xpm-2013-jan-29-la-na-nn-bp-pleads-guilty-to-manslaughter-in-2010-gulf-oil-spill-20130129-story.html
[416] Principles for Purposeful Business. The British Academy. Published 2019. thebritishacademy.ac.uk/publications/future-of-the-corporation-principles-for-purposeful-business
[417] Leape S et al. The 5Ps of company purpose are much more than a mission statement. McKinsey. mckinsey.com/capabilities/strategy-and-corporate-finance/our-insights/more-than-a-mission-statement-how-the-5ps-embed-purpose-to-deliver-value

suppliers, communities, and shareholders.[418] A company's purpose should act as its North Star. Therefore, leaders should have a consistent voice, portray a clear purpose, a coherent strategy, and a long-term view.[419]

PATAGONIA: THE FUTURE OF OWNERSHIP[420][421][422]

The owner of the Patagonia clothing brand announced in 2022 that all the profits would go towards saving the planet. The company transferred 98 percent of its stocks to a nonprofit and 2 percent to a special trust with decision-making power. The nonprofit will use 100 percent of the revenue to tackle climate change, protect biodiversity and the environment, and help communities switch from fossil fuels. The founder said that instead of "going public," the company was "going purpose" and planned to use its wealth to protect nature.

However, the Patagonia founder's family could, reportedly, potentially save over USD 1 billion in taxes through the announced donations, revealing disparities in how wealthy individuals navigate the tax system. Despite that, this is a significant move for a billion-dollar company, and it remains to be seen if others follow.

Legislation often outlines the primary responsibilities of boards and CEOs, which historically hasn't included sustainability. Owners play a significant role in defining the company's purpose, which has hereto commonly been

[418] Business Roundtable Redefines the Purpose of a Corporation… Business Roundtable. Published 19 August 2019. businessroundtable.org/business-roundtable-redefines-the-purpose-of-a-corporation-to-promote-an-economy-that-serves-all-americans

[419] The power of capitalism. BlackRock. Published 16 February 2022. blackrock.com/corporate/investor-relations/larry-fink-ceo-letter

[420] Gelles D. Billionaire No More: Patagonia Founder Gives Away the Company. The New York Times. Published 14 September 2022. nytimes.com/2022/09/14/climate/patagonia-climate-philanthropy-chouinard.html

[421] Armstrong M. Company given away to support the fight to save our planet and tackle the climate crisis. World Economic Forum. Published 23 September 2022. Accessed 19 December 2022. weforum.org/agenda/2022/09/the-size-company-given-away-to-save-the-planet-earth/

[422] Kaplan J, Kay G. Patagonia founder's big donation potentially saves him over $1 billion in taxes. Business Insider. Published 16 September 2022. businessinsider.com/patagonia-big-climate-donation-saves-1-billion-in-taxes-yvon-chouinard2022-9?r=US&IR=T

to create financial profit for shareholders but is increasingly recognising the importance of ESG impacts and creating value for all stakeholders. This shift is evident as shareholders start to demand sustainability, influencing company policies through voting rights and dialogue with management or even divesting from companies that lag in sustainable practices, thereby nudging them towards greener operations to maintain investor support.

The understanding and interpretation of corporate purpose have been evolving. Companies have begun to look further into the future, aiming to create long-term value as they impact their external world. In 1970, Nobel Prize-winning economist Milton Friedman stated that "there is one and only one social responsibility of business—to use its resources and engage in activities designed to increase its profits." He also said that people might fulfill their "social responsibilities" in their own time and with their own money.[423]

However, now only 7 percent of Fortune 500 CEOs believe that their company should focus first on profits without the distraction of social goals.[424] Moreover, a 2021 study reported that most managers and frontline employees in the US found that a company's purpose should receive more weight than profit. However, the study also showed that more than half of the participants believed their organisation's purpose statement did not drive actual impact.[425]

Reporting on Purpose (simplified indicators)	
What to report	How to report
Setting purpose (WEF Common metrics and GRI 2)	• Explain how the company's purpose, values, goals, and strategies align with sustainability.

[423] Friedman M. A Friedman doctrine - The Social Responsibility of Business Is to Increase Its Profits. The New York Times. Published 13 September 1970. nytimes.com/1970/09/13/archives/a-friedman-doctrine-the-social-responsibility-of-business-is-to.html

[424] Gast A et al. Purpose: Shifting from why to how. McKinsey. Published 22 April 2020. mckinsey.com/capabilities/people-and-organizational-performance/our-insights/purpose-shifting-from-why-to-how

[425] Purpose before profits? Employees say, 'yes, please'. McKinsey. Published 21 January 2021. mckinsey.com/featured-insights/coronavirus-leading-through-the-crisis/charting-the-path-to-the-next-normal/purpose-before-profits-employees-say-yes-please

Governing Body

The highest governing body of a company is responsible for making strategic decisions and overseeing management. A vital aspect of this is ensuring positive and sustainable long-term value creation, with purpose as its engine. Diverse boards improve problem-solving and creativity by providing new perspectives[426] to identify blind spots and improve competency in environmental, social, and economic areas. They can better contribute to more effective, equitable, and inclusive decision-making, considering all stakeholders' interests and being aligned with the company's purpose.

Demands for increased board diversity have been noticeable in recent years. Norway became the first country to introduce binding quotas, in force from 2008, requiring that the boards of publicly listed companies, and later unlisted midsize to large companies, comprise at least 40 percent women. Failure to comply with the legislation can result in the dissolution of the company. The very strict sanction is probably instrumental in ensuring that companies abide by the law.[427] Other countries have followed Norway's lead, but the penalties for not complying with the quota are variable and sometimes nonexistent.

[426] Ciavarella A. Board Diversity and Firm Performance Across Europe. SSRN. Published 7 December 2017. doi:10.2139/ssrn.3084114

[427] Klesty V, Fouche G. Norway proposes 40% gender quota for large and midsize unlisted firms. Reuters. Published 19 June 2023. reuters.com/markets/europe/norway-proposes-40-gender-quota-large-mid-size-unlisted-firms-2023-06-19

CHAPTER FIVE

ADDITIONAL DETAILS: EU DIRECTORS' GENDER BALANCE

In 2022, women constituted 31.5 percent of board members and 8 percent of board chairs in EU-listed companies.[428] The EU passed legislation targeting gender balance on corporate boards, mirroring initiatives in Norway, Iceland, and France. By 2026, targets require 40 percent of non-executive or 33 percent of all director positions to be held by the underrepresented gender, promoting fair, transparent, and neutral candidate assessments. Originally proposed by the EU in 2012, this legislation, debated for over a decade, still faces opposition from some EU countries, which argue such decisions should be domestic.[429]

In 2021, Nasdaq approved its Board Diversity Rule, requiring companies listed in the US stock exchange to have one director who identifies as female, a member of an underrepresented racial or ethnic minority, or LGBTQ+ or explain why they do not in their disclosures. Republican attorney generals and others opposed the rule, but institutional investors and Nasdaq-listed firms supported it. The SEC and Nasdaq argued that the rule is not a quota but a disclosure requirement that provides standardised information. A US court upheld the rule.[430]

The board structure varies by company depending on factors like industry, size, and regulations. Independent board members are preferred because they are more likely to provide a higher level of corporate governance to stake-

---

[428] Gender balance on corporate boards. European Council. Published June 2022. consilium.europa.eu/en/policies/gender-balance-corporate-boards
[429] Council approves EU law to improve gender balance on company boards. European Council. Published 17 October 2022. consilium.europa.eu/en/press/press-releases/2022/10/17/council-approves-eu-law-to-improve-gender-balance-on-company-boards
[430] Godoy J. US court upholds Nasdaq board diversity rule. Reuters. Published 19 October 2023. reuters.com/sustainability/boards-policy-regulation/us-court-upholds-nasdaq-board-diversity-rule-2023-10-18

holders.[431] Independence means making impartial decisions without influence from management or external factors. A board member is considered independent if they have no significant financial, employment, or ownership ties to the company, management, or major shareholders.[432] The definition of independence may differ by country and industry.

ADDITIONAL DETAILS: NOMINATION COMMITTEES

Nomination committees have become more popular recently, particularly after the 2008 financial crisis. They are intended to help ensure a good mix of skills, experience, and backgrounds on boards. Their primary responsibility is to assess whether candidates are suitable, leading to a more diverse board.[433] If a nomination committee is weak, there is a risk of appointing unsuitable candidates, leading to various risks. The Nordic countries all emphasise nomination committees to improve governance and the selection of board members.

There has been increased focus on female representation within governance bodies in recent years. A 2015 meta-analysis found a positive relationship between female board representation and accounting returns. This was especially relevant in countries with solid shareholder protections. Moreover, an increased number of female board members had a positive impact on monitoring and strategy involvement—two of the main responsibilities of boards.[434]

Even though this conversation on gender and the success that has followed in some cases is laudable, we must also focus on other forms of diversity within the governing body. These include age, minority or vulnerable groups, and

[431] Segal T. Evaluating the Board of Directors. Investopedia. Published 29 December 2021. investopedia.com/articles/analyst/03/111903.asp

[432] Powell S. Independent Director. Corporate Finance Institute. Published 9 March 2023. corporatefinanceinstitute.com/resources/career/independent-director

[433] Pirzada K, Mustapha MZ, Alfan EB. Antecedents of Ethnic Diversity: The Role of Nomination Committees. SSRN. Published 1 April 2017. doi:10.2139/ssrn.2976235

[434] Post C, Byron K. Women on Boards and Firm Financial Performance: A Meta-Analysis. Acad Manage J. 2015; 58(5):1546-1571. doi:10.5465/amj.2013.0319

different backgrounds relating to education, profession, and other relevant aspects.

Reporting on Governing Body (simplified indicators)	
What to report	**How to report**
Diversity of governance bodies and employees (GRI 405)	• Ratios of gender, age, minority and vulnerable groups among board members.
Nomination and selection of the highest governance body (GRI 2)	• Description of the board nomination and selection process and how diversity and relevant competencies are considered.

ESG-linked Remuneration and Incentives

Remuneration is one of the most debated topics in corporate governance; stakeholders demand increased transparency, but directors wish for privacy in their financial affairs.[435] Including ESG indicators in remuneration and incentive systems means aligning management goals with sustainability objectives. This can boost motivation towards responsible business practices. ESG indicators in such an incentive system could be any of those mentioned in this book. It would all depend on the company, its industry, materiality and executive and board focus to align with its core business and financial fundamentals.

By giving financial bonuses for achieving ESG targets, companies can ensure long-term value creation and reduce risks.[436] In the US, Europe, and Canada, 77 percent of firms had ESG indicators as part of their 2022 incentive plans, up from 68 percent in 2021. Being measured based on ESG performance could incentivise managers to make faster progress towards sustainability, benefiting both the company and the environment.[437]

[435] King IV Remuneration Governance. Deloitte South Africa. deloitte.com/za/en/pages/africa-centre-for-corporate-governance/articles/kingiv_remuneration_governance.html
[436] UN PRI. Integrating ESG issues into executive pay. UN PRI. Published June 2012. unpri.org/download?ac=1878
[437] Kuk K et al. Global study on ESG incentives in executive compensation. WTW. Published 4 January 2023. wtwco.com/en-BE/insights/2023/01/global-study-on-esg-incentives-in-executive-compensation

Incentive systems can increase productivity and motivation but may also cause unfair treatment and unethical decision-making. For instance, a company could set a goal that has already been reached or alter the goal to receive a bonus. Incentives must be ethically balanced to strike a fair and equitable outcome and promote productivity and ethical behaviour to achieve long-term success. Some incentive systems lead to excessive risk-taking, as seen during the financial crisis of 2007-2009. Therefore, companies should review their incentive structures, especially for top executives' stock options.[438]

To successfully link ESG with remuneration, a company must define its ESG strategy and identify relevant indicators. These indicators should be linked to remuneration to incentivise progress on material ESG topics, as it is pointless to incentivise topics where a company has no impact. Before proceeding, the company must ensure adequate data and expertise to support ESG-linked remuneration. It also needs to establish a governance framework that can be verified by receiving third-party assurance on key performance indicators (KPIs) and results. The framework should be reviewed, adjusted, and reported annually to promote transparency.[439]

ADDITIONAL DETAILS: SCHNEIDER ELECTRIC AND MARATHON PETROLEUM

According to reports, Schneider Electric's sustainability efforts have yielded positive results, including reducing CO_2 emissions by 10 percent, launching a Sustainability School, and avoiding 440 million tonnes of CO_2 emissions. Their external annual sustainability scores have improved, and this score is included in the company's short-term incentive plan for executives and 64,000 employees.[440]

---

[438] OECD. Risk Management and Corporate Governance. OECD; 2014. doi:10.1787/9789264208636-en
[439] Deloitte. Incorporating ESG performance in executive remuneration - A practical guide. Deloitte. Published 2023. deloitte.com/content/dam/Deloitte/dk/Documents/audit/Deloitte-ESG-brochure-for-the-%20Nordics.pdf
[440] Schneider Electric closes 2022 with strong Sustainability Impact results. Schneider Electric. Published 16 February 2023. se.com/ww/en/about-us/newsroom/news/press-releases/schneider-electric-closes-2022-with-strong-sustainability-impact-results-63eb57e413f0d16fb60800b4

Marathon Petroleum awarded a CEO bonus of USD 272,000 for meeting environmental goals despite causing 23 oil spills, one of which was a significant spill of 1,400 barrels. Reportedly, the company used an indicator that wrongly measured the number of spills rather than the total amount of oil spilt, leading to the wrong incentives.[441]

Reporting on Remuneration (simplified indicators)	
What to report	How to report
Remuneration policies (GRI 2)	• Senior executives' pay structure and performance pay.
The process to determine remuneration (GRI 2)	• Process and outcome of the company's remuneration policy.

Stakeholder Engagement and Analysis

Organisations do not exist in isolation. Rather, they significantly impact the surrounding community and environment. Therefore, they have a responsibility to acknowledge those impacts and work together with affected communities.[442] By understanding the needs and expectations of stakeholders, companies can mitigate risks, build trust, and create long-term value for themselves and society.

Stakeholders fall into two categories: internal (employees, managers, board members, and shareholders) and external (suppliers, customers, governments, trade unions, civil society organisations, and the local community). Companies must identify and understand their needs and expectations through two-way communication to engage stakeholders. Stakeholder analysis will assess and prioritise the stakeholders' importance and level of influence.

[441] Clouse C. Does linking ESG performance to executive pay actually make a difference? GreenBiz. Published 2 February 2022. greenbiz.com/article/does-linking-esg-performance-executive-pay-actually-make-difference

[442] Noland J, Phillips R. Stakeholder Engagement, Discourse Ethics and Strategic Management. International Journal of Management Reviews. 2010;12(1):39-49. doi:10.1111/j.1468-2370.2009.00279.x

Company stakeholders

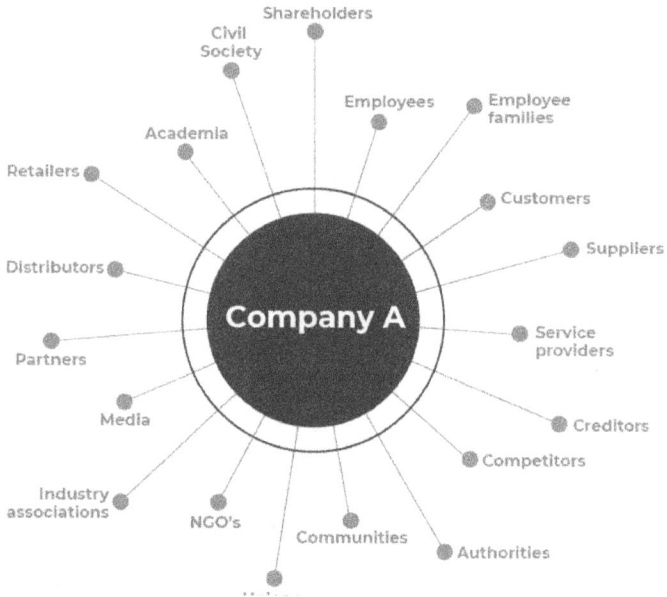

Image 5.2. Stakeholders are many. Source: Author

Maintaining a good relationship with stakeholders is critical. Best practices include open communication, active listening, addressing stakeholder concerns, and considering their interests in decision-making. Engaging stakeholders through regular meetings, surveys, and feedback builds trust and understanding. Stakeholder engagement enables companies to understand their impacts better and prioritise actions to address them.[443] By combining active, effective engagement with materiality analysis, governing bodies better understand the long-term value creation of their operations and pursue relevant stakeholder-centred practices.

---

[443] Defining the 'G' in ESG. World Economic Forum. Published June 2022. weforum.org/docs/WEF_Defining_the_G_in_ESG_2022.pdf

HOW TO CONDUCT A STAKEHOLDER ASSESSMENT

Stakeholder assessments are created using focus groups, interviews, or various sampling methods. Although the assessment has descriptive or strategic purposes, the active participation of stakeholders is required if the impacts are unknown. The use of a specific method of stakeholder analysis depends on its context. A typical stakeholder analysis involves:[444, 445]

- Identifying stakeholders to be impacted.
- Understanding the needs and concerns of each stakeholder, e.g., through interviews and collecting data.
- Review and contextualise the data to identify common themes and possible conflict areas.
- Adjusting the project or operations based on the outcome of the analysis.

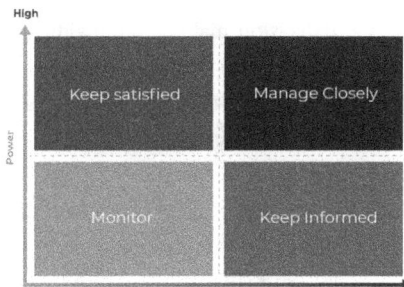

Image 5.3. Categorising stakeholders. Source: Forbes Advisor, Image: Author

[444] Reed MS et al. Who's in and why? A typology of stakeholder analysis methods for natural resource management. Journal of Environmental Management. 2009; 90(5):1933-1949. doi:10.1016/j.jenvman.2009.01.001
[445] Hooray L, Bottorff C. What Is A Stakeholder Analysis? Everything You Need To Know. Forbes Advisor. Published 7 August 2022. forbes.com/advisor/business/what-is-stakeholder-analysis

---

ADDITIONAL DETAILS: SPINNING GOLD

In 2014, a journal article "Spinning Gold: The Financial Returns to Stakeholder Engagement" showed that companies with increased stakeholder support had better financial value. The article analysed 26 gold mines owned by 19 publicly-traded companies over 15 years between 1993 and 2008. The study also looked at over 50,000 stakeholder events from media reports and developed a scale to measure the degree of stakeholder conflict or cooperation for these mines.[446]

Reporting on Stakeholders (simplified indicators)	
What to report	**How to report**
Stakeholder engagement and materiality (GRI 2 and WEF Common metrics)	• Explain how stakeholders are identified and engaged, the goals, and methods for meaningful engagement.

Ethical Behaviour

Ethics guide behaviour and decision-making in individuals, organisations, and society by determining right from wrong. Ethical conduct builds trust and promotes responsibility and long-term success by adhering to codes of conduct, ensuring fair business practices, respecting human rights, protecting the environment, promoting transparency and accountability, and encouraging responsible decision-making. Unethical behaviour harms reputations, relationships, and the environment. Companies promote ethical behaviour through six tools to create a culture of ethics that promotes sustainable business practices:

• Establish an ethics committee.

---

[446] Henisz JW, Dorobantu S, Nartey LJ. Spinning Gold: The Financial Returns to Stakeholder Engagement. Strategic Management Journal. 2014; 35(12):1727-1748. dx.doi.org/10.1002/smj.2180

- Create a code of conduct.

- Provide ethics training to employees.

- Establish a reporting mechanism.

- Conduct regular audits.

- Implement a rewards and recognition system to incentivise ethical behaviour.

Having a code of conduct promotes ethical behaviour in a company. It ensures that employees understand what is expected of them and promotes ethical behaviour and integrity within the organisation. Investors and customers may review the document before working with the company. A code often includes the other five tools mentioned in the previous paragraph and guidelines that ensure employees act according to the company's values and mission. The code of conduct should cover policies on anti-discrimination, harassment, and bribery, explain what happens if employees break these rules, and provide reporting mechanisms for employees.[447]

The relationship between competitive behaviour (antitrust), corruption, political engagement, and lobbying is complex and affects ethical behaviour. Companies that engage in anti-competitive practices risk violating antitrust legislation and damaging the company's reputation.[448] Political engagement and lobbying are legitimate ways for companies to engage with policymakers but can also create potential conflicts of interest and ethical lapses.

Competitive Behaviour (Antitrust)

Anti-competitive behaviour refers to actions that restrict the impact of market competition and encourage collaboration among potential rivals. Examples include fixing prices, coordinating bids, creating market or output restrictions, imposing geographic quotas, or allocating customers, suppliers,

---

[447] OECD. Codes of Corporate Conduct, OECD Working Papers on International Investment 2001/06. OECD Publishing. Published May 2001. dx.doi.org/10.1787/206157234626

[448] Chen J. Understanding Antitrust Laws. Investopedia. Published 2 May 2022. investopedia.com/ask/answers/09/antitrust-law.asp

geographic areas, and product lines.[449]

Anti-competitive behaviour negatively affects society. This happens as companies limit the positive impacts of market competition, i.e., they become too dominant in a specific geographic or product market. Consequences of this behaviour include price increases, decreases in the quality of service, and monopolisation. It holds back innovation by preventing other companies—which could potentially supply innovative products, services, or processes—from entering the market. Cartels are one example (albeit extreme) of entities that carry out anti-competitive behaviour.

Anti-competitive practices are illegal in most countries. Companies participating in such practices can face fines and regulatory or legal action. Big Tech companies recently came under scrutiny regarding anti-competitive behaviour. The EU is becoming more assertive in their competition regulation, and Big Tech will likely spend more resources on lawyers to tackle these regulations.

It has been reported that from 2021 to 2022, the EU opened twelve investigations, mainly into US tech companies. One investigation examined Meta's influence in the online classified ads market.[450] Additionally, competition authorities in India, the country's competition watchdog, have investigated Apple and Google over alleged abuse of the app market. Also, Amazon and Flipkart have been accused of anti-competitive practices involving promoting and prioritising certain sellers on their websites.[451]

Collaboration for sustainability has faced challenges due to concerns about anti-competition legislation. Businesses engaging in collaborative efforts for sustainability fear violating antitrust legislation. There is a growing demand for authorities to address this issue by adjusting legal frameworks to offer clear guidance for companies that seek cooperation to advance sustainability

---

[449] Global Sustainability Standards Board (GSSB). GRI 206: Anti-competitive Behaviour 2016. GRI. globalreporting.org/how-to-use-the-gri-standards/gri-standards-english-language
[450] Arcieri K. Big Tech unlikely to face major US legislation in 2023, but EU threats loom. S&P Global. Published 12 January 2023. spglobal.com/marketintelligence/en/news-insights/latest-news-headlines/big-tech-unlikely-to-face-major-us-legislation-in-2023-but-eu-threats-loom-73689665
[451] Ganguly S, Vengatill M. India panel recommends digital competition act to rein in Big Tech. Reuters. Published 22 December 2022. reuters.com/technology/india-panel-recommends-digital-competition-act-rein-big-tech-2022-12-22

goals.[452]

MATERIALITY IN COMPETITIVE BEHAVIOUR (ANTITRUST)

Industries where competitive behaviour is particularly relevant include extractives and mineral processing, construction materials, oil and gas, media and entertainment, internet media and services, semiconductors, software and IT services, telecommunication services, airlines, and rail transportation.

Corruption

Corruption occurs when people abuse power to gain personal benefits, such as bribing officials for special treatment or giving contracts to their friends and family. This has been happening for centuries and remains a big problem worldwide. Bribery and corruption cause significant social and environmental harm.[453] Corruption undermines democracy, human rights, and the rule of law, resulting in market distortions, reduced quality of life, and the spread of organised crime, terrorism, and other threats to human security, according to the UN Convention against Corruption.[454]

Corruption affects people unequally, hinders efforts to reduce poverty, and leads to weak economic growth.[455] Studies show that corruption over time has decreased productivity and negatively impacted economic performance.[456]

[452] ICC Task Force on Competition and Sustainability. When chilling contributes to warming. ICC. Published 10 November 2022. iccwbo.org/news-publications/policies-reports/how-competition-policy-acts-as-a-barrier-to-climate-action

[453] Morrow D et al. Understanding ESG Incidents: Key Lessons for Investors. Published December 2017. Sustainalytics. connect.sustainalytics.com/hubfs/INV%20-%20Reports%20and%20Brochure/Thought%20Leadership/UnderstandingESGIncidents_KeyLessonsforInvestors.pdf

[454] United Nations. United Nations Convention against Corruption. Adopted 31 October 2003. treaties.un.org/doc/Publication/MTDSG/Volume%20II/Chapter%20XVIII/XVIII-14.en.pdf

[455] United Nations against Corruption. United Nations. Published 2004. unodc.org/documents/brussels/UN_Convention_Against_Corruption.pdf

[456] Uberti LJ. Corruption and growth: Historical evidence, 1790–2010. Journal of Comparative Economics. 2022; 50(2):321-349. doi:10.1016/j.jce.2021.10.002

The WEF believes that corruption results in a 5 percent loss of global GDP each year,[457] although this statistic has been deemed unfounded by the CMI U4 Anti-corruption Resource Centre.[458]

Corruption hurts society through political, social, and environmental costs, including a lack of freedom, mistrust in governments, reduced efforts to tackle climate change, and other economic costs.[459] Corporate corruption festers when governments are seen as weak. According to the 2022 UN Report on the SDGs, almost one in six businesses globally face requests for bribe payments from public officials.[460]

One way to combat corruption is to increase the transparency of financials, decision-making, and other information for relevant stakeholders. Solely making data available will not fulfil the requirements of transparency. They must be easily accessible, understandable, and usable for affected stakeholders. Transparency is a long-term commitment and effort, and there are ways for companies to promote transparency within the organisation.

UN CONVENTION AGAINST CORRUPTION

The UN Convention against Corruption, implemented in 2005, is a global anti-corruption treaty that focuses on preventing, criminalising, and enforcing regulations against corruption and promoting international cooperation and asset recovery. The Convention was created through negotiations and had 189 parties as of November 2021. Related to this, in 2014, over 250 companies and investors signed the Anti-Corruption Call to Action, an appeal launched by the private sector urging governments to promote anti-corruption

---

[457] Transparency and Anti-Corruption. World Economic Forum. weforum.org/communities/gfc-on-transparency-and-anti-corruption

[458] Wathne C, Stephenson MC. The credibility of corruption statistics. CMI. U4 Issue 2021:4. u4.no/publications/the-credibility-of-corruption-statistics.pdf

[459] What is corruption? Transparency International. transparency.org/en/what-is-corruption

[460] United Nations. The Sustainable Development Goals Report 2022. United Nations; 2022. unstats.un.org/sdgs/report/2022

measures and establish good governance.[461, 462]

ADDITIONAL DETAILS: PARMALAT

Parmalat was a food and beverage company in Italy that declared insolvency in 2003. Despite claiming a strong financial position, the company was deeply in debt. Parmalat's owner was jailed for false accounting and market manipulation. The case highlighted the importance of having experienced and qualified board members, as many of Parmalat's board members were friends or relatives of the owner with no international company leadership experience.[463]

Political Engagement and Lobbying

Lobbying is an activity to influence policies, legislation, or regulations for specific outcomes. With the rise of digital technologies and social media, lobbying has become more complex. Beyond traditional communication methods between public officials and lobbyists, influences now include grassroots movements, industry associations, NGOs, and think tanks. Transparency is required as companies are urged to disclose their industry association memberships and ensure alignment with their ESG goals. The WEF actively encourages corporate partners to navigate this dynamic responsibly.

Corruption and lobbying do not necessarily go hand in hand. It can, however, lead to political corruption with powerful groups influencing legislation or regulations contrary to the public interest.[464] It can be a positive force in democracy—for example, if people aim for improved environmental standards or labour rights. Abuse of lobbying activities can slow down sustainable development as people or companies lobby for policies that can result in inaction on climate change or have adverse health outcomes.

[461] United Nations Convention against Corruption. United Nations Office on Drugs and Crime. unodc.org/unodc/en/corruption/tools_and_publications/UN-convention-against-corruption.html
[462] Anti-Corruption Call to Action. UN Global Compact. unglobalcompact.org/take-action/action/anti-corruption-call-to-action
[463] di Castri S, Benedetto F. There is Something About Parmalat (on Directors and Gatekeepers). SSRN. Published 1 November 2005. doi:10.2139/ssrn.896940
[464] Lobbying. OECD. oecd.org/corruption/ethics/lobbying

Lobbying and political contributions are essential factors for evaluating the political responsibility of companies. Companies must disclose the types and purposes of their contributions and costs to ensure transparency. In 2020, only 23 out of 41 countries analysed by the OECD had governance arrangements to address lobbying risks. However, more countries realise the importance of this issue, with seven countries designing, considering, or revising regulations on lobbying.[465]

Reporting on Ethical Behaviour (simplified indicators)	
What to report	How to report
Legal actions for anti-competitive behaviour, antitrust, and monopoly practices (GRI 206)	• Number and results of legal actions on anti-competitive, antitrust, or monopoly violations.
Anti-corruption (WEF Common metrics and GRI 205)	• Proportion of employees and stakeholders trained on anti-corruption policies and total corruption incidents and initiatives.
Association of strategy and lobbying policies (WEF Common metrics and GRI 415)	• Company's public policy participation and lobbying strategy, focusing on key issues and differences from goals and policies.
Monetary losses due to unethical behaviour (WEF Common metrics and SASB)	• Monetary losses from legal cases on unethical behaviour, including fraud, insider trading, or malpractice.

Cybersecurity

Cybersecurity protects computer systems, networks, and information from unauthorised access, theft, or damage. Evidence shows that financial institutions with weak risk governance are less prepared for and, therefore, more vulnerable to cyberattacks,[466] emphasising the need for robust risk governance. In the context of ESG, companies must maintain robust cybersecurity measures as information security breaches affect their reputation and financial

---

[465] OECD. Lobbying in the 21st Century: Transparency, Integrity and Access. OECD; 2021. doi:10.1787/c6d8eff8-en

[466] The effect on bank rating. S&P Global. Published 24 May 2021. insight.spglobal.com/cyber-risk-insights/page/6

stability.

The need for solid cybersecurity is on the rise. In recent years, accelerated digitalisation and remote working arrangements have increased exposure to cyber risks and could lead to even more complex cyberattacks and trigger higher financial losses.46 Cyber risks result in the loss of sensitive data, business interruption, and reputational damage, all of which are major ESG concerns.

Cybercrime examples include digital ad fraud, data hacks, and ransomware attacks. They are becoming more common and might increase by 15 percent annually in the next few years, costing an estimated USD 10.5 trillion annually. In 2021, cybercrime caused about USD 6 trillion of damage globally, with only about 10 percent of cases reported. Many industries, such as healthcare, finance, manufacturing, and government, are targets of cybercrime.[467] Cybercrime is popular because it can be cheap, relatively easy, and very profitable.[468]

News reports on cybercrime often focus on large global companies. Yet cybercrimes pose an even bigger risk to small and medium-sized companies. The damage is much more serious because these companies do not have as many resources to combat cybercrime. For example, a mid-sized steel product manufacturer in Texas filed for bankruptcy in 2019 due to a ransomware attack that rendered its software system unusable.[469]

There are ways for companies to manage cybersecurity risks, such as adopting a proactive approach, including regular risk assessments, robust security protocols, employee training, and incident response plans. They should also have adequate insurance coverage and build partnerships with cybersecurity experts to monitor and assess their security level.

---

[467] Morgan S. 2022 Cybersecurity Almanac: 100 Facts, Figures, Predictions And Statistics. Cybercrime Magazine. Published 19 January 2022. cybersecurityventures.com/cybersecurity-almanac-2022
[468] Bloomberg, J. Cybercrime: So simple anyone can do it. Forbes. Published 6 January 2019. forbes.com/sites/jasonbloomberg/2019/01/06/cybercrime-so-simple-anyone-can-do-it/?sh=19fa3b95401a
[469] Aiyer B et al. New survey reveals $2 trillion market opportunity for cybersecurity technology and service providers. McKinsey. Published 27 October 2022. mckinsey.com/capabilities/risk-and-resilience/our-insights/cybersecurity/new-survey-reveals-2-trillion-dollar-market-opportunity-for-cybersecurity-technology-and-service-providers

Reporting on Data Security (simplified indicators)	
What to report	How to report
Approach to identifying and addressing data security (SASB)	• Explain how cyber vulnerabilities are detected and dealt with, such as the frequency and source of attacks.

Oversight of Risks and Opportunities

In chapter one, "Our Global Challenges," we explored various risk categories and the notion that these risks can also manifest as opportunities. Building on that foundation, this chapter emphasises the critical role of risk management in safeguarding businesses' operations, reputation, and financial performance.

Beyond identifying potential threats, companies must recognise and seize opportunities that contribute to their long-term stability and success. This involves a holistic integration of environmental, social, and economic considerations into risk assessment frameworks. ESG risks are not static; they vary significantly across industries and can evolve over time, necessitating a dynamic and informed approach to risk management.

The board of directors is ultimately responsible for risk management and should have oversight, while the management is responsible for managing the risks daily based on the board's risk appetite. Risk appetite is the level of risk an organisation is willing to accept or tolerate to pursue its objectives.

After the 2008 financial crisis, the OECD found in its 2014 report that numerous companies have begun to place greater emphasis on risk management. Yet, this increased focus is often not mirrored in the formalisation of procedures, with exceptions primarily seen in the financial sector and among companies that have recently experienced significant risk management failures. It seems that the prevailing view among most companies is that risk management should continue to be the purview of line managers.[470]

Risks need to be identified, understood, and appropriately managed. Risk

---

[470] OECD. Risk Management and Corporate Governance. OECD; 2014. doi:10.1787/9789264208636-en

management is the process of forecasting and evaluating risks and identifying procedures to avoid or minimise their impact. The process involves identifying, evaluating, and managing sustainability risks and integrating these into the company's risk management with senior-level accountability and the highest governing body oversight. Organisations often use enterprise risk management (ERM) systems, such as the ERM framework by the Committee of Sponsoring Organisations of the Treadway Commission (COSO).

While analysing risks, the severity of impacts and financial loss should be considered. The cost of breaches is often high and underestimated, internally and externally. Risk management failures result when governance bodies do not realise the extent of the risk they are taking. Examples include financial risk-taking, environmental catastrophes, and accounting fraud.[471]

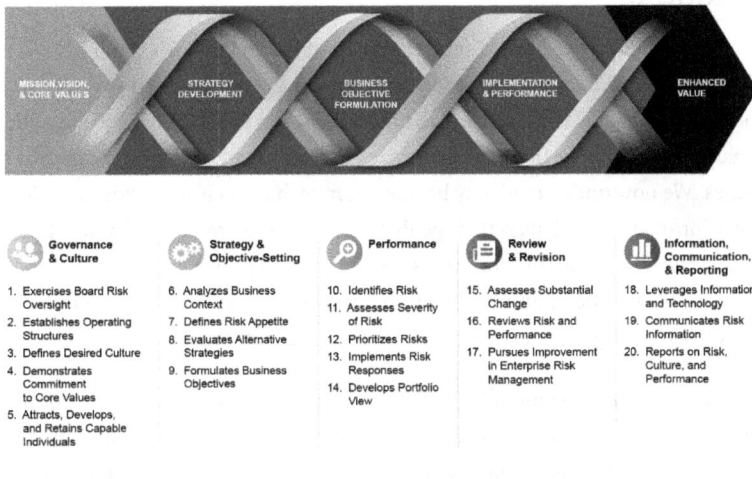

Governance & Culture	Strategy & Objective-Setting	Performance	Review & Revision	Information, Communication, & Reporting
1. Exercises Board Risk Oversight	6. Analyzes Business Context	10. Identifies Risk	15. Assesses Substantial Change	18. Leverages Information and Technology
2. Establishes Operating Structures	7. Defines Risk Appetite	11. Assesses Severity of Risk	16. Reviews Risk and Performance	19. Communicates Risk Information
3. Defines Desired Culture	8. Evaluates Alternative Strategies	12. Prioritizes Risks	17. Pursues Improvement in Enterprise Risk Management	20. Reports on Risk, Culture, and Performance
4. Demonstrates Commitment to Core Values	9. Formulates Business Objectives	13. Implements Risk Responses		
5. Attracts, Develops, and Retains Capable Individuals		14. Develops Portfolio View		

Image 5.4. COSO's Enterprise Risk Management Framework. Source: COSO[472]

Companies recognise the increasing need to assess and report ESG risks more frequently. Doing so helps identify risks, which in turn affects future value creation. Ignoring these risks increases the chance of experiencing ESG-related

---

[471] OECD. Risk Management and Corporate Governance. OECD; 2014. doi:10.1787/9789264208636-en
[472] COSO was not part of the team preparing the report and does not endorse its content. Compliance Risk Management: Applying the COSO ERM Framework. COSO. Accessed 9 February 2024. coso.org/Shared%20Documents/Compliance-Risk-Management-Applying-the-COSO-ERM-Framework.pdf

incidents such as corruption, safety hazards, or emission scandals. Companies that face high to severe incidents experience an average 6 percent decrease in market capitalisation. Integrating ESG indicators into decision-making processes improves risk management and helps companies address various ESG-related issues.[473]

| Reporting on Risk Management (simplified indicators) ||
What to report	How to report
Integration of risks and opportunities (WEF Common metrics)	• Describe company-specific material risks and opportunities, how they've changed, and the company's response.

Endnote

In this chapter, we examined several aspects of the Governance pillar of ESG by looking at corporate governance, governing purpose and governing body, ESG-linked remuneration and incentives, stakeholder engagement and analysis, ethical behaviour, cybersecurity, and oversight of risks and opportunities. We now understand why businesses must have a clear purpose to guide decision-making and align their goals and values. Integrating ESG indicators into performance metrics incentivises employees to prioritise sustainable and responsible practices, ultimately improving ESG performance, enhancing reputation, mitigating risks, and generating long-term value.

We also know that maintaining a dialogue with stakeholders is key to a company's success. Businesses can improve their reputation, relationships, and trust by understanding their stakeholders' needs and expectations. Furthermore, overseeing risks and opportunities enables companies to anticipate and respond to potential challenges or opportunities, thereby reducing the likelihood of financial or reputational damage and seizing opportunities that lead to growth and increased profitability. In the next chapter, we will examine the last of the four pillars of ESG: Prosperity.

---

[473] Morrow D et al. Understanding ESG Incidents: Key Lessons for Investors. Published December 2017. Sustainalytics. connect.sustainalytics.com/hubfs/INV%20-%20Reports%20and%20Brochure/Thought%20Leadership/UnderstandingESGIncidents_KeyLessonsforInvestors.pdf

CHAPTER SIX

Prosperity: Sustainable Growth

The ESG framework has evolved to encompass prosperity as its fourth pillar, focusing on promoting economic growth and development in a way that benefits individuals and society, while in harmony with nature.

The WEF defines prosperity as a part of the ESG framework, which includes employment and wealth generation, innovation and R&D, community and social vitality, and, inevitably, taxes, which reflects the subchapters in this chapter. This broader definition of ESG reflects the growing recognition that businesses are responsible for contributing to the economic development of their communities, not only focusing on environmental and social impacts.

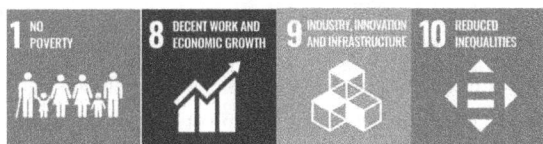

Image 6.1. UN SDGs material to the Prosperity pillar. Source: UN, see footnote 34

MATERIALITY IN PROSPERITY

Prosperity is essential to all sectors. However, specific industries, such as polluting industries and sectors relying on low-paid labour, face criticism for their negative impact on local communities. Commercial banks can provide financial inclusion to underserved groups, such as low-income populations and small businesses, through responsible lending and extending credit.

Employment and Wealth Generation

Companies contribute to employment and wealth generation by creating jobs, paying fair wages, providing employee benefits, retaining their workforce, being profitable, and paying dividends. Companies stimulate economic growth through their operations and investments. Additionally, paying their taxes is a way to contribute to essential public services that allow businesses and markets to operate successfully and support local, regional, and national economies.

The creation and sustainment of job opportunities hinge on several factors. These include business-friendly policies, which should be carefully balanced while facilitating ease of doing business to avoid harm to individuals and communities. Additionally, governance quality, marked by low levels of corruption, and access to additional financing are important elements in this process.[474]

Despite companies being sources of employment, there have been limited endeavours to contribute to overall wealth generation. Even with substantial profits, companies often offer low wages to workers, primarily benefiting bosses, owners, and shareholders rather than fostering widespread economic prosperity. CEO-to-median-worker pay ratios have skyrocketed over the last decades, and in 2022, Walmart and McDonald's reportedly paid more than

[474] OECD. The Geography of Firm Dynamics: Measuring Business Demography for Regional Development. OECD Publishing; 2017. oecd.org/cfe/the-geography-of-firm-dynamics-9789264286764-en.htm

half their workers less than USD 15 an hour, while CEOs receive millions of dollars.[475]

Furthermore, capital income has increased by two-thirds and productivity gains by 25 percent since the 1990s, yet wages have only increased by 11 percent.[476] There is a debate about whether this is fair, and we can also question whether these trends are good in the long term for society or even businesses that operate within those societies.

Low-income groups are more vulnerable to wage decline than higher-income groups. As a result, wealth is becoming less concentrated among low-income groups. In the six largest European countries, the lowest 20 percent of income households had to increase their expenditure by 50 percent more than the highest 20 percent due to higher energy and food prices in 2022.[477] Real wages are declining as inflation increases, leading to an imbalance in the power relationship between employers and employees.

In 2020, 225 million full-time jobs were lost, four times more than in the 2008 financial crisis. Women and young people were the most negatively affected, which in turn caused adverse impacts on the progress made towards closing gender gaps in the workforce.[478] In 2022, unemployment rates have recovered slower for young people (15-24 year old) than other age groups. About 73 million young people were unemployed in 2022, 6 million more than before Covid-19.[479] The decline in employment threatened business stability by elevating the risk of financial losses and reducing the customer base's purchasing power.

Good working conditions and employment provisions are equally important.

[475] Sainato M. Most workers at large retail and food firms get less than $15 an hour—study. The Guardian. Published 19 April 2022. theguardian.com/us-news/2022/apr/19/how-much-retail-food-companies-pay-workers-per-hour

[476] Manyika J et al. A new look at how corporations impact the economy and households. McKinsey. Published 31 May 2021. mckinsey.com/capabilities/strategy-and-corporate-finance/our-insights/a-new-look-at-how-corporations-impact-the-economy-and-households

[477] Employment Outlook 2022 - Tackling the cost-of-living crisis. OECD. oecd.org/employment-outlook/2022

[478] United Nations. The Sustainable Development Goals Report 2021. United Nations; 2021. unstats.un.org/sdgs/report/2021

[479] Recovery in youth employment is still lagging, says ILO. ILO. Published 11 August 2022. ilo.org/global/about-the-ilo/newsroom/news/WCMS_853078/lang--en/index.htm

Millions of informally employed people must often endure poor working conditions, which only worsened in 2020 and have since persisted. The number of workers living in extreme poverty has stagnated after some progress before 2019.[480] Poverty and high living costs are pushing people into taking any job for low pay that does not provide job security or social protection.

Big corporations moving into smaller communities can bring benefits such as employment opportunities and better access to education and healthcare. However, multinational companies have often gone to developing countries or regions in dire situations, even in the US or Europe, to exploit cheap labour and natural resources with little regulation or government oversight. These are often countries with high poverty levels and lacking infrastructure and social services. Negative impacts can include environmental damage, economic exploitation through low wages, cultural vandalism, driving small local businesses out of operation, social displacement, and more.[481]

Companies risk their reputations when exploiting them as more people and the media pay attention. However, counting on the media alone to hold businesses accountable has challenges like corrupt governments, lack of transparency, and threats to press freedom. These broader issues should be addressed, emphasising the need for clear rules and cooperation to make companies act responsibly. For example, Greenpeace called out Nestlé in a 2010 campaign regarding their palm oil supplier, which was destroying rainforests and tribal ancestral lands. Nestlé began phasing out this problematic source and claimed to have responsibly sourced palm oil in 2013.[482]

[480] ILO. World Employment and Social Outlook: Trends 2023. Geneva: International Labour Office; 2023. ilo.org/wcmsp5/groups/public/---dgreports/---inst/documents/publication/wcms_865332.pdf
[481] Muthuri JN, Moon J, Idemudia U. Corporate Innovation and Sustainable Community Development in Developing Countries. Business & Society. 2012; 51(3):355-381. doi:10.1177/0007650312446441
[482] Ionescu-Somers A, Enders A. How Nestlé dealt with a social media campaign against it. Financial Times. Published 3 December 2012. ft.com/content/90dbff8a-3aea-11e2-b3f0-00144feabdc0

| Reporting on Employee and Wealth Generation (simplified indicators) ||
What to report	How to report
Absolute number and rate of employment (WEF)	• Number and rate of employee hires and turnover, with diversity information.
Economic value (GRI 201)	• Economic value generated and distributed, including revenue, costs, wages, and payments to capital providers, governments, and communities.
Government financial assistance (GRI 201)	• Total monetary value, including tax relief, subsidies, grants, and awards.
Financial investment contribution (WEF Common metrics)	• Total capital expenditure and share repurchases.
Infrastructure investments and services supported (GRI 203)	• Description of investments and services, commercial, in-kind or pro bono, with positive and negative impacts on communities and economies.
Significant indirect economic impacts (GRI 20^3)	• Indirect economic impacts and their effects on stakeholders, compared to external benchmarks and policies.

Innovation and R&D: Better Products and Services

Innovation is the process of translating ideas or inventions into new or improved products, services, or processes that bring value to the market. Research and Development (R&D) is a subset of activities within innovation, referring to the investigative activities, systematic research, and experimentation a company conducts to improve existing products or create new ones. Innovating and conducting R&D contribute to prosperity by driving economic growth, creating jobs, improving productivity, and advancing knowledge and skills, ultimately leading to an enhanced quality of life.

According to reports, the top spenders in R&D globally include Amazon

(USD 73 billion), Alphabet (USD 40 billion), and Meta (USD 35 billion), representing 25-43 percent of their revenue for 2022.[483] Even for small and new companies, devoting a sensible ratio to innovation and R&D can benefit them in the medium and long term as they can see a return on their investments. Transparent reporting about these activities can help investors and other stakeholders get a glimpse into companies' future ambitions.[484]

Innovating and conducting R&D allows us to better understand the impact of our actions on the planet and society and to develop new, more sustainable technologies, practices, and systems. The circular economy alone, for example, is estimated to create a USD 4.5 trillion opportunity through innovation, employment, and better waste management.[485] Continued investment in research and innovation ensures an easier transition to a more sustainable future. It helps ensure economic growth and development with environmental protection and social progress, promoting long-term sustainability.

Technological or product innovation contributing to lower pollution or GHG emissions is essential to mitigate climate change and environmental degradation. This type of innovation includes products or services that increase energy efficiency or scale up renewable energy solutions—for example, wind or solar energy. The storage of renewable energy is also a challenge for innovators since mining for materials commonly found in batteries is not the most sustainable solution in the long term.[486]

Service innovation involves the development of new ways to use typical products. An example is the mobility service of car sharing, which has risen gradually in the past few years and will likely continue to rise. Globally, users of this service are expected to grow from 53 million in 2023 to over 64 million users in 2028, with revenues projected to have a growth rate of 4.3 percent

[483] Irwin-Hunt A. Top 100 global innovation leaders. fDi Intelligence.19 June 2023. fdiintelligence.com/content/feature/global-innovation-leaders-2022-edition-82527

[484] World Economic Forum. Measuring Stakeholder Capitalism. Towards Common Metrics and Consistent Reporting of Sustainable Value Creation. World Economic Forum; 2020. weforum.org/docs/WEF_IBC_Measuring_Stakeholder_Capitalism_Report_2020.pdf

[485] McGinty D. 5 Opportunities of a Circular Economy. World Resources Institute. Published 3 February 2021. wri.org/insights/5-opportunities-circular-economy

[486] Jurgens J. Technological innovations can help us meet climate goals. World Economic Forum. Published 25 May 2022. weforum.org/agenda/2022/05/3-ways-technological-innovation-can-help-us-meet-climate-goals

each year.[487]

Image 6.2. Innovation can be conceptualised in multiple ways; here are three types of sustainable innovation for businesses. Source: Adams et al. (2015)[488]

Social innovations are new ideas that meet social needs, create social relationships, and form new collaborations: innovations such as products, services, or models addressing unmet needs.[489] Rising living costs, deteriorating mental health, and social isolation of the elderly all highlight the importance of social innovation.

Fortunately, entrepreneurs have harnessed technology to benefit their immediate communities. For example, a business in Nairobi, Kenya, uses 3D printing technology to print everyday objects for local people. The 3D printers are made of recycled materials and are cheaper than those made in China and the US. Kenyans designed the printers to withstand the warm climate.[490]

Similarly, financial institutions can use innovative approaches to design their

[487] Car-sharing - Worldwide. Statista. statista.com/outlook/mmo/shared-mobility/shared-rides/car-sharing/worldwide

[488] Richard Adams, Sally Jeanrenaud, John Bessant, Patrick Overy, David Denyer. 2012. Innovating for Sustainability: A Systematic Review of the Body of Knowledge. Network for Business Sustainability. Retrieved from: nbs.net/systematic-review-innovating-for-sustainability

[489] Employment, Social Affairs & Inclusion. European Commission. 11 September 2020. ec.europa.eu/social/main.jsp

[490] Srinivasan R. Opinion: The Global South Is Redefining Tech Innovation. Wired. Published 7 November 2019. wired.com/story/opinion-the-global-south-is-redefining-tech-innovation

products, such as small non-collateral loans for rural female daily wage earners, helping them set up micro-businesses and helping with gender equality. Although microlending is not a new concept, it is being transitioned as a part of the corporate sustainability agenda. We can also explore new products, such as insurance coverage for typhoon-prone areas or lower interest rate loans to rebuild a typhoon-affected area, as a way to eradicate poverty.

ADDITIONAL DETAILS: BLOCKCHAIN AND CRYPTOCURRENCIES

Blockchains can support sustainability by enabling secure and decentralised systems to manage resources, such as improving supply chain transparency, promoting fair trade practices,[491] and tracking carbon credits.[492] Cryptocurrencies, or crypto, like Bitcoin, facilitate fast and low-cost transactions on the blockchain and can serve as a hedge against inflation and government control.[493]

However, they consume significant amounts of energy, with Bitcoin reportedly using more electricity annually than Sweden or the UAE.[494] Further, crypto has been considered to have a Ponzi scheme element (and is sometimes tied to money laundering), where investors are promised high returns without clear explanation or legitimacy, leading to financial losses for later investors.[495]

In 2023, developments occurred in further mainstreaming cryptocurrencies with big names from the traditional financial industry

[491] Friedman N, Ormiston J. Blockchain as a sustainability-oriented innovation? Opportunities for and resistance to Blockchain... Technological Forecasting and Social Change. 2022; 175:121403. doi:10.1016/j.techfore.2021.121403

[492] Chen D. Utility of the Blockchain for Climate Mitigation. The JBBA. 2018; 1(1). doi:10.31585/jbba-1-1-(6)2018

[493] Tambe N, Jain A. Advantages and Disadvantages of Cryptocurrency in 2023. Forbes. Published 5 May 2023. forbes.com/advisor/in/investing/cryptocurrency/advantages-of-cryptocurrency

[494] Lacaille R. Can cryptocurrencies become friendlier to people and planet? World Economic Forum. Published 24 May 2022. weforum.org/agenda/2022/05/can-cryptocurrencies-become-environmentally-friendly

[495] Chipolina S. Two Estonians accused of $575mn crypto fraud. Financial Times. Published 21 November 2022. ft.com/content/7785c7c0-7175-43e2-ad43-e46b27bdcd4a

Citadel Securities, Fidelity, and Charles Schwab backing a new exchange called ESX Markets.[496] The European Union's leadership council approved a new regulatory framework for cryptocurrencies, set to take effect in 2024, marking a significant move towards comprehensive cryptocurrency regulation, a widely advocated change.[497]

Automation and its impact on employment have been debated since the Industrial Revolution. Although automation can increase productivity and decrease labour costs, it raises questions about the future of work, particularly regarding manual work, decision-making, and knowledge work. The potential result is a loss of approximately 85 million jobs globally while also creating 97 million new ones from 2020 to 2025. However, this shift will require significant reskilling efforts for employees to adapt.[498]

Innovation in the environment and nature can be risky, as it may have unintended consequences. Attempts to influence solar radiation through geoengineering, for example, could create a cooling effect on the planet and have been discussed as an approach to reduce global warming. However, this approach means manipulating the atmosphere on a global scale, possibly leading to international conflicts and increased UV radiation, with risks to human health and biodiversity being largely unknown.[499]

Innovation involves operational risks and high costs that can impede progress. For instance, Google Glass, despite initial excitement, failed to capture the market due to its high cost, leading to wasted resources.[500] Similarly, carbon capture, utilisation, and storage (CCUS), despite its promise to reduce CO_2

[496] Yang Y, Doherty K. Crypto Exchange Backed by Citadel Securities, Fidelity Goes Live. Bloomberg. 20 June 2023. bloomberg.com/news/articles/2023-06-20/crypto-exchange-backed-by-citadel-securities-fidelity-goes-live

[497] Markets in Crypto-Assets Regulation (MiCA). ESMA. Accessed 8 February 2024. esma.europa.eu/esmas-activities/digital-finance-and-innovation/markets-crypto-assets-regulation-mica

[498] Recession and Automation Changes Our Future of Work, But There are Jobs Coming, Report Says. WEF. Published 20 October 2020. weforum.org/press/2020/10/recession-and-automation-changes-our-future-of-work-but-there-are-jobs-coming-report-says-52c5162fce/

[499] UNEP. One Atmosphere: An independent expert review on Solar Radiation Modification research and deployment. UNEP; 2023. wedocs.unep.org/20.500.11822/41903

[500] Weidner JB. How and Why Google Glass Failed. Investopedia. Published 13 December 2022. investopedia.com/articles/investing/052115/how-why-google-glass-failed.asp

emissions, face slow adoption due to the significant expenses associated with its implementation.[501] [502]

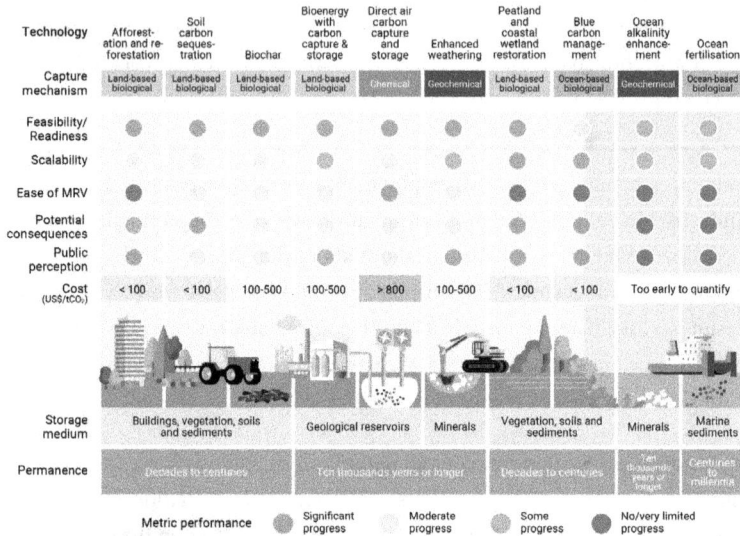

Technology	Afforest-ation and re-forestation	Soil carbon seques-tration	Biochar	Bioenergy with carbon capture & storage	Direct air carbon capture and storage	Enhanced weathering	Peatland and coastal wetland restoration	Blue carbon manage-ment	Ocean alkalinity enhance-ment	Ocean fertilisation
Capture mechanism	Land-based biological	Land-based biological	Land-based biological	Land-based biological	Chemical	Geochemical	Land-based biological	Ocean-based biological	Geochemical	Ocean-based biological
Feasibility/Readiness										
Scalability										
Ease of MRV										
Potential consequences										
Public perception										
Cost (US$/tCO₂)	< 100	< 100	100-500	100-500	> 800	100-500	< 100	< 100	Too early to quantify	
Storage medium	Buildings, vegetation, soils and sediments				Geological reservoirs	Minerals	Vegetation, soils and sediments		Minerals	Marine sediments
Permanence	Decades to centuries				Ten thousands years or longer		Decades to centuries		Ten thousands years or longer	Centuries to millennia

Metric performance — Significant progress · Moderate progress · Some progress · No/very limited progress

Image 6.3. The coloured circles indicate the level of progress for different metrics based on the current development of the technology. Green corresponds to progress being close to the target levels required for wider adoption, whereas red indicates no progress or limited progress towards the target. Geographical context may influence the applicability, and the technology is changing fast, which can influence scalability and costs. Source: UNEP[503]

Despite the obvious learning opportunity for those involved, examples here highlight the delicate balance between innovation's benefits and its economic and environmental drawbacks, like misallocated R&D funds and higher emissions. Nonetheless, the advantages of innovation, particularly when considering the pressing issue of a sustainable future, far surpass its risks, and companies that fail to innovate risk falling behind and eventually going out of business.

[501] What is carbon capture and storage? National Grid. Accessed 19 December 2023. nationalgrid.com/stories/energy-explained/what-is-ccs-how-does-it-work

[502] Baylin-Stern A, Berghout N. Is carbon capture too expensive? IEA. Published 17 February 2021. iea.org/commentaries/is-carbon-capture-too-expensive

[503] Emission gap report 2023. UNEP. Published 20 November 2023. Accessed 12 February 2014. unep.org/resources/emissions-gap-report-2023

Reporting on Research and Development (simplified indicators)	
What to report	How to report
R&D expenses (WEF Common metrics)	• Total cost for research and development.
Social value generated (WEF Common metrics)	• Revenue from sustainable products and services.

Community and Social Vitality

According to the WEF, community and social vitality, which leads to taxes being paid, are core disclosure metrics on prosperity. Community vitality is the health and strength of the community or society in the broadest terms. Companies contribute financially to increase the community vitality where they operate or elsewhere. This can be achieved through direct or indirect investments, such as community investment and taxes.

Companies prioritising social good as a part of their business model can reap benefits. For example, 80 percent of consumers are more likely to recommend a company that improves its local community. Direct contributions to local communities are one way to do this, rather than merely compensating for social or environmental impacts. BLQK Coffee, for example, allocates 25 percent of profits to direct community investment.[504]

Community investment allows businesses to benefit society and their short- and long-term operations. For example, Microsoft invested USD 500 million in affordable housing in Seattle in 2019. Prudential Financial invested USD 180 million to support global youth with limited access to education, training, or job opportunities.[505] When companies support capacity-building or improve service access, they invest in a better social environment for their operations.

Companies can further impact the economy and society through financial

[504] Morgan B. 20 Companies That Use Their Profits For Social Good. Forbes. Published 26 October 2021. forbes.com/sites/blakemorgan/2021/10/26/20-companies-that-use-their-profits-for-social-good
[505] JUST Capital. 6 Companies Making a Big Investment in Their Communities. JUST Capital. Published 24 September 2019. justcapital.com/news/companies-making-a-big-investment-in-their-communities

investments and investments in infrastructure and services. This can, in turn, support the company's growth and the economy. Indirect economic impacts (or externalities) are negative or positive and do not have to be monetary. Positive indirect impacts include increased knowledge and skills in business operations.[506] Negative indirect impacts include economic impacts of pollution and contributing to price increases on essentials, which then become too expensive for low-income groups.[507]

Why Communities Invest in Economic Development

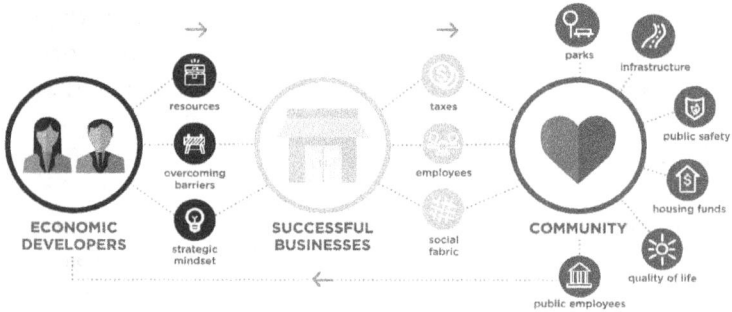

Image 6.4. Why companies invest in economic development. Source: California Association for Local Economic Development (CALED)

Despite good intentions, community investment carries both reputational and financial risks. For instance, poorly planned and managed projects can lead to conflict with the community. This often stems from issues like corruption or the exclusion of certain groups during the investment planning process.[508] This could reflect poorly on the company and cause harm to the community. Significant conflict and disagreements may cause a project to break down, meaning the investment is lost. This investment is usually for the community

[506] World Economic Forum. Measuring Stakeholder Capitalism. Towards Common Metrics and Consistent Reporting of Sustainable Value Creation. World Economic Forum; 2020. weforum.org/docs/WEF_IBC_Measuring_Stakeholder_Capitalism_Report_2020.pdf

[507] Global Sustainability Standards Board (GSSB). GRI 203: Indirect Economic Impacts 2016. GRI. globalreporting.org/how-to-use-the-gri-standards/gri-standards-english-language

[508] IFC. Strategic Community Investment: A Good Practice Handbook for Companies. IFC. Published June 2010. ifc.org/wps/wcm/connect/Topics_Ext_Content/IFC_External_Corporate_Site/Sustainability-At-IFC/Publications/Publications_Handbook_CommunityInvestment__WCI__1319576907570

closest to the company, but it can also target underserved areas.[509]

Companies must identify and engage with stakeholders to invest strategically in communities and increase community vitality. This ensures input from affected stakeholders and helps to build trust, respect, and local ownership. Participatory methods in community engagement are essential to setting a foundation for successful investment. Companies should also understand the local context through a socioeconomic assessment to identify potential challenges.[510]

ADDITIONAL DETAILS: CONNECTIVITY

Around 2.7 billion people worldwide lack internet access, e.g., 60 percent in Africa and 10-20 percent in Europe. The lack of affordability of internet connections in low-income countries is a significant obstacle to bridging the gap. To tackle this issue, the ITU Partner2Connect Digital Coalition has reportedly mobilised USD 29.2 billion to improve internet infrastructure and access.[511] Connecting people to the internet contributes to education, skills development, economic opportunities, and productivity gains.[512]

Taxes

Tax evasion (the illegal act of deliberately underreporting income) and avoidance (the legal practice of using methods within the law to minimise tax liability, sometimes deemed unethical) by businesses and individuals may pro-

[509] Fontinelle A. Community Investing 101. Investopedia. Published 25 August 2021. investopedia.com/articles/basics/12/community-investing.asp

[510] IFC. Strategic Community Investment: A Good Practice Handbook for Companies. IFC. Published June 2010. ifc.org/wps/wcm/connect/Topics_Ext_Content/IFC_External_Corporate_Site/Sustainability-At-IFC/Publications/Publications_Handbook_CommunityInvestment__WCI__1319576907570

[511] ITU. Measuring digital development: Facts and Figures. ITU; 2022. itu.int/hub/publication/d-ind-ict_mdd-2022

[512] United Nations. Achieving universal and meaningful digital connectivity - Setting a baseline and targets for 2030. United Nations. itu.int/itu-d/meetings/statistics/wp-content/uploads/sites/8/2022/04/UniversalMeaningfulDigitalConnectivityTargets2030_BackgroundPaper.pdf

vide short-term gains to themselves. Still, the hidden costs can harm not only the society but also the taxpayers. Tax evasion and sometimes tax avoidance (even though not illegal) pose regulatory, legal, and reputational risks for companies.

Unpaid taxes could have been used to build hospitals, schools, and roads and help impoverished people. This leads to decreased revenues for governments and municipalities and a higher burden on those who do pay fair taxes, ultimately increasing the inequality gap. Tax evasion and avoidance must be addressed to ensure a fair and just society and avoid the negative impact on communities.[513]

According to reports, Google paid EUR 965 million in 2019 to French authorities after allegations of tax fraud in 2015, with EUR 500 million as a penalty and EUR 465 million in "additional taxes."[514] Further, and as recently as in October 2023, the US Internal Revenue Service (IRS) claimed Microsoft owed the government USD 29 billion in unpaid taxes over transfer pricing claims.[515] These instances highlight a broader issue of large companies navigating complex tax landscapes, leading to significant disputes and allegations.

Similarly, tax practices in certain jurisdictions present another example of how major corporations manage their tax obligations to maximise benefits. In 2021, it was reported that Amazon paid no corporation tax in Luxembourg, which has its sales unit for several European countries, despite a record sales income of EUR 44 billion. A Fair Tax Foundation CEO called Amazon's tax avoidance "astounding," allowing them to dominate the market while smaller, responsible taxpayers suffer.[516]

Governments enforce regulations that require companies to pay and dis-

[513] OXFAM International. Inequality and poverty: the hidden costs of tax dodging. Oxfam International. Published 25 May 2022. oxfam.org/en/inequality-and-poverty-hidden-costs-tax-dodging

[514] The Associated Press. Google pays France over $1 billion to settle tax case. NBC News. Published 12 September 2019. nbcnews.com/tech/tech-news/google-pays-france-over-1-billion-settle-tax-case-n1053106

[515] Harshberger C. IRS's $28.9 Billion Tax Claim Against Microsoft, Explained. Bloomberg Tax. Published 13 October 2023. news.bloombergtax.com/daily-tax-report/irss-28-9-billion-tax-claim-against-microsoft-explained

[516] Neate R. Amazon had sales income of €44bn in Europe in 2020 but paid no corporation tax. The Guardian. Published 4 May 2021. theguardian.com/technology/2021/may/04/amazon-sales-income-europe-corporation-tax-luxembourg

close taxes. The OECD's Pillar Two Global Anti-Base Erosion Rules ensure that multinational corporations earning over EUR 750 million pay taxes in all countries in which they operate.[517] The EU also mandates public country-by-country reporting (CBCR) from 2021, which obliges multinational companies to report their income tax payment in every EU country where they operate. Since companies operate globally, this transparency ensures that they pay taxes to the governments where they earn their profits.[518]

General Anti-Avoidance Rules (GAAR) and Specific Anti-Avoidance Rules (SAAR) are regulatory approaches against unethical tax practices within legal bounds. GAAR disallows practices considered tax avoidance, allowing tax authorities to revoke a tax benefit or impose a higher tax liability.[519] SAAR targets tax avoidance practices.[520] Tax authorities implement both approaches in various forms worldwide.

When a company contributes to the community and social vitality by paying taxes, the community gives back. Companies build a more robust customer and employee base in blossoming communities. This is due to an increasingly skilled workforce (potentially due to better access to education, partially paid with company taxes) and a more extensive customer base. The people within the community have the resources and purchasing power to trade with the company.[521]

Companies increase their trustworthiness by being transparent about their official societal contributions, such as taxes. Investors and stakeholders are increasingly interested in a company's ESG practices, making transparency in tax payments essential. By providing reliable information about tax payments

---

[517] Further progress on two-pillar solution: OECD releases consultation document... OECD. Published 20 December 2022. oecd.org/tax/beps

[518] KPMG International. KPMG Tax Impact Reporting. Published January 2022. assets.kpmg/content/dam/kpmg/xx/pdf/2022/01/tax-impact-reporting-2022-web-new.pdf

[519] Waerzeggers C, Hillier C. Introducing a General Anti-Avoidance Rule (GAAR) - Ensuring That a GAAR Achieves Its Purpose. IMF Legal Department; 2016. imf.org/external/pubs/ft/tltn/2016/tltn1601.pdf

[520] Shome P. Specific Anti-avoidance Rules (SAAR). In: Shome P, ed. Taxation History, Theory, Law and Administration. Springer Texts in Business and Economics. Springer International Publishing; 2021:329-347. doi:10.1007/978-3-030-68214-9_28

[521] World Economic Forum. Measuring Stakeholder Capitalism. Towards Common Metrics and Consistent Reporting of Sustainable Value Creation. World Economic Forum; 2020. weforum.org/docs/WEF_IBC_Measuring_Stakeholder_Capitalism_Report_2020.pdf

in sustainability reporting, companies demonstrate that they are trustworthy and law-abiding.

Third-party firms provide tax impact reporting and advisory services to help companies reduce regulatory risk and accurately report their tax footprint. These firms increasingly avoid engaging in aggressive tax strategies, which exploit tax legislations, incentives, and shell companies in tax havens to minimise tax liability.

While legal, such aggressive strategies are considered unethical and can damage a company's reputation, both the service providers and their clients, if caught or information leaks. Tax strategies become illegal when they involve fraud, evasion, or deliberate misrepresentation, crossing legal boundaries. Aggressive but legal strategies may push the limits of tax legislation, exploiting loopholes or minimising liabilities. The distinction often lies in the intent and methods used—ethical compliance versus intentional deception.

Reporting on Social Vitality and Taxes (simplified indicators)	
What to report	**How to report**
Total Social Investment (WEF Common metrics)	• Social impact investments.
Total taxes paid (WEF Common metrics)	• Total taxes paid, including corporate, property, VAT or purchase tax, employee taxes, and other types. • Taxes paid by location.

Endnote

In this chapter, which concluded our examination of the four pillars of ESG, we examined the following aspects of prosperity: employment and wealth generation, innovation and R&D, community and social vitality, and taxes.

We now understand why businesses should consider the wealth generation of individuals and their communities, as it directly affects their financial performance. Furthermore, greater wealth means people are more likely to buy the company's goods and services, which boosts revenue. We have also seen why investment in research and development is necessary for businesses to remain competitive by developing new products and technologies, improving efficiency, reducing costs, and increasing profitability.

In this world, nothing can be said to be certain except death and taxes, which, we now know, is why responsible tax practices are essential because taxes are a major source of government revenue. Conversely, tax avoidance limits a government's ability to provide public goods and services. Noting that the allocation of government revenue and its responsible management is a topic deserving its own book for debate. Businesses also need monetary profits to cover costs, invest in growth, provide returns to shareholders, allocate resources to benefit stakeholders, and pay taxes.

The next chapter examines integrating sustainability into a company's strategy and vision.

Sustainability Integration: From Silos to Synergy

Having gained an understanding of the four pillars of ESG, we next turn to how to integrate sustainability into a company's business model and core operations. This chapter will examine step-by-step integration of sustainability, ESG scores and ratings, and life cycle thinking—value and supply chain management. Additionally, we will demystify the "greenwashing" concept, what it means in practice, and how companies can avoid being caught in greenwashing claims—noting that the prefix "green" can also be replaced by other colours of the rainbow.

In business, silos refer to divisions or groups that operate independently without sharing information or targets with each other. Although this might seem to make each division work more efficiently—and sometimes it can—when it comes to integrating sustainability, synergy is key. Even within executive teams, silos can exist.

Integrating sustainability into a company's strategy and vision involves careful planning, execution, and communication with key stakeholders, opening up consistent communication channels to identify gaps and issues that must be addressed. It must align with the company's values, culture, and purpose to build trust and ensure credibility while never losing sight of its core products, services, and financial fundamentals.

A 2023 survey of executives revealed a consensus among CEOs and CFOs on prioritising cost management-focused growth, technology, and talent to navigate the business landscape. In this survey, environmental sustainability and the customer received the lowest priority.[522] This backdrop sets the stage for exploring the integration of sustainability into business models and operations. The presence of sustainability officers and other passionate individuals within a company cannot make up for the absence of a strong commitment to sustainability from CEOs, CFOs, and other executives at the top level.

Typically, around 80 percent of revenue growth is attributed to core products and services, making a focus on these areas 20 percent more likely to achieve above-peer growth.[523] Considering this, it's clear that while ESG integration can enhance a company's performance and reputation, it cannot serve as a cure-all for weak business fundamentals. This underscores the importance of solidifying these fundamentals as a prerequisite for leveraging the full benefits of ESG integration.

Step-by-Step Integration

Business Models, Visions, Strategies, and Structures

A business model outlines how a company creates, delivers, and captures value through its activities and stakeholder relationships. A well-defined business model clarifies a company's value proposition, targeting customer segments and revenue streams. It also outlines how it will acquire and allocate resources, manage relationships and critical processes, and compete in the market. A transparent business model provides structure and direction and facilitates decision-making and executing strategies.

A good business model increases resilience—essential for companies to thrive in today's rapidly changing global economy. In a business context, resilience refers to the ability of a company to withstand and adapt to challenges, disruptions, and unexpected events. Antifragility goes beyond mere resilience. It refers to an organisation's ability to survive and thrive in the face of stressors and shocks. Antifragile organisations can adapt and evolve in response to

[522] CFO Perspective on the 2023 CEO Survey. Gartner. Accessed 12 February 2024. gartner.com/en/articles/what-matters-to-ceos-and-cfos-right-now

[523] Birshan M et al. Choosing to grow: The leader's blueprint. McKinsey. Published 7 July 2022. mckinsey.com/capabilities/growth-marketing-and-sales/our-insights/choosing-to-grow-the-leaders-blueprint

stressors and take advantage of them to become stronger.[524]

Companies need a deep understanding of their risks and opportunities and a clear management strategy to build resilience. This includes incorporating sustainability into their business models and operations, using the ESG framework, and developing contingency plans for potential operational disruptions. By doing so, companies mitigate risks and capitalise on emerging opportunities, leading to long-term value creation.

Integrating ESG into a business model requires a systematic approach: the consideration of ESG risks and opportunities, the integration of ESG principles into core business strategies and decision-making, the alignment of stakeholders' expectations, and the regular evaluation of ESG performance. The success of the ESG integration process also depends on the leadership of senior management, the support of relevant policies and systems, and the necessity of materiality assessments. As with any organisation-wide initiative, establishing clear roles and team workflows will allow for the seamless integration of ESG strategies.

Ambition is the drive or determination to achieve success, progress, or goals. In the corporate world, ambition transcends the tangible aspects of strategies, policies, and reports, embedding itself more as an intangible, cultural essence—a feeling experienced through the actions and attitudes of a company's people rather than through written documents. This intangible nature of ambition suggests that without a foundational level of ambition, businesses may risk stagnation or failure and divide the leaders from the laggards.

CEOs and sustainability executives frequently receive the most praise when initiatives succeed, yet the pivotal middle managers are critical to the success of sustainability efforts. How this group drives sustainability will vary with a company's sustainability maturity. Recent research ranks managers in four sustainability levels. Level one managers should introduce sustainability, level two managers need to integrate it into daily operations, level three involves accelerating efforts and transparency, and level four focuses on building a

---

[524] Taleb NN. Antifragile: Things That Gain from Disorder. Random House Trade; 2014.

strong, lasting sustainability base and forming key partnerships.[525]

Transitioning to the consideration of "sustainable by design" for new companies adds a new layer to this dynamic. By integrating sustainability into their foundational decisions, these companies can preemptively sidestep the costs of later transitions. Although more than 50 percent (varies by region and industry) of new companies face challenges within their initial years, exploring whether a sustainability-focused strategy impacts their success remains intriguing.

Building the next Amazon, Citibank, Google, etc., would require over thirty years. While new companies may be sustainable by design, established incumbents are far more likely to wield greater immediate influence. The transformative impact of emerging companies on a significant scale might only materialise after 2050, when we, as a society, should have achieved most of the sustainability objectives.

Image 7.1. An organisational hierarchy from a sustainability perspective. Optimising for accountability and decision-making power. Source: Author

---

[525] Winston A, Polman P, Seabright J. Middle Management Is the Key to Sustainability. Harvard Business Review. November 2023. hbr.org/2023/11/middle-management-is-the-key-to-sustainability

A Business Model

All components of a business model must work together and should describe a current state and a strategy for a desired state.[526]

Component	Details
Vision and mission	A company's purpose and goals for all employees.
Value proposition	How a product or service benefits customers.
Customer segments	Groups of customers with similar needs to target.
Customer relationships	Understanding customer needs and delivering value through communication.
Channels: marketing and communication	Methods used to promote products, build brand awareness, and gather feedback.
Revenue streams	Sources of income (sales, licensing, commission, etc.).
Cost structure	Types of expenses incurred to operate and produce goods or services.
Key resources	Tangible and intangible assets required to operate and produce.
Key activities	Critical activities for the company's function.
Key partnerships	Relationships with other organisations or individuals.
Key processes	Core activities for delivering value and achieving objectives.
Competitors	Competition from similar or replaceable products or services.
Ownership structure	Owners and the value they bring.
Geography	Current and future geographic markets.
Why now	Why the business is necessary or relevant today.
Timeline and what next	Timeline and actions from the current to the desired state.

Standards and Frameworks

In the sustainability context, a standard is a set of criteria a company must

---

[526] Author's models inspired by books such as The Business Model Canvas, Blue Ocean Strategy, The Founder's Dilemmas, Zero to One, The Personal MBA, and others.

meet. Industry organisations or regulatory bodies usually develop and maintain standards to establish a minimum level of ESG performance. In contrast, a framework is a more flexible, high-level set of guidelines that provides a structured approach to ESG performance but allows for more discretion in implementation. Companies use standards and frameworks to help them improve their ESG performance and communicate their efforts to stakeholders.

When companies are starting out or reassessing their approach to sustainability, selecting one or two frameworks to structure the evaluation process and pinpoint the appropriate language, methods, and metrics is appropriate. Consider exploring recommendations from industry peers, market leaders, and relevant associations. While some standards are obligatory, others vary based on company size and industry. Adopting a particular standard can be influenced by personal preference or alignment with the company's values and objectives. Furthermore, some regulations prescribe standards and note who applies them.

Navigating the Landscape

Efforts to classify the plethora of frameworks, standards, international agreements, and sustainability goals have resulted in diverse categorisations, recognising that many entities span multiple domains. While we use EU regulations as a reference point, we acknowledge the presence of other regional or country-specific regulations that could be applied similarly, aiming to assist readers globally in contextualising and applying their specific regulations. Our approach simplifies this complex landscape into three distinct categories. This structured classification is one attempt to provide an overview of this ecosystem. What would your categorisation look like?

Reporting frameworks and guidelines	Standards, principles, and regulatory guidance	International agreements and sustainability goals	Rating Agencies and Sustainability Indices
CDP	CSRD	EU Sustainable Finance Action Plan	Bloomberg
CDSB	EFRAG	GHG Protocol	Corporate Knights
GRI	ESRS	Kunming-Montreal GBF	CSR Hub
IFC	EU Taxonomy	Kyoto Protocol	EcoVadis
<IR>	Equator Principles	Paris Agreement	EPI (Yale)
PRI	FASB	SBT	Fitch Ratings
TCFD	IASB	SDGs	FTSE Russell
TNFD	IFRS	UNCBD	GGEI
UNEPFI	ISSB	UNCHE	GRESB
Value Reporting Foundation	ISO	UNFCCC	ISS ESG
WBCSD	OECD	UN Global Compact	LESG (Refinitiv)
	PCAF	UNCED	Moody's
	SASB		MSCI
	SFDR		Morningstar
			RepRisk
			S&P
			Sustainalytics

Some of the main players will be mentioned here to give insight into the number of groups and regulatory bodies that publish reporting standards. These include the European Sustainability Reporting Standard (ESRS), the World Economic Forum's International Business Council (WEF IBC), the International Financial Reporting Standards Foundation (IFRS), the US Securities and Exchange Commissions (US SEC), and the European Financial Reporting Advisory Group (EFRAG). Some of the world's most impactful asset managers and institutional investors support these reporting standards.

Thankfully, some leading organisations are working together towards comprehensive corporate reporting and aligning their methodologies.[527] These are the CDP (originally the Carbon Disclosure Project), the Climate Disclosure Standards Board (CDSB), the Global Reporting Initiative (GRI), the International Integrated Reporting Council (IIRC), and the Sustainability Accounting

---

[527] Statement of Intent to Work Together Towards Comprehensive Corporate Reporting. Integrated Reporting. integratedreporting.org/resource/statement-of-intent-to-work-together-towards-comprehensive-corporate-reporting

Standards Board (SASB).[528] SASB and TCFD (not a part of the collaboration mentioned earlier) are on the rise in terms of use and attention.[529] According to an annual survey of sustainability reporting in 2022, the most commonly used standards were GRI and TCFD.[530]

Despite further work required to align methodologies and standards, new reporting proposals and regulations are entering this crowded and complex space. Although they may help with reporting comparability, they complicate the space further. Among these developments are three significant reporting proposals from the International Sustainability Standards Board (or ISSB under IFRS), EFRAG, and the US SEC. They share similarities, such as benchmarking to TCFD, but they have additional requirements and components. The ISSB tried to address this complexity by announcing in 2023 that they would enable a phase-in approach to reporting, where companies will start with climate change reporting for the first year before moving on to tackling other topics.[531]

Let's explore the main frameworks and standards from which each company will identify sustainability topics and indicators for its materiality assessment and further integration of sustainability into its business model. Although even more are on the way, I hope a universal framework will emerge with the ability to compare companies while allowing for industry-specific adjustments.

The Task Force on Climate-Related Financial Disclosures (TCFD), established by the Financial Stability Board (FSB) in 2015, has completed its mission and has been succeeded by the International Financial Reporting Standards (IFRS). It developed a framework to help companies disclose climate risks and opportunities to investors, lenders, and insurers. TCFD also

---

[528] World Economic Forum. Measuring Stakeholder Capitalism: Towards Common Metrics and Consistent Reporting of Sustainable Value Creation. World Economic Forum; 2020. weforum.org/docs/WEF_IBC_Measuring_Stakeholder_Capitalism_Report_2020.pdf

[529] SASB and TCFD report fastest growth in usage in the last two years. Corporate Disclosures. Published 28 February 2023. corporatedisclosures.org/content/top-stories/sasb-and-tcfd-report-fastest-growth-in-usage-in-the-last-two-years.html

[530] Big shifts, small steps. KPMG. Published October 2022. assets.kpmg.com/content/dam/kpmg/se/pdf/komm/2022/Global-Survey-of-Sustainability-Reporting-2022.pdf

[531] ISSB decides to prioritise climate-related disclosures to support initial application. IFRS. Published 4 April 2023. ifrs.org/news-and-events/news/2023/04/issb-decides-to-prioritise-climate-related-disclosures-to-support-initial-application

suggests metrics and targets to measure and address these risks.

The Task Force on Nature-related Financial Disclosures (TNFD) helps businesses understand the risks and opportunities of nature loss. Many businesses need more information to assess how nature loss affects financial performance and long-term risks. The TNFD aims to provide this information so businesses can integrate biodiversity risks and opportunities into their governance, risk management, and strategy. The TNFD comprises thirty-four members, including financial institutions and companies, with approximately USD 19.4 trillion combined assets.

SASB Standards apply to multiple industries and focus on the issues most important to a company's value and financial performance. These standards cover environmental, social, human, business, and governance topics. Each industry standard includes, on average, six disclosure topics, accounting metrics, technical protocols, and activity metrics. SASB also created the Sustainable Industry Classification System (SICS) to group similar companies with shared sustainability risks and opportunities, making it easier to compare them.

The Global Reporting Initiative (GRI) is a sustainability reporting standard created in 1997. GRI standards fall into universal, sector, and topic categories, depending on a company's industry and relevant material topics. Each category has a numerical designation code: one digit for universal standards, two digits for sector standards, and three digits for topic standards. The GRI provides instructions for linking with other reporting efforts like TCFD and SASB. As of 2022, about 80 percent of the world's largest companies use the GRI for reporting.[532]

The EU's Corporate Sustainability Reporting Directive (CSRD) and its accompanying **European Sustainability Reporting Standards (ESRS)** require companies to disclose certain environmental, social, and governance information.[533] The ESRS provides guidelines for general and specific topics, such as climate change and business conduct. The regulations came into force in

---

[532] Four-in-five largest global companies report with GRI. GRI. Published 21 October 2022. globalreporting.org/news/news-center/four-in-five-largest-global-companies-report-with-gri/
[533] First Set of draft ESRS. EFRAG. efrag.org/lab6

January 2023 for large publicly listed companies (with over 500 employees). Still, they will soon apply to companies with over 250 employees, EUR 40 million in turnover, or EUR 20 million in total assets. By 2026, even smaller companies will be included. Reports for all company groups are expected the year after the regulations start applying, i.e., reports for large companies will be due in 2025 for the financial year of 2024.[534] The Sustainable Finance Disclosure Regulation (SFDR) is a similar regulation for financial disclosures.

CDP (originally known as the Carbon Disclosure Project) is a global platform that enables companies, cities, regions, and investors to disclose information about climate change, water security, and deforestation. It was created in 2000 to meet the growing demand for climate performance disclosures. CDP helps businesses identify and manage the risks and opportunities associated with these issues, which stakeholders use. In 2021, over 13,000 companies—representing more than 64 percent of global market capitalisation and 1,100 cities, states, and regions—disclosed data through CDP.[535]

The **<IR> (Integrated Reporting) framework** helps companies report their information in a more comprehensive way that shows they are part of a more extensive system.[536] The framework has "content elements" on which companies report, including an organisational overview and external environment, governance, business model, risks and opportunities, strategy and resource allocation, performance, outlook and basis of preparation and presentation.[537] Over 2,500 businesses have used this framework since the International Integrated Reporting Council created it in 2013.[538]

In 2020, the **World Economic Forum (WEF)** collaborated with the big four

---

[534] Sustainable economy: Parliament adopts new reporting rules for multinationals. European Parliament. Published 11 October 2022. europarl.europa.eu/news/en/press-room/20221107IPR49611/sustainable-economy-parliament-adopts-new-reporting-rules-for-multinationals

[535] CDP reports a record number of disclosures and unveils new strategy to help... CDP. Published 14 October 2021. cdp.net/en/articles/media/cdp-reports-record-number-of-disclosures-and-unveils-new-strategy-to-help-further-tackle-climate-and-ecological-emergency

[536] Frequently Asked Questions. Integrated Reporting. integratedreporting.org/FAQS

[537] Value Reporting Foundation. Transition to Integrated Reporting. Integrated Reporting. Published September 2021. integratedreporting.org/wp-content/uploads/2022/08/Transition-to-integrated-reporting_A-Getting-Started-Guide.pdf

[538] IIRC publishes revisions to International <IR> Framework to enable enhanced reporting. Integrated Reporting. Published 19 January 2021. integratedreporting.org/news/iirc-publishes-revisions-to-international-framework-to-enable-enhanced-reporting

accounting firms to publish a white paper called **Measuring Stakeholder Capitalism.**[539] The paper aims to establish consistent and common metrics for companies to report on their sustainable value creation towards society and the planet. The paper has four pillars: governance, planet, people, and prosperity. Each pillar outlines topics, core metrics, and disclosures that align with existing standards, such as the SDGs, GRI, TCFD, SASB, and CDSB. The core metrics are mainly quantitative and already reported by companies, while expanded metrics and disclosures have a broader value chain scope.[540]

Materiality Assessment

Armed with relevant standards and frameworks and aiming to comply with regulations, a company conducts a materiality assessment, remembering single, double, and dynamic materiality. A materiality assessment systematically identifies and prioritises positive and negative sustainability topics, identifying factors within the topics most relevant to the organisation or stakeholders. A materiality assessment uses the elimination method to find the most significant risks and opportunities. There are three main factors to consider when conducting a materiality assessment. These factors may be conducted in any sequence or simultaneously.

1. **Internal:** Involve different groups like the board, managers, and employees to bring different perspectives and insights.

2. **External:** Engage with external stakeholders through surveys or conversations to understand what they find necessary.

3. **Science and best practices:** Use standards and frameworks like SASB, GRI, and other tools and data sets provided by ESG data providers to explore ESG indicators that can affect a given industry positively or negatively, based on science and best practices.

The information undergoes analysis and evaluation based on its potential

[539] Measuring Stakeholder Capitalism Towards Common Metrics and Consistent Reporting of Sustainable Value Creation. WEF. September 2020. weforum.org/docs/WEF_IBC_Measuring_Stakeholder_Capitalism_Report_2020.pdf
[540] World Economic Forum. Measuring Stakeholder Capitalism: Towards Common Metrics and Consistent Reporting of Sustainable Value Creation. World Economic Forum; 2020. weforum.org/docs/WEF_IBC_Measuring_Stakeholder_Capitalism_Report_2020.pdf

significance to the organisation and its stakeholders, factoring in strategic priorities, business risks, and opportunities. This analysis produces a list of ESG indicators ranked in order of materiality and guides the development of the organisation's sustainability strategy and reporting. A materiality assessment empowers organisations to focus on critical ESG indicators and improve transparency and accountability.

Internal and external stakeholder engagement in this process is a prerequisite. Incorrect or misguided materiality focus prevents value creation and harms the company in the short and long term. A few challenges may arise when conducting a materiality assessment. These include conducting the assessment in isolation from the business, failure to involve senior management, the approach not reflecting the complexity of the business, and misidentification of key stakeholders or their insufficient involvement.

A company builds its materiality profile from the viewpoints of different stakeholders. When the company has determined key ESG issues, it chooses the corresponding ESG indicators from relevant frameworks and guidelines. Those material indicators will become the basis for determining a baseline, setting targets, and making an action plan.

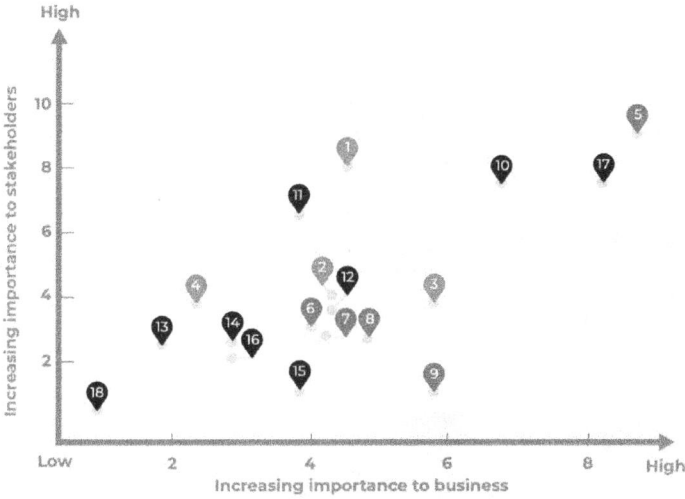

Image 7.2. Stakeholder assessment mapping. Image: Author

Governance

1. Corporate governance
2. Data security and privacy
3. Business ethics
4. Innovation and responsible technology

Environment

5. Climate change and GHGs
6. Water
7. Operational waste
8. Environmental protection
9. Circular design and lifecycle management

Social

10. Human rights and working conditions in the supply chain
11. Talent
12. Employee health and safety and labor rights
13. Employee wellbeing
14. Community impact
15. Economic empowerment
16. Digital inclusion
17. Inclusion and diversity
18. Critical human needs and disaster relief

Indicators	Group	Bjarki	Eydís	Lucile	Nína	Thomas
GHG emission Scope 1, 2, 3	3.0	3	3	3	3	3
GHG intensity	2.0	2	2	2	2	2
Operational sites, significant impacts, and protected and restored habitats	2.4	3	2	2	2	3
IUCN Red List species	2.0	2	2	2	2	2
Total water withdrawal, consumption, discharges, recycled or reused	1.4	2	1	1	2	1
Commodity use of marine resources	1.0	1	1	1	1	1
(add others as neccessary)	0.0	0	0	0	0	0
Diversity and inclusion	1.6	2	1	1	2	2
Wage levels and pay equality	2.2	2	3	1	2	3
Training and education	1.8	2	2	2	2	1
The number of unfilled skilled positions	2.0	2	2	2	2	2
(add others as neccessary)	0.0	0	0	0	0	0
Setting Purpose	1.8	1	2	2	3	1
Remuneration policies	2.0	2	1	2	2	3
The process to determine remuneration	1.4	1	1	2	1	2
Legal actions for anticompetitive behaviour, antitrust, and monopoly practices	1.0	1	1	1	1	1
Anticorruption	1.8	2	2	1	2	2
Integration of risks and opportunities	3.0	3	3	3	3	3
(other optional)	0.0	0	0	0	0	0
R&D expenses	3.0	3	3	3	3	3
Social value generated	3.0	3	3	3	3	3
(other optional)	0.0	0	0	0	0	0
Environmental - weight	32%	35%	31%	32%	32%	32%
Social - weight	21%	22%	23%	18%	21%	21%
Governance - weight	30%	27%	29%	32%	32%	32%
Prosperity - weight	16%	16%	17%	18%	16%	16%
Total	100%	100%	100%	100%	100%	100%

Image 7.3. Stakeholder survey example. Source: Author.

Sector Classification Systems

Sector classification systems are good tools when applying materiality. The main ones are ICB, SICS, DJSI, and NACE, but GICS (Global Industry Classification Standard), developed by MSCI and S&P Dow Jones Indices, is the most widely used.[541] Sustainability service providers rely on different systems.

Sectors	Industry Groups (each group breaks into 69 industries and then 158 sub-industries)
Energy	Energy at the industry group level, but equipment and services and oil, gas, and consumable fuels at the industry level.
Materials	Materials at the industry group level, but chemicals, construction materials, containers & packaging, metals & mining, and paper & forest products at the industry level.
Industrials	Capital goods, commercial and professional services, and transportation.
Consumer Discretionary	Automobiles and components, consumer durables & apparel, consumer services, and retailing.
Consumer staples	Food and staples retailing, food, beverage, tobacco, household and personal products.
Health care	Equipment & services, pharmaceutical, biotechnology and life science.
Financials	Banks, diversified financials, insurance.
Information technology	Software and services, hardware and equipment, semiconductors and semiconductor equipment.
Communication services	Telecommunication services, media and entertainment.
Utilities	Utilities at the industry group level, but electric, gas, multi, water utilities, and independent power and renewable electricity producers at the industry level.
Real estate	Equity investment trusts (REIT) and real estate management and development.

Baselines

Establishing baselines as early as possible in their sustainability journey is essential in measuring a company's ESG progress towards its goals and targets.

---

[541] The Global Industry Classification Standard. MSCI. msci.com/our-solutions/indexes/gics

This common reference point enables stakeholders to understand the company's current ESG performance and progress towards its goals. The reference point is typically set in the past, such as in 2009[542] (typical for governments) or 2018 (for businesses).[543] The baseline also helps benchmark the organisation's performance against peers and industry standards.

Updating or refining baselines signifies a dedication to continuous improvement and adapting to evolving standards. However, maintaining stakeholder trust is contingent on transparency. Articulating the reasons for baseline adjustments, detailing methodologies, and explaining the impact on reported data fosters openness, ensuring credibility and accountability in the sustainability reporting process.

Baselines have garnered some controversy for several reasons. Sometimes, they are set too low or manipulated to make progress look better, such as when companies choose a convenient year for comparison. Inaccurate or incomplete data also creates a false impression of progress, even when a company's sustainability performance has not improved. Thus, accurate, reliable data must be used to ensure the validity and effectiveness of sustainability initiatives.

Goals and Targets

To achieve sustainability goals, companies must set ambitious and specific targets aligned with their ESG strategy and grounded in their material ESG risks and opportunities. Goals are broad, long-term, qualitative, and specific to the company's materiality profile and ambition levels. It is essential to understand one's organisation and business, capital structure, cash flow, customers, and other aspects of a business model to identify appropriate levels of ambitions and be realistic about what is achievable.

To achieve its goals and a meaningful impact, good ESG targets are SMART: specific, measurable, achievable, relevant, and time-bound. Industry best

---

[542] Targets and performance. UK Parliament. 2023. parliament.uk/about/sustainability/targets-and-performance
[543] Sustainability reporting guidelines 2021/2022. UK Government. Published 2021. gov.uk/official-documents

practices must be followed and aligned with international environmental goals, climate and environmental science, and ESG standards.

First, set ultimate goals such as being net zero by 2030, achieving biodiversity recovery by 2040, or a specific gender ratio in the workplace by 2030. Then, set interim goals such as reducing car fleet emissions by 50 percent by 2026 or achieving biodiversity recovery in an operational site by 2027. Goals should be short-, medium-, and long-term,[544] where medium-term goals contribute towards reaching the company's long-term goals. However, real action, not only setting goals, is necessary.

Action Plans and Scenarios

Companies need to make action plans to achieve their objectives, which can be done using scenario analysis. Practical action plans include setting clear goals, identifying the necessary steps, assigning responsibilities, establishing timelines, considering obstacles, developing contingency plans, and regularly reviewing and adjusting the plan. Effective communication and collaboration among team members are essential. A clear plan increases accountability, measures progress, and enables effective strategy adjustments.

Scenario planning is beneficial when making action plans to achieve business objectives because it helps prepare for a range of possible future situations. Businesses identify potential risks and opportunities by considering different scenarios and their potential impacts and develop plans to respond accordingly. This allows more flexibility and adaptability in uncertainty, enabling better decision-making and achieving objectives effectively.

Businesses may encounter challenges when setting ambitious sustainability goals. For example, they may find that achieving these goals requires significant investment, such as upgrading industrial equipment and machinery. This leads to a lengthy discussion on the company's financial sustainability, the owners' risk appetite, and group dynamics. As a result, decisions and deliberations may take months or years to finalise, which can delay formulating an

---

544 EFRAG Project Task Force on European sustainability reporting standards (PTF-ESRS). [Draft] ESRS E4 - Biodiversity and ecosystems. Published April 2022. efrag.org/Assets/Download?assetUrl=%2F-sites%2Fwebpublishing%2FSiteAssets%2FED_ESRS_E4.pdf

action plan. Companies must consider the financial implications of their sustainability goals and ensure they have the necessary resources to achieve them.

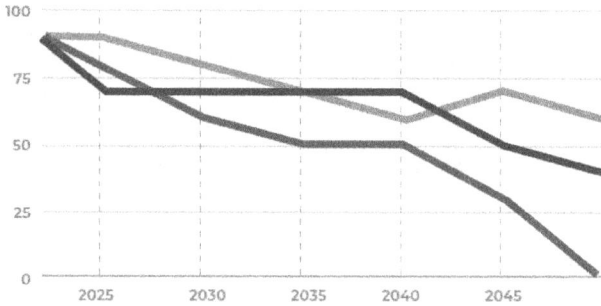

Image 7.4. A hypothetical scenario and optimisation mapping, e.g., net zero by 2050. Source: Author

Sustainability Policies

Sustainability policies help companies make accountable and transparent decisions by setting clear objectives and actions. When policies are integrated into the company's culture, it can lead to better sustainable performance. To make policies, companies should understand their materiality profile and stakeholder views and use standards and frameworks. They should also reflect baselines, targets, and an action plan to achieve them. Once a company has done all this, it can communicate its sustainability efforts to the world. A common pitfall is that policies are statements of regulatory compliance or general good intentions that are so vague as to be impractical and useless.

There is a best-practice framework for designing good corporate policies. It involves defining the company's purpose, values, and priorities, considering legal and regulatory requirements, and engaging with stakeholders. The framework should also align policies with the company's overall business model, core strengths, and strategy, set clear objectives and targets, and provide a plan for implementation, monitoring, and reporting.

Policies must remain relevant, practical, and holistic. This requires reviewing and updating policies regularly to align with the company's ESG performance and sustainability goals. Involving employees, customers, and other stakeholders in the policy design process builds trust, ensures accountability, and enhances the policy's overall acceptance. This policy should be visible to all stakeholders to uphold transparency and responsibility, holistic in a way that avoids purpose washing, where "businesses claim and promote a sense of purpose as a reputational tool to gain market share."[545]

Sustainability Policy Example	
Introduction	Explain the company's business, purpose, and importance.
Environmental	Identify critical issues and how the company will manage material risks and opportunities with key targets and indicators.
Social	
Governance	
Prosperity	
Financing	Explain how long-term goals will be funded.
Reporting	Describe how reports will be made, including guidelines, checks, and how often.
Oversight	Explain who's in charge of ESG indicators, how the company ensures responsibility, and if there are incentives.
Review	Explain how and how often the policy will be reviewed.

Reporting

Reporting on sustainability progress is not only legislated in most cases but required by companies' internal and external stakeholders. It includes positive and negative impacts and progress towards targets and is typically published annually. It exists either as a standalone document or increasingly (and preferably) as part of a general annual report. Authorities require certain organisations to publish sustainability reports, such as those registered on stock exchanges or operating within the EU.[546]

---

[545] Granger A. Research among business leaders warns of 'purpose wash.' Published 18 May 2020. prca.org.uk/ResearchLeadersWarnPurposeWash
[546] Corporate sustainability reporting. European Commission. finance.ec.europa.eu/capital-markets-union-and-financial-markets/company-reporting-and-auditing/company-reporting/corporate-sustainability-reporting_en

The increasing importance of sustainability reporting is apparent when viewing developments over recent decades. As reporting has shifted from primarily voluntary to ever more mandatory, the landscape is evolving rapidly with the increased number of standards, maturing stakeholder demands, and more understanding that this information is as relevant as financial information. Aside from a few countries not included in the report, 96 percent of the world's 250 biggest companies have sustainability reports. This number will grow as regulations for reporting non-financial information increase.[547]

Sustainability reporting should not be a mere "tick-the-box" exercise; it should be taken seriously, approached consistently, and a reliable report produced. Proper reporting ensures accountability and accessibility for external stakeholders to track progress. Reports should be published in a format accessible long-term, like PDF files, to avoid information being easily removed and forgotten.

Companies should prioritise a robust annual reporting process, dedicating ample resources while primarily focusing on investing in fundamental sustainability initiatives. Simultaneously, effective communication with all relevant departments is essential, encouraging timely participation and information sharing on performance and plans.

Sustainability reporting varies across companies, which makes comparisons of ESG or sustainability performance challenging. Each company must report in a way that informs its stakeholders and complies with relevant legislation and regulations. Companies may consult with stakeholders to determine which externalities or impacts are significant. Stakeholders are now demanding information on sustainability risks and opportunities, as the impacts of climate change affect companies' assets, operations, and reputation.[548]

The quality and scope of the reports depend on the standards or frameworks used and the amount of information made public. A 2019 survey showed that

[547] KPMG International. Big Shifts, Small Steps: Survey of Sustainability Reporting 2022. KPMG. Published October 2022. assets.kpmg/content/dam/kpmg/xx/pdf/2022/10/ssr-small-steps-big-shifts.pdf
[548] Bernow S et al. More than values: The value-based sustainability reporting that investors want. McKinsey. Published 7 August 2019. mckinsey.com/capabilities/sustainability/our-insights/more-than-values-the-value-based-sustainability-reporting-that-investors-want

investors could not easily rely on sustainability reports because the variety of frameworks and indicators did not necessarily enable them to make informed decisions. This is why executives and investors want to simplify and reduce the number of frameworks and standards. When investors evaluate sustainability reports, they look for three main characteristics:[549]

- **Materiality:** See previous discussion on materiality and materiality assessments.

- **Consistency:** Sustainability reporting varies greatly, making comparing companies or tracking progress difficult. Companies must invest time in establishing transparent reporting practices and explaining any changes.

- **Reliability:** Reliable sustainability information is essential to avoid allegations of greenwashing and to support progress towards sustainability. Around 97 percent of investors surveyed wished for some degree of third-party audit for sustainability reports, and 67 percent would want to have them audited with the same enthusiasm as financial audits.

Assurances and Audits

Many companies have third-party audits to reassure stakeholders that a company is serious about sustainability. These audits have pros and cons. The main benefit is that it provides an independent assessment of a company's sustainability performance, which helps build trust and identify areas for improvement. Additionally, third-party audits can help benchmark and demonstrate sustainability leadership. Assurance statements might be boring, but they also provide important information.

On the downside, third-party assurance can be time-consuming and expensive, considering internal and external costs. Although assurance methods are uniform between providers, what they assess is not, which can lead to inconsistencies between assurance statements. Ultimately, companies must evaluate

---

[549] Bernow S et al. More than values: The value-based sustainability reporting that investors want. McKinsey. Published 7 August 2019. mckinsey.com/capabilities/sustainability/our-insights/more-than-values-the-value-based-sustainability-reporting-that-investors-want

the potential benefits and drawbacks of third-party assurance or verification and engage with stakeholders to determine the best approach for their ESG performance.

Sustainability assurance requirements vary across reporting frameworks. ISSB doesn't require it, but the company's country of domicile may. SEC's draft climate disclosure rule only needs it for Scope 1 and 2 emissions. EFRAG requires a certain level of assurance that will increase over time, moving from limited assurance to reasonable assurance from 2026 to 2028.[550] [551] Liability in assurances and audits is nuanced and situational, potentially impacting both the auditor, for the accuracy and fairness of their report, and the company, for truthfully representing its sustainability practices, underscoring the complex interplay of accountability in these evaluations.

ADDITIONAL DETAILS: EXAMPLE OF AN ASSURANCE STATEMENT

We have reviewed A-Co's Sustainability Report for 2022, which follows the GRI Standards, using the International Standard on Assurance Engagements (ISAE) 3000. We reviewed the report to confirm that it complies with A-Co's stated sustainability reporting framework. We obtained evidence by performing procedures and concluded that, in our opinion, the sustainability information disclosed in the report is presented in all material respects per A-Co's stated sustainability reporting framework based on GRI. Our opinion is based on our agreed-upon terms and should not be used or relied on by any other parties.

---

[550] KPMG. Comparing sustainability reporting proposals: ISSB, EFRAG and SEC. KPMG. Published November 2022. assets.kpmg/content/dam/kpmg/xx/pdf/2022/06/comparing-sustainability-reporting-proposals-talkbook.pdf
[551] Limited assurance vs reasonable assurance. ICAEW. icaew.com/technical/audit-and-assurance/assurance/process/scoping/assurance-decision/limited-assurance-vs-reasonable-assurance

ESG Scores and Ratings

ESG ratings for sustainability and ESG in credit ratings are separate concepts. Credit ratings are used to determine the creditworthiness of a borrower and are crucial for lenders in setting appropriate interest rates and estimating default probability.[552] ESG information is then used as an additional layer to further estimate a company's credit quality further and focuses on financial materiality and cash flow consequences. It is closely linked to financial risks rather than sustainability risks.[553] Therefore, it is essential to distinguish ESG ratings for sustainability from ESG in credit ratings.

The use of ESG in credit ratings is dynamic and varies between credit rating providers. ESG credit factors are commonly defined as ESG considerations that can impact an issuer's ability and willingness to fulfil its financial obligations. ESG-related rating actions refer to cases where ESG credit factors played a role in modifying a credit rating, credit outlook, or CreditWatch status upwards or downwards. The use of ESG factors in credit ratings has developed somewhat over the last few years and is anticipated to continue developing.

Companies seek sustainability, or ESG, scores or ratings beyond third-party audits to demonstrate their commitment and provide stakeholders with subjective and objective assessments of their ESG impact. These scores can show sustainability leadership, or lack thereof, and attract or discourage investment from ESG-focused investors. Despite potential benefits, obtaining a rating is optional and sometimes controversial due to the emergence of "shadow-ratings" from public data compilations, leading to a "pay to play" scenario. Concerns over cost, resource allocation, and the accuracy of these ratings further complicate companies' decisions on whether to pursue them.

ESG scores and ratings, while aiming to assess ESG performance, face criticism for inconsistency, subjectivity, and difficulty of comparison. Variations arise from different methodologies among agencies, including the emphasis on certain ESG indicators and reliance on public information or easily

---

[552] ESG in credit ratings and ESG ratings. PRI. Published 6 March 2023. unpri.org/credit-risk-and-ratings/esg-in-credit-ratings-and-esg-ratings/11071.article

[553] Ray D. How sustainability risks factor into credit ratings. Nordea. Published 9 November 2022. nordea.com/en/news/how-sustainability-risks-factor-into-credit-ratings

improved metrics over impactful ones. One element is how much weight they give to specific ESG indicators. Despite some of them using the same underlying methodology and pursuing the same objective, they will still generate different results if they rely on different underlying data. Research suggests that the majority of disagreements between ESG ratings are due to such differences.[554]

To address these criticisms, companies and rating providers need to improve transparency and consistency, focusing on the impact of their ESG objectives. With increased regulations on ESG reporting, an audit mechanism must be in place.[555] The EU's proposal to regulate the ESG rating sector in 2022 was not favoured by leading ESG providers, who preferred an industry-supported code of conduct.[556]

In June 2023, the EU presented a proposal for a regulation on transparency and integrity of the ESG rating activities. It aims to improve the reliability, comparability, and transparency of ratings and enhance the quality of information. It, on the other hand, does not aim to harmonise the existing methodologies but solely to increase their transparency.[557] All companies providing ESG ratings that wish to operate in the EU must comply with certain requirements and be authorised by the European Markets Authority (ESMA); noncompliance could lead to fines of up to 10 percent of their annual net turnover. This has caused some uproar among professionals, while others say regulations are long overdue.[558]

Companies must embrace transparency and honesty when disclosing their ESG performance to prevent fraud. They should prioritise meaningful sustainability initiatives over boosting their ESG scores. While ESG reporting is not as regulated as financial disclosure, manipulating ESG scores or ratings

[554] Berg F, Kölben JF, Rigobon R. Aggregate Confusion: The Divergence of ESG Ratings. Review of Finance. Vol 26. Issue 6. November 2022. doi.org/10.1093/rof/rfac033

[555] Emerging Fraud Risks to Consider: ESG. Deloitte. Published July 2022. deloitte.com/us/en/pages/center-for-board-effectiveness/articles/emerging-fraud-risks-to-consider-esg.html

[556] Andrew T. Leading ESG data providers reject EU regulation proposals. ETF Stream. Published 17 August 2022. etfstream.com/news/leading-esg-data-providers-reject-eu-regulation-proposals

[557] Lalucq A. Environmental, Social and Governance (ESG) rating activities: Commission proposal for a Regulation on their transparency and integrity. European Parliament. 23 September 2023. europarl.europa.eu/legislative-train/theme-an-economy-that-works-for-people/file-esg-rating

[558] Meager E. EU's new ESG rating framework will be major overhaul. Capital Monitor. 27 September 2023. capitalmonitor.ai/regions/europe/eus-new-esg-ratings-framework-will-be-major-overhaul

can have significant repercussions. Companies must commit to transparency, disclosures, and continuous improvement to mitigate these risks.

ADDITIONAL DETAILS: TESLA AND CREDIT SUISSE

Tesla was removed from S&P Global's 500 sustainability index due to poor performance in social and governance aspects of the ESG framework. The company faced criticism for deaths related to self-driving cars, poor working conditions, and a lawsuit related to discrimination and harassment.[559] Tesla led the transformation of electrifying the car manufacturing industry, forcing others to follow. Oil companies, arms manufacturers, and similar companies have ticked the necessary boxes and often remain on such indices. Additionally, Elon Musk argued that he may have done more for the environment than anyone else in the world.[560]

Credit Suisse's ESG ratings decreased in 2022 across various rating agencies due to negative governance issues, CEO resignations, financial losses, and poor investment performance. Different rating agencies have varying opinions on the bank's status, with some rating it adequately and others rating it poorly.[561]

Life Cycle Thinking: Value and Supply Chain Management

Companies are responsible for sustainability across their entire supply and value chains, from raw materials to end-of-life. Life cycle thinking involves considering an operation's and product's or service's environmental and social impacts from beginning to end, from raw materials to disposal. This approach

---

[559] Norton L. This is Why Tesla's ESG Rating Isn't Great. Morningstar UK. Published 22 May 2022. morningstar.co.uk/uk/news/221629/this-is-why-teslas-esg-rating-isnt-great.aspx

[560] Dang S. Elon Musk curses out advertisers who left X over antisemitic content. Reuters. 30 November 2023. reuters.com/technology/elon-musk-curses-out-advertisers-who-left-x-over-antisemitic-content-2023-11-29

[561] Mackintosh J. Credit Suisse Shows Flaws of Trying to Quantify ESG Risks. The Wall Street Journal. Published 17 January 2022. wsj.com/articles/credit-suisse-shows-flaws-of-trying-to-quantify-esg-risks-11642435816

helps companies make more sustainable decisions by understanding the impact of their choices on people and the planet. Most of the impact on the environment and natural resources comes from companies' supply chains.[562]

Companies must address these impacts, as unethical practices have been tolerated for too long and more issues are coming up as attention and the spotlight is directed to these issues. Workers' conditions and environmental waste are the most common issues in less-regulated countries. Suppliers may operate where regulations do not exist or are not enforced. At the same time, companies may demand products or services that surpass the supplier's production capacity, leading to heavy overtime and decreased safety.[563]

Failure to consider a product's entire life cycle can lead to unexpected costs and missed opportunities for innovation, cost savings, and reaching customers who value sustainability. In December 2023, a provisional agreement was reached on the new EU Corporate Sustainability Due Diligence Directive (CS3D or CSDDD), which will enforce this approach through fines and compliance orders. The CSDDD poses rules that are set to enter force in 2027 for large companies within the EU regarding potential adverse impacts on the environment and human rights throughout their business chains, both with upstream business partners and downstream activities relating to distribution or recycling.[564]

Ensuring suppliers meet specific standards and requirements helps companies meet ethical and social responsibilities. Germany, for example, implemented a new supply chain act in 2023, which makes large companies responsible for human rights and environmental violations within their supply chain. The CS3D is more extensive than the German regulation and has a broader scope on environmental and social issues that companies must address in their value

---

[562] Bové AT, Swartz S. Starting at the source: Sustainability in supply chain. McKinsey. Published 11 November 2016. mckinsey.com/capabilities/sustainability/our-insights/starting-at-the-source-sustainability-in-supply-chains

[563] Villena VH, Gioia DA. A More Sustainable Supply Chain. Harv Bus Rev. Published 1 March 2020. hbr.org/2020/03/a-more-sustainable-supply-chain

[564] Corporate sustainability due diligence: Council and Parliament strike deal to protect environment and human rights. European Commission. consilium.europa.eu/en/press/press-releases/2023/12/14/corporate-sustainability-due-diligence-council-and-parliament-strike-deal-to-protect-environment-and-human-rights/

chain.[565]

Companies can choose sustainable suppliers or work more closely with existing suppliers to promote sustainability in their supply chain. They should set long-term sustainability goals and encourage their suppliers to do the same.[566] Goals may include recycling more, improving safety, or using renewable energy. They can also involve downstream actors and incentivise consumers with discounts on environmentally friendly products.[567] Collaborating with supply chain partners can drive green innovation strategies because relationships between partners can influence green innovation performance.[568]

Image 7.5. A supply chain. Image: Author

Supplier codes of conduct are policies companies use to inform suppliers about sustainable procurement policies. These codes outline shared prin-

[565] The German Supply Chain Act. Norton Rose Fulbright. Published February 2023. nortonrosefulbright.com/en/knowledge/publications/ff7c1d04/the-german-supply-chain-act

[566] Villena VH, Gioia DA. A More Sustainable Supply Chain. Harv Bus Rev. Published online 1 March 2020. Accessed 28 November 2022. hbr.org/2020/03/a-more-sustainable-supply-chain

[567] Dilmengani C. 7 Ways to Improve Your Supply Chain Sustainability in 2023. AI Multiple. Published 24 january 2022. research.aimultiple.com/supply-chain-sustainability

[568] Yang Z, Lin Y. The effects of supply chain collaboration on green innovation performance: An interpretive structural modelling analysis. Sustainable Production and Consumption. 2020; 23:1-10. doi:10.1016/j.spc.2020.03.010

ciples suppliers should follow, covering human rights, labour rights, and environmental impact. Implementing these codes is often challenging for large companies with complex supply chains. Hence, internal policies, audits, supplier engagements, integration of sustainability criteria, and procurement processes are necessary to ensure their impact. Companies like Nordea Bank and Volvo have supplier codes of conduct that use the UN Global Compact, ILO, and OECD Guidelines for Multinational Enterprises to set obligations and requirements for their suppliers.[569] [570]

A life-cycle assessment (LCA) is a tool that helps companies understand the sustainability impact of their product, service, or operations from "cradle to grave." Companies can make informed decisions and better market their products by identifying areas where negative sustainability impact can be reduced.[571] Strict requirements must be met to use LCAs for marketing, including peer reviews and verifications. Life cycle costing assessments (LCCAs) evaluate a product's total cost over its life cycle, including production, use, and disposal costs. LCCAs can be added to LCAs to provide a more comprehensive assessment of a product's sustainability and economic impacts.

Although LCAs have been criticised, they remain valuable when performed correctly. Criticisms include incomplete or inaccurate data, a lack of standardisation, and little consideration of broader social or environmental concerns. If done correctly, an LCA still has the potential to provide valuable information for decision-making when combined with other methods and approaches. LCAs have four phases and are executed with various tools and databases.[572]

1. **Defining the scope:** The study's intended use and system boundaries are set, and the level of detail required for the LCA, methodology used, assumptions, and limitations are determined.

[569] Nordea. Nordea Supplier Code of Conduct. Nordea. nordea.com/en/doc/nordea-supplier-code-of-conduct-2019.pdf

[570] Volvo Group. Volvo Group supplier code of conduct. Volvo Group. Published 2019. volvogroup.com/content/dam/volvo-group/markets/master/suppliers/our-supplier-requirements/Code-of-conduct.pdf

[571] Life Cycle Assessment - an overview. ScienceDirect Topics. sciencedirect.com/topics/earth-and-planetary-sciences/life-cycle-assessment

[572] ISO 14040:2006(en), Environmental management - Life cycle assessment - Principles and framework. ISO. iso.org/obp/ui/#iso:std:iso:14040:ed-2:v1:en

2. **Inventory analysis:** Data is collected on the inputs and outputs of the system to be analysed, such as raw materials and emissions.

3. **Impact assessment:** The environmental impacts of the system are measured, including climate change, ecological footprint, water footprint, human toxicity, energy footprint, acidification, and more.

4. **Interpretation:** The study results are evaluated to provide relevant conclusions and recommendations for informed decision-making based on the initial LCA goal and scope.

International organisations offer tools for sustainable supply chain management, such as the UN Global Compact's guidance documents (Decent Work Toolkit for Sustainable Procurement, Guide to Traceability, Practical Guide for Continuous Improvement)[573] and the Sustainable Development Report's interactive SDG country progress map.[574]

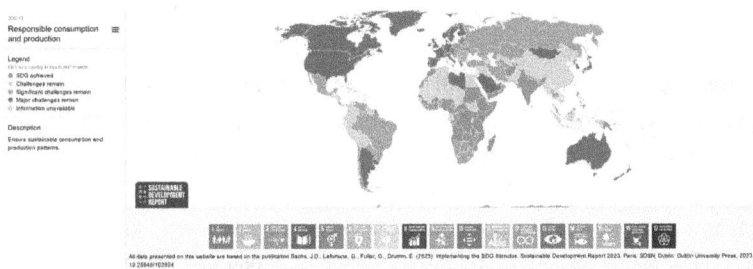

Image 7.6. Value chain mapping using the UN SDGs. Source: The Sustainable Development Report[575]

The Washing Machine: Green and All the Colours of the Rainbow

We often see claims like "sustainable", "natural", "eco-friendly", "organic", "climate neutral", and "ethical" in our daily lives. However, are these phrases

[573] Supply Chain Sustainability. UN Global Compact. unglobalcompact.org/what-is-gc/our-work/supply-chain
[574] Overall score. Sustainable Development Report. dashboards.sdgindex.org/map
[575] Sachs et al. (2022): From Crisis to Sustainable Development: the SDGs as Roadmap to 2030 and Beyond. Sustainable Development Report 2022. dashboards.sdgindex.org/map/goals/sdg12

always used accurately? This is where the term "greenwashing" comes in. It was initially used in the 1960s to describe false environmental claims made by hotels to save costs by reusing towels.[576] Today, "greenwashing" refers to inaccurate or exaggerated claims about sustainability. Prefixes like "pink", "blue", "climate", "social", and "rainbow" can also be used in the same way for specific topics. Here, we use "greenwashing" as an umbrella term to capture all those prefixes.

Greenwashing arises when exaggerated or false environmental claims are made about a product, service, or company for marketing purposes. It poses a reputational and legal risk for companies as it can result in negative publicity, loss of customer trust, and legal action. It also undermines the efforts of companies committed to sustainability, harming the entire industry's credibility. A well-known example is the highly reported Volkswagen emission case, where the results of emission tests were altered, and actual nitrogen oxide emissions were forty times over the allowed limit.[577]

The difference between greenwashing and fraud is not always obvious. Greenwashing is making exaggerated or false environmental claims for marketing purposes, while fraud involves intentionally deceiving consumers or stakeholders for financial gain. Greenwashing can be intentional and unintentional, with companies sometimes making legitimate claims but misleadingly presenting them. Such issues may emerge when internal miscommunication occurs, sometimes due to a disconnect between marketing or PR teams and their sustainability teams.

Some companies mislead customers by cherry-picking parts of their services or products that fit their narrative, using misleading statistics, or simply lying to cover up wrongdoings. The ultimate responsibility for this lies with themselves. Regulators and other stakeholders must hold companies accountable for their sustainability claims. This will empower consumers to make informed decisions and ultimately lead to progress in solving environmental issues. In 2021, the EU Commission found that 42 percent of environmental

---

[576] Orange E, Cohen AM. From Eco-Friendly to Eco-Intelligent. The Futurist. 2010; 44(5):28-32. proquest.com/docview/736165378/abstract/92982016FF0A4E44PQ/1
[577] Hotten, Russel. Volkswagen: The scandal explained. BBC. Accessed 10 Feb 2024. bbc.com/news/business-34324772

claims in sectors like garments and cosmetics were potentially misleading, underscoring the growing issue of 'greenwashing' amid rising consumer demand for eco-friendly products.[578]

Greenwashing is a real risk for companies as investors and other stakeholders hold them accountable for their ESG disclosures.[579] Policies are being developed to address these risks and improve the reliability of financial products.[580] Companies caught greenwashing risk government authorities taking action, such as in the reported case of HSBC, whose ads were banned in the UK. In 2023, the EU proposed a new legislation called the Directive on Green Claims, which outlines how companies should support their environmental claims. It mandates greater transparency and aims to prevent misleading statements.[581]

In a 2023 report looking into 148 instances of greenwashing found that 106 were by banks and financial services companies, increasing by 70 percent globally in a year. The European Banking Federation said the report comprised allegations rather than verified greenwashing. The jump might be due to increased scrutiny of banks and their sustainability commitments rather than deliberate misrepresentation.[582]

Companies such as BP and ExxonMobil have also been publicly accused of greenwashing. ExxonMobil was called out on advertising potential algae biofuels while at the same time having no company-wide net-zero targets. BP was reportedly accused of misleading public consumers in their claims of dedication to low-carbon energy even though BP dedicated only fragments of their operations to the cause. BP is still an oil and gas company with most of their spending going towards fossil fuels.[583]

---

[578] Screening of websites for 'greenwashing': half of green claims lack evidence. ICPEN. Published 29 January 2021.icpen.org/news/1146

[579] Andrews P. Greenwashing and the Mis-Selling of ESG. Nasdaq. Published 24 August 2022. nasdaq.com/articles/greenwashing-and-the-mis-selling-of-esg

[580] ESAs launch joint Call for Evidence on greenwashing. European Banking Authority. Published 15 November 2022. eba.europa.eu/esas-launch-joint-call-evidence-greenwashing

[581] Green claims. European Commission. environment.ec.europa.eu/topics/circular-economy/green-claims_en

[582] Banks behind 70% jump in greenwashing incidents in 2023. Reuters. Published 3 October 2023. reuters.com/sustainability/banks-behind-70-jump-greenwashing-incidents-2023-report-2023-10-03

[583] Robinson D. 10 Companies Called Out For Greenwashing. Earth.Org. Published 17 July 2022. earth.org/greenwashing-companies-corporations/

Using the SDGs misappropriately is called "rainbow-washing" or "SDG-washing." Companies have used the SDGs questionably by claiming to work towards them and presenting this information to stakeholders as if they have operationalised them. In reality, they use SDGs in their reports to create some sense of legitimacy in the eyes of stakeholders, failing to account for minimal—or any—environmental or social performance.[584]

As the sustainability discussion matures, other greenwashing variations have been defined. Greencrowding is built on believing we can hide in a crowd to avoid discovery. Greenlighting occurs when company communications spotlight a mainly green feature to draw attention away from other damaging activities. Greenshifting occurs when companies imply or shift the blame to the consumer and companies change their targets before they are achieved.[585]

ADDITIONAL DETAILS: DEUTSCHE BANK'S DWS

DWS, a German asset management company owned by Deutsche Bank, was reportedly sued for greenwashing allegations in 2022. Investigations for investment fraud were conducted, and the CEO resigned following whistleblower allegations of misleading investors. DWS labelled EUR 459 billion in assets as "ESG-integrated," while the accurate number was around EUR 100-150 billion.[586] This incident was a wake-up call for the industry, highlighting the need for accurate and factual information.

Endnote

In this chapter, which follows the discussion on ESGP, we focused on how companies can holistically integrate these aspects into their business model.

---

[584] Emma GM, Jennifer MF. Is SDG reporting substantial or symbolic? An examination of controversial and environmentally sensitive industries. Journal of Cleaner Production. 2021; 298:126781. doi:10.1016/j.jclepro.2021.126781

[585] Greenwashing is growing increasingly sophisticated, says Planet Tracker. Planet Tracker. Published January 10, 2023.planet-tracker.org/greenwashing-growing-increasingly-sophisticated-says-planet-tracker

[586] Schiffler A. DWS and the Global Crackdown on Greenwashing. Morningstar UK. Published 19 September 2022. morningstar.co.uk/uk/news/226564/dws-and-the-global-crackdown-on-greenwashing.aspx

We have established that integrating ESGP can benefit companies' cash flow, value and reputation if it concentrates on materially significant issues. Nonetheless, recent studies suggest that such integration does not necessarily lead to improved performance if the company's business and financial fundamentals are weak. Therefore, while these business and financial fundamentals should be the primary focus, integrating ESGP considerations is also essential and should never be overlooked.

We have learned that, in general, fostering synergy across departments is often considered more beneficial for companies than working in silos within departments. However, achieving effective synergy can be challenging and may require a supportive organisational culture, effective communication channels, and leadership that encourages collaboration.

As companies embark on integrating ESGP, they must carefully select appropriate frameworks and standards and comprehend the relevant legislation and regulations specific to their industry. Establishing baselines, setting SMART targets, formulating action plans, devising policies, and communicating these efforts to stakeholders are essential steps in this process. Though this journey may be complex and costly, the potential benefits are substantial. However, companies should be vigilant against the pitfalls of superficial compliance, which can lead to greenwashing, and ensure their integration efforts are genuine and impactful.

In the next chapter, we will see that when it comes to sustainability, money really does talk!

CHAPTER EIGHT

Sustainable Finance: Money Talks

This chapter examines why money really does talk when it comes to sustainability. Here, we will examine the basics of sustainable finance, EU regulations, labelled fixed-income financing, transparency and disclosures (allocation and impact), labelled equity, sustainable insurance, pension funds, central banks, and more.

Further, there were many possible ways to construct this chapter, and we concentrated, perhaps disproportionately, on labelled financing. Understanding the nature of the green, social, and sustainability-linked labels can help grasp the broader concepts of sustainable finance and how investors categorise their portfolios. Armed with the additional understanding of previous ESGP chapters, it becomes easier to understand ESG investments and ESG funds, which cover much of the same topics previously discussed.

Sustainable finance exists to support long-term economic growth by channelling financial resources towards climate mitigation and adaptation, nature protection, and social cohesion, and addressing the financial risks posed by the range of ESG issues by integrating ESG criteria.[587] It can channel finances to companies and projects that do bad and make them stop, do less bad and improve them, and do good and create positive impacts. It matters because it aligns investment decision-making and can help advance urgent goals such as the Paris Agreement and the Kunming-Montreal Global Biodiversity Frame-

---

[587] Overview of sustainable finance. European Commission. 2021. finance.ec.europa.eu/sustainable-finance/overview-sustainable-finance_en

work. Further, it recognises that ESG factors are not just ethical concerns but are critical to financial stability and fiduciary duty.

As we move towards ESG 2.0, we must look in the rearview mirror to identify unsustainable financial products and practices. Index provider MSCI has spearheaded a shake-up by stripping thousands of funds of their ESG ratings.[588] Even though most people acted with the best information and not with malice, much has changed and will continue to. Sustainable finance continues to be scrutinised by all stakeholders.

Basics of Sustainable Finance

Sustainable finance has grown significantly, with no single best approach in place. The field is marked by various, often competing, standards and methodologies. While certain practices may dominate temporarily, shifts in the organisations setting these standards—due to mergers, acquisitions, or closures—can change how sustainable investments are classified and carried out.

Financial markets and their subset capital markets are any place or system that provides buyers and sellers the means to trade financial instruments, including bonds, equities, currencies, and derivatives. They can advance sustainable development and unsustainable activities by supporting sovereigns, municipalities, companies, and investors in financing, investments, and capital allocation.

For instance, the world's 60 largest banks contributed USD 669 billion in fossil fuel financing in 2022, which many consider showing a lack of commitment and incentivising unsustainable practices. For comparison, global investments in renewable energy totalled USD 499 billion in the same year.[589] [590] In February 2024, Barclays set an example and publicly announced their plan to halt direct financing of new oil and gas projects and further set a USD 1 trillion

[588] Johnson S. Hundreds of funds to be stripped of ESG rating. Financial Times. Published 24 March 2023. ft.com/content/fc920b7b-ed17-4927-92fe-c238f22725cd
[589] Global landscape of renewable energy finance 2023. IRENA. Published February 2023. irena.org/Publications/2023/Feb/Global-landscape-of-renewable-energy-finance-2023
[590] Banking on Climate Chaos - Fossil Fuel Financing Report 2023. RAN. Published 12 April 2023. ran.org/wp-content/uploads/2023/04/BOCC_2023_vF.pdf

ESG and transition finance target.[591]

Investor groups, such as the Institutional Investors Group in Climate Change, with over 400 members with assets worth over USD 65 trillion (approximately 65 percent of total assets under management globally),[592] are addressing sustainability issues, showcasing the magnitude of the sustainable finance industry.[593]

The distinct perspectives of younger generations and women increasingly shape the evolving landscape of financial markets. Generations from Gen X onwards, including millennials and Gen Z, are redefining investment priorities with a strong emphasis on sustainability and values-driven investing. Concurrently, women, who now control a third of global wealth, are growing their financial influence at unprecedented rates, but they still have a long way to go.[594]

From 2016 to 2019, women's wealth grew annually by 6.1 percent, compared to 4.1 percent for men. The investment decisions of these younger generations and women are informed, purposeful, and increasingly autonomous, challenging traditional norms and biases in the finance sector and suggesting a transformative future, especially for sustainable finance.[595]

Green bonds have been a significant building block in the sustainable finance market by creating a new asset class with a simple name, and some have dubbed it as one of the most successful marketing and branding stunts in recent financial market history.[596] They have gained widespread popularity and support since the first green bond was issued by the World Bank in 2008. They have, despite criticism, remained largely unchanged in practice ever since and

[591] Barclays focuses capital and resources on supporting energy companies to decarbonise. Barclays. Published 9 February 2024. home.barclays/news/press-releases/2024/01/barclays-focuses-capital-and-resources-on-supporting-energy-comp
[592] McIntyre et al. The Tide Has Turned. BCG. Published 15 May 2023. bcg.com/publications/2023/the-tide-has-changed-for-asset-managers
[593] IGCC. About Us. IGCC. Accessed 9 February 2024. iigcc.org/about-us
[594] Gelfand A. The ESG Generation Gap: Millennials and Boomers Split on Their Investing Goals. Stanford Business. Published 10 November 2022. gsb.stanford.edu/insights/esg-generation-gap-millennials-boomers-split-their-investing-goals
[595] Zakrazewski A. et al. Managing the Next Decade of Women's Wealth. BCG. Published 9 April 2020. bcg.com/publications/2020/managing-next-decade-women-wealth
[596] I heard an influential person in sustainable finance say this in public meeting. I'll leave it to you to interpret this in the positive or negative or remain neutral to the comment.

are only growing in popularity. The most interesting about their development is that it was market-based and not regulated, meaning the trust between market actors allowed their growth.

The financial cost of achieving the net-zero transition involves investing USD 275 trillion in physical assets for energy and land-use systems from 2021 to 2050. Annual investments must increase by as much as USD 3.5 trillion to achieve the transition, equivalent to nearly half of global corporate profits in 2020. Considering the USD 5.7 trillion allocated in 2021, an annual investment of USD 9.2 trillion is needed, and most of the investments are required in the next five to ten years. Of the USD 9.2 trillion, private financial institutions may contribute up to USD 3.5 trillion annually between 2022 and 2050, commercial banks USD 2-2.6 trillion, and asset managers, private equity, and venture capital funds may add up to USD 1.5 trillion.[597] [598]

ADDITIONAL DETAILS: GREENIUM

Greenium, a portmanteau of "green premium," describes the higher price investors are willing to pay for sustainable financial products over conventional ones and continues to be debated. For example, instead of the issuer paying a 3.5 percent interest rate (or yield), the investor might agree to a lower 3.4 percent when financing green or sustainable activities.

The issuer would then pay less interest over the lifetime of a bond, and the investor would receive less return. The investor might agree to this because the issuers of green bonds are perceived as less risky and have better creditworthiness. The instrument is perceived as less risky and finances more future-proof assets.[599] [600]

[597] Azoulay M et al. Financing the net-zero transition: From planning to practice. McKinsey. Published 13 January 2023.
mckinsey.com/capabilities/risk-and-resilience/our-insights/financing-the-net-zero-transition-from-planning-to-practice
[598] Krishnan M et al. The net-zero transition: What it would cost, what it could bring. McKinsey. Published January 2023. mckinsey.com/capabilities/sustainability/our-insights/the-net-zero-transition-what-it-would-cost-what-it-could-bring
[599] D'Incau F et al. Identifying the 'greenium'. UNDP. Published 25 April 2022. undp.org/blog/identifying-greenium
[600] Larcker DF, Watts EM. Where's the greenium? Journal of Accounting and Economics. 2020; 69(2):101312. doi:10.1016/j.jacceco.2020.101312

> [601] Investors are willing to pay for sustainable investments but don't pay extra for more impact, i.e., it doesn't matter if an investment saves 0.5 or 5 tonnes of CO2. Emotional, rather than calculated, valuation drives their willingness to pay, according to a 2022 study.[602]

While these figures represent significant investments, unchecked climate change could, as previously mentioned, cost the global economy USD 178 trillion over fifty years or up to 50 percent of global GDP between 2070 and 2090, making the financial investments necessary for a net-zero transition all the more crucial to consider.[603] This underscores the economic imperative of investing in net-zero transitions not just as a cost but as a vital step to avoid far greater losses and secure a sustainable future.

Developing countries, or the Global South, require significant investment volumes to support sustainable development and address climate change. The annual investment gap of USD 4 trillion for them to achieve the SDGs by 2030 signifies that investors from developed markets need to allocate more funds to these countries.[604] Lack of information, reputational, and ESG risks prevent institutional investors from allocating larger amounts to the Global South and emerging and frontier markets. Therefore, improving data infrastructure, especially for disclosing ESG,[605] in addition to de-risking mechanisms and increasing the size of investments or ticket sizes.

While innovative initiatives offer promising starts to tackling environmental challenges, market forces alone cannot overhaul the vast physical infrastructure required for change. Almost half of the emission reductions needed by

[601] Löffler KU, Petreski A, Stephan A. Drivers of green bond issuance and new evidence on the "greenium." Eurasian Econ Rev. 2021; 11(1):1-24. doi:10.1007/s40822-020-00165-y
[602] Heeb F et al. Do Investors Care about Impact? The Review of Financial Studies. 2023; 36(5):1737-1787. doi:10.1093/rfs/hhac066
[603] Deloitte research reveals inaction on climate change could cost the world's economy USD 178 trillion by 2070. Deloitte. Published 23 May 2022. deloitte.com/global/en/about/press-room/deloitte-research-reveals-inaction-on-climate-change-could-cost-the-world-economy-us-dollar-178-trillion-by-2070.html
[604] World Investment Report 2023. UNCTAD. Published 5 July 2023. unctad.org/publication/world-investment-report-2023
[605] Drivers of investment flows to emerging and frontier markets. Mobilist. Published 14 June 2022. mobilistglobal.com/research-data/drivers-of-investment-flows-to-emerging-and-frontier-markets

2050 for net-zero targets hinge on technologies not yet commercially viable,[606] necessitating significant government action to foster innovation and investment in clean energy. Blended financing is a strategy which combines public funds and private investments to support sustainability projects in the Global South. For example, public funds are used to de-risk investments, attracting private capital to projects that might otherwise seem too risky or not profitable enough.[607]

A Marshall Plan-like effort may be essential to catalyse these investments. The Marshall Plan was a US-sponsored program implemented following the end of World War II, granting USD 13 billion in foreign aid to European countries that had been physically and economically devastated by World War II so they could be rebuilt. In the context of a sustainable future, we could see the creation of such a plan at a much larger scale from the Global North for investing not only in itself but in the Global South to put us on an accelerated and much faster-paced path to a sustainable future.

As of 2022-2023, the sustainable finance landscape has encountered challenges amidst higher interest rates and inflation. Marking a clear deviation from the earlier optimistic projections in a near-to-zero-interest-rate environment—a situation we might never experience again. It is becoming evident that transitioning to a sustainable future will likely be more costly than anticipated.

According to one study, the cost of electricity for solar photovoltaics and onshore wind will increase by 11 to 25 percent, respectively, with financing costs accounting for one-third.[608] Ørsted, an energy company, experienced a 25 percent drop in shares following the announcement of write-downs of its offshore wind project in the US, which was due to supplier delays, problems negotiating US tax credits, and an increase in interest rates.[609] This underscores the

[606] World Energy Outlook 2021: Executive summary. IEA. Accessed 9 February 2024. iea.org/reports/world-energy-outlook-2021/executive-summary

[607] Blended finance: How setting up a financial intermediary can accelerate sustainable development. WEF. 3 April 2023. weforum.org/agenda/2023/04/blended-finance-financial-intermediation-can-accelerate-sustainable-development

[608] Schmidt TS, Steffen B, Egli F, Pahle M, Tietjen O, Edenhofer O. Adverse effects of rising interest rates on sustainable energy transitions. Nature Sustainability Vol II. September 2019. nature.com/articles/s41893-019-0375-2.epdf

[609] Ørsted shares crash by 25 percent on US problems. The Local. 31 August 2023. thelocal.dk/20230831/orsted-shares-crash-by-25-percent-on-us-problems

need to re-evaluate future projections, risk pricing, and acceptable returns and highlights that fundamental finance principles still steer the direction of sustainability projects despite potential environmental objectives.

ADDITIONAL DETAILS: (PREFIX) INVESTING

Below is a list of sustainable finance's most common investing strategies. Although the below concepts have different prefixes, they all involve ESG considerations but with different weights on financial returns, risk management, and impact.

- Sustainable investing refers to a range of practices in which investors aim to achieve financial returns while promoting long-term sustainable development.
- Impact investing, a USD 1.2 trillion market,[610] is to positively impact society or the environment beyond making profits,[611] following principles described later in labelled financing and the EU taxonomy, for example. It is also known as thematic investing.[612] The Gates Foundation is one of the most well-known impact investment funds. Engine No. 1, a hedge fund backed by BlackRock, recently won three board seats at ExxonMobil, aiming to reduce Exxon's carbon footprint and increase shareholder value. Exxon's share price rose substantially after years of underperformance following the campaign.[613]
- ESG investing evaluates corporate behaviour and screens investments based on a company's ESG score. It aims to choose companies that perform better than others. The ESG evaluation complements traditional financial analysis by identifying a company's ESG risks and opportunities. ESG investing's

[610] GIIN. Sizing the Impact Investing Market. GIIN; 2022. thegiin.org/assets/2022-Market%20Sizing%20Report-Final.pdf
[611] Impact Investing Marketing Map. UNPRI. Published 20 August 2018. unpri.org/thematic-and-impact-investing/impact-investing-market-map/3537.article
[612] ESG, SRI, and Impact Investing: What's the Difference? Investopedia. 28 November 2022. investopedia.com/financial-advisor/esg-sri-impact-investing-explaining-difference-clients
[613] Phillips M. Exxon's Board Defeat Signals the Rise of Social-Good Activists. The New York Times. Published 9 June 2021. nytimes.com/2021/06/09/business/exxon-mobil-engine-no1-activist.html

primary objective is financial returns.[614] Some investors look for companies with high ESG scores, while others focus on specific industries.[615]

Responsible investing means considering ESG indicators when deciding where to invest and trying to affect companies or assets through active ownership, so investing in both good ESG performance and laggards. Socially Responsible Investing (SRI) has focused on positive social impacts and ethical criteria in recent years. Investors can have different goals. Some prioritise financial return and only consider ESG issues, while others aim for both financial returns and positive impact.[616]

THE OUTPERFORMANCE OF SUSTAINABLE FINANCE INVESTMENTS

A meta-study of over 2,200 individual studies from 1970 to 2014 found strong support for the business case for ESG investing, with approximately 90 percent of studies revealing a nonnegative relationship between ESG factors and corporate financial performance (CFP). More significantly, the vast majority of these studies report positive outcomes.[617]

Morningstar has also found that ESG investments often outperform, suggesting that investors may not have to choose between sustainability and profit.[618]

[614] Krull P. ESG Investing Is Not Sustainable Investing. Forbes. Published 4 January 2022. forbes.com/sites/peterkrull/2022/01/04/esg-investing-is-not-sustainable-investing

[615] ESG 101: What is Environmental, Social and Governance? MSCI. msci.com/esg-101-what-is-esg

[616] What is responsible investment? PRI. 2023. unpri.org/introductory-guides-to-responsible-investment/what-is-responsible-investment/4780.article

[617] Friede et al. Journal of Sustainable Finance & Investment 5(4):210-233. Published October 2015. doi: 0.1080/20430795.2015.1118917

[618] Kolostyak S. Do ESG Stocks Outperform? Morningstar UK. Published 11 August 2021. morningstar.co.uk/uk/news/214249/do-esg-stocks-outperform.aspx

UN PRI—Responsible Investing

Responsible investing aims to reduce risks and promote responsible behaviour through active ownership. At the same time, sustainable investing seeks to create a positive long-term ESG impact alongside financial returns. According to the UN Principles for Responsible Investment (PRI), approaches to responsible investing are typically a combination of ESG incorporation and active ownership.

PRI encourages sustainable and socially responsible investment. Since its inception in 2006, more than 5,350 investors have signed up for the PRI's six principles as of 2024. By voluntarily committing to them, investors showed their intention to integrate ESG indicators into their decision-making and ownership practices, driving sustainability in the investment community.[619] The PRI also provides a framework to measure progress and engage with companies for sustainable business practices.[620]

1. **ESG Integration:** Factor ESG indicators into investment analysis, policies, and training, and evaluate managers based on ESG due diligence.

2. **Active Ownership:** Actively engage companies on ESG indicators, collaborate with others, and develop engagement capabilities.

3. **ESG Disclosure:** Ask companies to disclose ESG information and integrate it into financial reports and standards.

4. **Industry Promotion:** Promote the Principles in "request for proposals" (RFPs), communicate ESG expectations, and support relevant tools, policies, and regulations.

5. **Collaboration:** Work with others to address emerging ESG issues, share resources, and develop collaborative initiatives.

6. **Reporting:** Disclose how we integrate ESG indicators, report progress on implementing the Principles, and communicate with beneficiaries.

---

[619] About the PRI. PRI. unpri.org/about-us/about-the-pri
[620] UN PRI. What are the Principles for Responsible Investment? PRI. unpri.org/about-us/what-are-the-principles-for-responsible-investment

By incorporating ESG indicators into their investment process, investors can better evaluate risks and opportunities and make more informed decisions. A 2022 study of investors in Europe, the Middle East, and Africa found that, in over two-thirds of cases, ESG issues uncovered during due diligence could be a deal breaker.[621]

ADDITIONAL DETAILS: AUSTRALIA'S CLIMATE RISK TO ITS SOVEREIGN DEBT

In 2020, the Australian government published a plan to achieve net-zero emissions by 2050. The plan suggested that not responding to climate change could cause sovereign debt costs to triple. There is a growing Greenium for sovereign issuers who issue green bonds, causing a penalty for climate laggards.[622] A report by FTSE Russell in 2021 suggested that if the world's efforts to fight climate change faced major obstacles, Australia would default on its sovereign debt by 2050.[623]

Responsible Ownership and Shareholder Engagement

Shareholder engagement means companies and investors discuss ESG to create long-term value. This requires a cooperative dialogue based on mutual understanding and a better flow of information, leading to deeper ESG knowledge and more informed investment decisions in the future.[624] Investors have several ways to communicate with the companies they own shares in, subject to legal restrictions and corporate governance policies, such as attending

---

[621] 2022 EMA ESG Due Diligence Study. KPMG. kpmg.com/xx/en/home/insights/2022/11/esg-due-diligence-in-deals.html
[622] Australia's long-term emissions reduction plan. Australian Government. dcceew.gov.au/climate-change/publications/australias-long-term-emissions-reduction-plan
[623] Anticipating the climate change risks for sovereign bonds. FTSE Russell. Published 16 June 2021. ftserussell.com/research/anticipating-climate-change-risks-sovereign-bonds-part-2
[624] Gond JP et al. How ESG engagement creates value for investors and companies. PRI; 2018. unpri.org/download?ac=4637

shareholder meetings. Replacing CEOs, shorting stocks, and other more aggressive communication methods are not discussed here, but they certainly are options.

Proxy voting, another form of communication, is when shareholders give their voting rights to others to make company decisions on their behalf. Shareholders can delegate their voting rights to proxy voting services, advocacy groups, or other shareholders on ESG issues, such as electing directors and approving transactions. It encourages companies to implement ESG practices. By supporting ESG-related proposals, shareholders support sustainable practices and encourage companies to follow ESG values.

Activist investors in the ESG space have positively impacted companies' ESG practices and investment outcomes. They tend to focus on companies with high ESG ratings, which have less room for improvement and may have fewer growth opportunities. Companies with a good ESG track record are also more likely to accept suggestions from investors.[625] This highlights the need for more shareholder engagement with companies with poor ESG performance.

EU-Driven Sustainable Finance

The EU has emerged as a leader in sustainable finance due to its strong commitment to promoting sustainability and combating climate change and has taken several steps to advance sustainable finance. This includes establishing the Sustainable Finance Action Plan and adopting the EU taxonomy, which sets out the criteria for determining whether economic activities are environmentally sustainable. The EU has also implemented regulations under the SFDR, requiring asset managers and institutional investors to disclose how they integrate ESG indicators into their investment decisions.

The need to transition to a more sustainable and resilient economy is the key factor in the EU's leadership in sustainable finance while addressing the risks and opportunities of climate change. The EU's regulatory and taxonomy approach is in the vanguard today. Still, several other countries, such as Co-

---

[625] Barko T, Cremers M, Renneboog L. Shareholder Engagement on Environmental, Social, and Governance Performance. J Bus Ethics. 2022; 180(2):777-812. doi:10.1007/s10551-021-04850-z

lombia, South Africa, Georgia, Russia, China, and South Korea, have already implemented such regulations or taxonomies. Hong Kong, UAE, the UK, Chile, and Mexico are also developing similar initiatives of their own.[626]

The UK has declared the development of a classification system for environmentally sustainable economic activities, named the UK Green Taxonomy.[627] The Association of Southeast Asian Nations (ASEAN) has also established its taxonomy, ASEAN Taxonomy for Sustainable Finance.[628] Discussions have also taken place in Canada, where there is a need to create a classification system to determine what is sustainable.[629]

The EU's sustainable finance standards could be problematic for emerging and developing countries. These countries often do not have the resources or ability to meet the EU's complex sustainability standards, or the EU's standards do not match the priorities of countries in the Global South. This creates a financial system where some countries are excluded from large pools of sustainable finance, making it harder for them to achieve sustainable development goals and deepen existing inequalities.

The emergence of different taxonomies worldwide has the potential for interoperability and increasing international mobilisation of sustainable capital. However, there is a risk that it may cause more complexity and confusion for international companies, mainly if the criteria differ. Therefore, future taxonomies must develop shared objectives, definitions, and principles to compare sustainable economic activities easily. Some countries are already trying to harmonise different taxonomies. For example, China and the EU have announced a joint initiative, known as the Common Ground Taxonomy-Climate Change Mitigation (CGT), to do just that.[630]

---

[626] Thür D. Green Taxonomies Around the World: Where Do We Stand? ECOFACT. Published 1 November 2022. ecofact.com/blog/green-taxonomies-around-the-world-where-do-we-stand

[627] UK Green Taxonomy—GTAG. Green Finance Institute. greenfinanceinstitute.co.uk/programmes/uk-green-taxonomy-gtag

[628] ASEAN Taxonomy. ASEAN Capital Markets Forum. Published 13 June 2022. theacmf.org/initiatives/sustainable-finance/asean-taxonomy

[629] Redefining ESG: A green taxonomy for Canada? Refinitiv. Published 30 January 2020. refinitiv.com/perspectives/future-of-investing-trading/redefining-esg-a-green-taxonomy-for-canada

[630] First green bonds under the new China-EU Common Ground Taxonomy (CGT). Crédit Agricole Corporate & Investment Bank. Published 12 July 2022. ca-cib.com/pressroom/news/first-green-bonds-under-new-china-eu-common-ground-taxonomy

CHAPTER EIGHT

EU SFDR—Disclosures and Articles 6, 8, and 9 Funds

The EU's Sustainable Finance Disclosure Regulation (SFDR) is a key component of the European Commission's flagship Sustainable Finance Action Plan. The action plan aimed to fulfil three goals: first, steer the flow of capital towards sustainable investments; second, incorporate environmental considerations into the financial system; and third, deploy these policies on a pan-European scale.[631] Since becoming applicable in 2021, the key aim of the SFDR has been to prevent the greenwashing of financial products and financial advice in the EU by mandating the disclosure of more sustainability-related information.[632]

The impact of the SFDR is significant as it mandates and levels the playing fields with financial market participants who offer sustainable investment products to provide information about their sustainability at a firm and product level. SFDR aims to ensure transparency and accountability of sustainable investments and prevent misleading information, thereby empowering investors to make investment choices in line with their sustainability goals.[633] Therefore, companies will no longer be able to present an environmentally responsible public image or overstate the sustainability characteristics of investment funds; instead, they must categorise and disclose them.

The SFDR, like the CSRD, requires organisations that fall within certain criteria to disclose certain information such as sustainability risk policy, sustainability risk remuneration policy, and principal adverse impact (PAI) of an investment. PAI is intended to help investors comprehend the negative effects of an investment on the environment and society in a standardised format. Organisations shall further disclose how they plan to address and prioritise negative impacts. The SFDR regulation outlines 14 key indicators to enhance standardisation: nine indicators related to the environment and five covering social factors.

---

[631] High-Level Expert Group on sustainable finance (HLEG). European commission. Published 28 October 2016. finance.ec.europa.eu/publications/high-level-expert-group-sustainable-finance-hleg_en
[632] What is the Impact of the EU Sustainable Finance Disclosure Regulation (SFDR)? S&P Global. Published 1 April 2021. spglobal.com/marketintelligence/en/news-insights/blog/what-is-the-impact-of-the-eu-sustainable-finance-disclosure-regulation-sfdr
[633] Sustainability-related disclosure in the financial services sector. European Commission. finance.ec.europa.eu/sustainable-finance/disclosures/sustainability-related-disclosure-financial-services-sector_en

The regulation establishes criteria for defining a sustainable investment and categorises funds or other financial products into Articles 6, 8, or 9 based on how they fare according to these criteria. The criteria consider the investment to have an environmental or social purpose, not cause significant harm to the environment or society, and have good governance principles. On top of assessing all relevant financial risks, financial actors and advisors should include sustainability risks that might have a relevant material negative impact on the return of an investment or advice in their due diligence processes.[634]

Article 6	Article 8	Article 9
Brown funds disclose ESG risks but don't aim for sustainability or positive impact. As a side note, "brown" to describe polluting companies and funds can be seen as perpetuating harmful racial attitudes[635] and that concept may disappear soon.	Light Green funds promote positive ESG impact and require good governance practices. Noncompliant opportunities may be excluded.	Dark Green funds aim for positive ESG impact without harming other sustainability goals. They go beyond Article 8 requirements.

EU Taxonomy and EU Green Bond Standard

The EU taxonomy, a key regulation in sustainable finance, promotes sustainable investments and aims to support the transformation of the EU economy to meet its Green Deal objectives, including its ultimate climate-neutrality goal by 2050. By providing a common language for sustainable investments, the EU taxonomy underscores the role of financial markets, which helps direct capital towards sustainable projects and prevents greenwashing.

Fundamentally, it lists economically sustainable activities and has six objec-

---

[634] Regulation (EU) 2019/2088 of the European Parliament and of the Council of 27 November 2019 on sustainability-related disclosures in the financial services sector. EUR-Lex. 27 November 2019. eur-lex. europa.eu/legal-content/EN/TXT/?uri=celex%3A32019R2088

[635] Mackenzie K. In Climate Terms, 'Brown' Is Always Bad—and That's a Problem. Bloomberg. Published 24 July 2020. bloomberg.com/news/articles/2020-07-24/in-climate-change-brown-is-always-bad-perpetuating-racism

tives against which to assess investments.[636] Companies are adjusting to report compliance with the EU taxonomy, and some companies were surprised to discover that not all their activities qualified.[637] The EU has created tools to help them align with the EU Taxonomy.[638] It is expected that best practices emerge in a few reporting cycles.

There are three criteria an economic activity must meet under the EU taxonomy to qualify as sustainable or "green." Firstly, make a **significant contribution** to one of the six objectives listed by complying with the technical screening criteria. The EU develops these criteria to evaluate if an activity meets an environmental objective. This prevents companies from simply claiming alignment with the EU taxonomy and ensures a significant contribution to its objectives. The six objectives are:

1. Climate change mitigation

2. Climate change adaptation

3. The sustainable use and protection of water and marine resources

4. The transition to a circular economy

5. Pollution prevention and control

6. Protecting and restoring biodiversity and ecosystems

The second criterion, **does no significant harm (DNSH),** means the activity should not harm the other five environmental objectives while contributing to at least one of them. A narrow focus on carbon emissions and climate change should be avoided, and consideration should also be given to other environmental aspects, such as biodiversity.[639] Reducing emissions, for example, should not significantly harm biodiversity.

---

[636] EU taxonomy for sustainable activities. European Commission. finance.ec.europa.eu/sustainable-finance/tools-and-standards/eu-taxonomy-sustainable-activities_en

[637] Ramel E, Gamsjäger L. A first look at companies' EU Taxonomy reporting. Nordea. Published 5 May 2022. nordea.com/en/news/a-first-look-at-companies-eu-taxonomy-reporting

[638] EU Taxonomy Calculator. European Commission. ec.europa.eu/sustainable-finance-taxonomy/wizard

[639] Humphreys N. What does it mean to "Do No Significant Harm"? Bloomberg. Published 4 March 2022. bloomberg.com/professional/blog/what-does-it-mean-to-do-no-significant-harm

The third criterion, **meeting minimum social safeguards,** means the activity should align with "the OECD Guidelines for Multinational Enterprises and UN Guiding Principles on Business and Human Rights, including the ILO Declaration on Fundamental Rights and Principles at Work, the eight ILO core conventions and the International Bill of Human Rights."[640]

One of the most political and controversial subjects the EU tackled when formulating the taxonomy framework was whether nuclear energy and gas activities should be classified as sustainable energy sources. It was heavily debated during the passage of the legislation, with just over half of the votes in favour of classifying them as sustainable, given that they fulfil several conditions specific to these activities.[641] The European Commission is being sued by environmental campaigners and NGOs such as Greenpeace, Client Earth, and WWF, who have announced that they will challenge the decision in the European Court of Justice.[642]

[640] EU Technical Expert Group on Sustainable Finance. Taxonomy: Final Report of the Technical Expert Group on Sustainable Finance. European Commission; 2020. finance.ec.europa.eu/system/files/2020-03/200309-sustainable-finance-teg-final-report-taxonomy_en.pdf

[641] Hancock A. EU parliament votes to designate gas and nuclear as sustainable. Financial Times. Published 6 July 2022. ft.com/content/0df04289-1014-406e-81c7-1e4a6b1ea5bc

[642] Rankin J. EU faces legal action after including gas and nuclear in 'green' investments guide. The Guardian. April 18.theguardian.com/environment/2023/apr/18/eu-faces-legal-action-gas-nuclear-green-investments-guide-european-commission

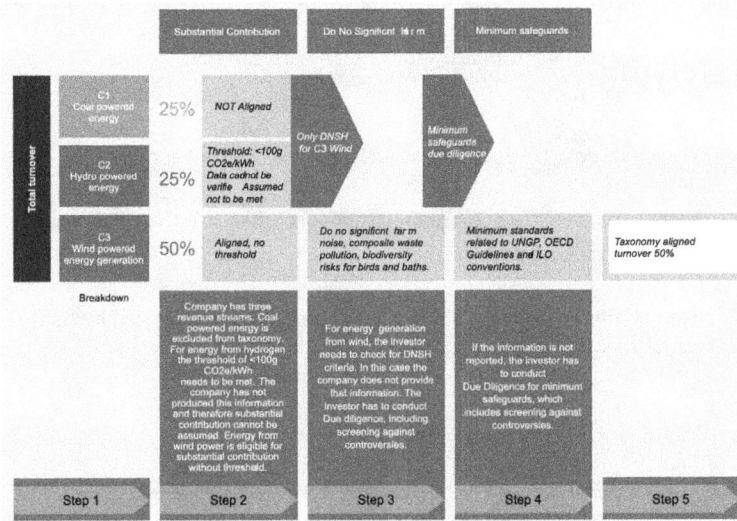

Image 8.1. Applying the taxonomy showing 3 economic activities. Source: EU TEG[643]

Another sustainable finance tool in the EU toolbox is the EU Green Bond Standard (EUGBS) adopted in October 2023. This tool better defines green bonds and what they should be financing in line with the technical screening criteria of the EU taxonomy. While similar to the ICMA's GBP, the EU implemented the standard to create uniformity among member states as a gold standard for green bonds.[644] GBP and EUGBS differ because GBP provides recommendations, while EUGBS imposes requirements. GBP outlines categories for green projects, while EUGBS uses the EU taxonomy to determine if the economic activity is green.[645] Under the EUGBS, four core components are required.

[643] EU Technical Expert Group on Sustainable Finance (EU TEG). March 2020. Accessed 12 February 2024. finance.ec.europa.eu/system/files/2020-03/200309-sustainable-finance-teg-final-report-taxonomy_en.pdf

[644] European green bond standard. European Commission. finance.ec.europa.eu/sustainable-finance/tools-and-standards/european-green-bond-standard_en

[645] EU Technical Expert Group on Sustainable Finance. TEG Report Proposal for an EU Green Bond Standard. European Commission; 2019. finance.ec.europa.eu/system/files/2019-06/190618-sustainable-finance-teg-report-green-bond-standard_en.pdf

1. **Taxonomy aligned:** Bonds should align with sustainable economic activity standards.

2. **Transparency:** Detailed reporting is required on financing use.

3. **External review:** Reviewers should be accredited to ensure EU regulation and taxonomy compliance.

4. **Supervision:** Reviewers need to be registered and supervised by ESMA for investor and market protection.[646]

Labelled Fixed-Income Financing

Labelled financing refers to funding projects, assets, and operations classified or labelled as Green, Social, Blue, Sustainability-Linked, Transition or any mix of those then labelled as sustainable. This market is sometimes called GSSSB, i.e., green, social, sustainability, sustainability-linked, and the B meaning bonds. However, I would like B to stand for blue, deserving its own label, given the increased interest in water and ocean-related activities and financing.

Other labels exist, which are variations of these main labels and generally follow their principles. They include Orange, created for the Global South and mainly focuses on financing gender equality, Rhino, which finances the increase of rhinos in Africa, and green Sukuks, Shari'ah-compliant securities backed by a specific pool of assets, and more. New labels may appear in the future, and some may fade away.

---

[646] European green bond standard. European Commission. finance.ec.europa.eu/sustainable-finance/tools-and-standards/european-green-bond-standard_en

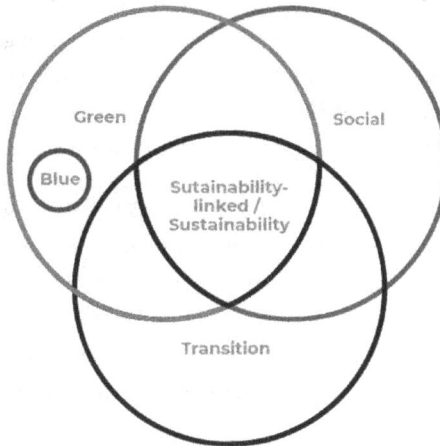

Image 8.2. The interrelation between Green, Blue, Social, Sustainability-linked, and Sustainability labels. Source: Author

Fixed income refers to an investment that provides a regular and predictable income stream over a specified period, typically through interest payments. Examples of fixed-income instruments include government and corporate bonds, certificates of deposits, preferred stocks, and mortgage- and asset-backed securities. In the case of bankruptcy, fixed-income investors are typically paid before common stockholders.

Companies, assets, and projects financed with labelled financing are intended to increase positive impacts, reduce negative impacts, mitigate risks, and, in general, contribute positively towards a sustainable future. Each financed project has risks, opportunities, and value chain issues and impacts that investors expect issuers to manage through policies, systems, and processes to mitigate negative impacts. Looking at green or any other label in isolation is increasingly difficult, as most projects and assets have environmental and social impacts. Therefore, in green bond issuances, for example, social and governance risks and impacts are increasingly considered, and vice versa for social bonds.

Labelled financing has experienced year-on-year growth, surpassing USD 1 trillion in issuance before declining by 23 percent in 2022. That was the first-ever decline in sustainable bond volume, attributed to a challenging macroeconomic environment and increasing interest rates, impacting global fixed-income markets. Nevertheless, the Nordic bond market grew by 3 percent during the same period, with green issuances driving the growth.[647] The total sustainability bond market is expected to exceed USD 900 billion in 2023, but not exceeding the total market size from when it peaked in 2021.[648]

It is projected to grow moderately in 2023 and 2024. Still, any growth and potential decline will depend heavily on the global interest rates and macro-economic conditions. Even though all labels are projected to increase, green will continue to dominate, mainly because of the Paris Agreement, Net Zero, energy transition, and biodiversity commitments globally—this will also depend heavily on how sovereigns act as they are behind large movements in the GSSSB market.

Social bonds experienced a sharp increase in allocated capital in recent years in response to the Covid-19 pandemic highlighting the urgency of social needs in society.[649] The market value for green bonds has grown to dominate the sustainable finance market. It has grown exponentially since its inception in 2008 and has expanded into a USD 2 trillion market in 2023.[650] There was a Sustainability Linked Bonds (SLB) issuance boom in recent years, with SLB issuance reaching over USD 100 billion in 2021, up from USD 9 billion the year before.[651] The market shrank by 25 percent in 2022, however, with the likely culprit being increased scrutiny of KPIs and ambitions and hence, credibility, forcing market players back to the SLB drawing board.

The International Capital Market Association (ICMA) has issued various voluntary guidelines and principles on green, social, sustainability-linked, and

[647] Ray D, Mylläri S. Sustainable finance markets: 2022, a year in charts. Nordea. Published 9 February 2023. nordea.com/en/news/sustainable-finance-markets-2022-a-year-in-charts

[648] Cochelin P, Popoola B, Sugrue D. Global Sustainable Bonds Issuance To Exceed 900 Billion. S&P Global. 14 September 2023. spglobal.com/esg/insights/featured/special-editorial/global-sustainable-bonds-2023-issuance-to-exceed-900-billion

[649] Baas D, Ho J. Navigating sustainable bond opportunities. Allianz. Published 15 November 2022. allianzgi.com/en/insights/outlook-and-commentary/navigating-sustainable-bond-opportunities

[650] Green and Social Bond Funds Impact Report 2022. Goldman Sachs Asset Management. Published 16 October 2023. gsam.com/content/dam/gsam/pdfs/international/en/articles/2023/green-and-social-bond-funds-impact-report-2022.pdf

[651] Murphy D. What are sustainability linked bonds and how can they support the net-zero transition? World Economic Forum. Published 11 November 2022. weforum.org/agenda/2022/11/cop27-sustainability-linked-bonds-net-zero-transition

sustainability financing to promote transparency and integrity in sustainable finance. In addition, it published a Climate Transition Finance Handbook as additional guidance for those seeking to utilise their climate transition strategy.[652] The Climate Bond Initiative has developed a standard to determine if financed projects align with the goals of the Paris Agreement, and the Chinese Green Bond Endorsed Project Catalogue provides criteria for green projects.[653]

The Principles

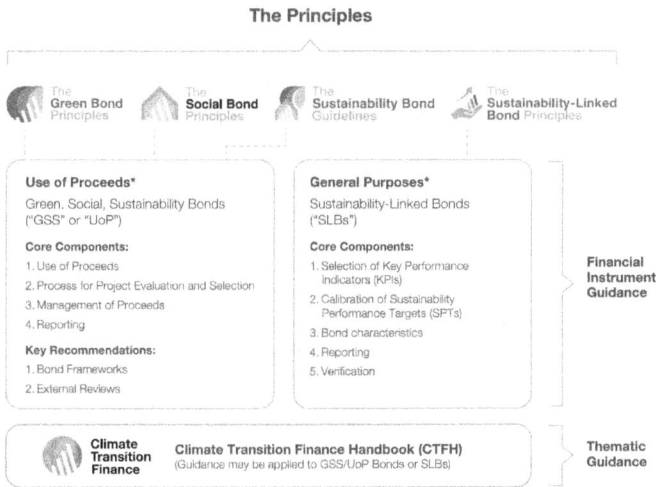

Under the GBP, SBP and SBG, an amount equal to the net bond proceeds is dedicated to financing eligible projects (Use of Proceeds Bonds) while under the SLBP, proceeds are primarily for the general purposes of an issuer in pursuit of identified KPIs and SPTs Sustainability-Linked Bonds). A bond that combines SLB and Use of Proceeds features should apply guidance for both types of bonds.

Image 8.3. An overview of the bond principles from ICMA. Source: ICMA[654]

Emerging regulations are intended to provide greater clarity, harmonisation, and decreased risk of greenwashing on sustainable debt instruments. In reality, they sometimes create confusion and considerable workload on all ends of a transaction. Examples include the EU taxonomy and EU Green Bond Standard (EUGBS), which determine the extent to which green bond projects, for example, are considered sustainable or green. According to the ICMA, 98

---

[652] The Principles, Guidelines and Handbooks. ICMA. icmagroup.org/sustainable-finance/the-principles-guidelines-and-handbooks

[653] Baas D, Ho J. Navigating sustainable bond opportunities. Allianz. Published 15 November 2022. allianzgi.com/en/insights/outlook-and-commentary/navigating-sustainable-bond-opportunities

[654] Green Bond Principles, p.9. ICMA. June 2021. Accessed 12 February 2024. icmagroup.org/assets/documents/Sustainable-finance/2022-updates/Green-Bond-Principles_June-2022-280622.pdf

percent of all global sustainable bonds in 2021 aligned with its principles and guidelines, with a total value of more than USD 998 billion.[655]

When creating a green bond, the issuer usually devises a "framework" outlining the financing and project details to create a labelled financial instrument. An independent party then reviews or gives a (second) opinion of the framework. In the framework, the issuer essentially forms her or his first opinion, and the investors or lenders form their (third) opinion, potentially adding a (fourth) opinion of verifiers. Anyone outside of the transaction can make up their (fifth) opinion on how sustainable the instrument is. While it is possible for an issuer to self-label, it is increasingly unacceptable in the financial market. In 2021, 86 percent of green bonds added to the Climate Bonds database had external reviews; most bonds without reviews originated in the US and China.[656]

Labelled instruments can finance general operations and equity investments, e.g., one company purchasing the equity of another company to either own it as a subsidiary or fully merge the two. When equity can be labelled as green, the equity in question, representing the underlying business, must be defined as a "pure player." The "pure player" definition has developed over the last several years; no hard and fast definition is in place, and it will continue to evolve. Typically, being a "pure player" means that 90 percent or more of the revenue is derived from sustainable products with a caveat that the other 10 percent is not from "dirty" or unethical products.[657] [658]

Issuing labelled financial instruments can be more expensive. This is due to internal and external costs, alongside additional requirements for transparency and reporting, coming on top of traditional costs such as underwriting and legal fees. The extra cost comes with its perks: issuers can access a larger investor base, improve sustainability efforts, enhance communication (e.g.,

[655] ICMA. Sustainable bonds based on GBP, SBP, SBG and SLBP in 2021. ICMA. icmagroup.org/assets/documents/Sustainable-finance/GBP-infographic.pdf

[656] Sustainable debt. Climate Bonds Initiative. 2021. climatebonds.net/files/reports/cbi_global_sot-m_2021_02h_0.pdf

[657] Bloomberg Barclays MSCI Global Green Bond Index. MSCI. Published 24 June 2021. msci.com/documents/10199/242721/Barclays_MSCI_Green_Bond_Index.pdf

[658] Climate Bonds Releases Updated Green Bonds Methodology. Climate Bonds Initiative. Published 6 July 2022. climatebonds.net/2022/07/climate-bonds-releases-updated-green-bonds-methodology

between treasury and sustainability teams), and boost their reputation, although a greenium is not guaranteed.

There is some discrepancy between the labelled financing market and the abundance of corporate sustainability standards and regulations, e.g. CSRD and ESRS in Europe and GRI, which directly affects various aspects of companies' sustainability activities and reporting and, hence, ESG integration by investors. I believe they have not yet been comprehensively integrated into labelled financing, particularly in how issuers are assessed, potential or real impacts of projects' evaluated, and general use of language. Achieving a more unified language and approach across the board remains important.

Labelled Financing Framework Based on the Green Bond Principles (GBP)

Labelled financing applies to financing or refinancing eligible projects meeting specific criteria outlined in a framework. The framework helps organisations issue sustainable financial instruments and communicate their sustainability goals to stakeholders. The framework can apply to different types of sustainable financing, including green, social, blue, and transition financing. The aim is to integrate sustainability considerations into financial decision-making systematically. However, sustainability-linked financing may require a different structure, as discussed.

	Framework description (adapted and simplified from GBP)
Introduction	Provide information about the company, its sustainability goals, and risk management.
Use of proceeds	Clearly state how bond proceeds will be used, including refinancing plans.
Project categories	Ensure that projects financed through the bonds align with environmental and social objectives.
Process for asset evaluation and selection	Communicate who takes decisions, governance around the financing, and relevant information about managing social and environmental risks.
Management of proceeds	Track net proceeds appropriately and exclude certain types of financing, such as gambling, fossil fuels, tobacco, and pornography.

Reporting	Provide annual updates on the use of proceeds, including a list and description of funded projects and expected impact.

Green Financing

Overall, green financing is essential in promoting sustainability and addressing climate change. The ICMA's Green Bond Principles (GBP) outline what types of projects are considered green, although those categories are indicative rather than definitive. The EU has established the EU Green Bond Standard, which is aimed to be the "gold standard" for green bonds. It aligns with the EU Taxonomy and aims to provide a common definition of green for investors and non-financial players.

Issuers ought to include the five environmental objectives of the GBP in their framework: mitigation, adaptation, natural resource conservation, biodiversity conservation, and pollution prevention and control. Green standards or certifications should be referred to when selecting projects. It is essential to grasp the entire impact across the value chain comprehensively. This involves evaluating both the physical and transition risks and considering the life cycle impact of the financed activities.

Green bonds garner praise for creating a new asset class and criticism for not addressing broader environmental impacts. A company emitting significant GHGs can issue a green bond dedicated to fostering biodiversity while doing nothing to address their emissions that contribute to climate change.[659] Practices, regulations, and standards have evolved, with increasing measures being implemented to mitigate risks in green bond issuances, though challenges persist.

---

[659] Wilkes T, Furness V. Explainer: Decoding COP27: the many shades of green bonds. Reuters. Published 9 November 2022. reuters.com/business/cop/decoding-cop27-many-shades-green-bonds-2022-11-09

Green Financing Examples (simplified)			
Project category	Example projects	Project category	Example projects
Renewable energy	Offshore wind farm, solar farm, nuclear plant, and hydropower.	Sustainable water and wastewater management	Sewerage systems, wastewater treatment plants, and water purification and recycling systems.
Energy efficiency	Energy efficient lighting systems, energy infrastructure and grid updates, and smart thermostats.	Terrestrial and aquatic biodiversity	Restoration of degraded lands, sustainable forest management, and river restoration.
Pollution prevention and control	Air pollution system installation, plastic waste reduction programs, and vapour recovery units.	Clean transportation	Renew vehicle fleet with EVs, public transportation systems, and installation of charging stations.
Environmentally sustainable management of living natural resources and land use	Restoration of degraded forests, reducing GHG from farming, and biodiversity protection and improvement.	Climate change adaptation	Coastal protection infrastructure, drought-resistant crops, and data infrastructure for early warning systems.
Circular economy adapted products, production technologies, processes, certified eco-efficient products	Reusable packing systems, textile recycling, and waste reduction and resource efficiency.	Green buildings	Sustainability certified (e.g., BREEAM, LEED), energy-efficient, and net-zero buildings.

ADDITIONAL DETAILS: THE FIRST GREEN BOND(S)

A report by the IPCC in 2007 showed a clear link between climate change and human activities, leading Swedish pension funds to become interested in incorporating environmental products into their portfolios. In partnership with SEB, a Swedish bank, the World Bank issued the first green bond in 2008. It aimed to finance climate-related projects to help fight global warming. The bond had a six-year maturity, an Aaa/AAA rating, and paid 0.25 percent higher interest rates than Swedish government bonds.[660] The World Bank created the Green Bond Principles alongside the bond issuance. It defined the scope of eligible projects and best practices for collaboration.[661] [662] This World Bank Green Bond is generally considered the first, although some friendly debate has occurred between that and the European Investment Bank's (EIB) climate awareness bond, which relied on a different structure.[663] Both institutions state they issued the first green bond.

Blue Financing

Blue finance refers to financing marine and ocean-based projects and activities that have positive environmental and economic impacts and contribute to the sustainable use of the ocean and water resources. Historically categorised under the green label, it is growing into its own label. Blue finance targets positive impacts such as reducing plastic pollution, upholding labour rights at sea, and ensuring sustainable fishing and farming practices, but also firmly

[660] World Bank and SEB partner with Scandinavian Institutional Investors to Finance "Green" Projects. World Bank. Published 6 November 2008. worldbank.org/en/news/press-release/2008/11/06/world-bank-and-seb-partner-with-scandinavian-institutional-investors-to-finance-green-projects
[661] 10 Years of Green Bonds: Creating the Blueprint for Sustainability Across Capital Markets. World Bank. Published 18 March 2019. worldbank.org/en/news/immersive-story/2019/03/18/10-years-of-green-bonds-creating-the-blueprint-for-sustainability-across-capital-markets
[662] From Evolution to Revolution: 10 Years of Green Bonds. World Bank. Published 16 November 2018. worldbank.org/en/events/2018/11/16/from-evolution-to-revolution-10-years-of-green-bonds
[663] Climate Awareness Bonds. EIB. eib.org/en/investor-relations/cab/index.htm

excludes practices harmful to the marine environment, such as destructive fishing, pollution, and activities threatening wildlife.[664]

The urgency to protect our oceans and harness their potential for sustainable development has never been more critical. The ocean remains an untapped reservoir of opportunity, pivotal for its ecological significance and vast potential to bolster global prosperity. The benefits of ocean-based investments, spanning across conserving mangrove habitats, scaling up offshore wind production, decarbonising international shipping, and sourcing ocean-based proteins, significantly outweigh the costs. With a projected net benefit of USD 8.2 to 22.8 trillion from a USD 2.0 to USD 3.7 trillion investment over three decades, underscoring a striking benefit-cost ratio and the importance of blue financing.[665]

Demand has outstripped supply since the first blue bond was issued in 2018, partly due to the market's lack of standardised issuing of blue bonds. According to the UN Environment Programme Finance Initiative (UNEP FI), investors sometimes fund activities in harmful industries such as deep-sea mining, which might not be their intention.[666] Recognising these challenges, stakeholders' growing commitment to refine and standardise blue financing, thereby nurturing a market that, while still in its infancy, shows promise for substantial growth akin to its green predecessors.

Global standardisation is coming. The ICMA, together with the International Finance Corporation (IFC), a member of the World Bank Group, UN Global Compact, UNEP FI, and the Asian Development Bank (ADB), developed and released a global practitioner's guide for bonds to finance the sustainable blue economy in September 2023.[667] Before this, issuers relied on guidelines such as the IFC's guidance for financing the blue economy, building on the GBP

[664] Recommended Exclusions for Financing a Sustainable Blue Economy. UNEP FI. Published June 2021. unepfi.org/publications/turning-the-tide-recommended-exclusions

[665] Konar M, Ding H. A Sustainable Ocean Economy for 2050: Approximating Its Benefits and Costs. Ocean Panel. Published May 2022. oceanpanel.org/wp-content/uploads/2022/05/Ocean-Panel_Economic-Analysis_FINAL.pdf

[666] Azizuddin K. Indian blue bond mining provisions draw market scepticism. Responsible Investor. Published 23 August 2022. responsible-investor.com/indian-blue-bond-mining-provision-draws-market-scepticism

[667] New Guidance on Blue-Themed Bonds to Help Unlock Finance for a Sustainable Ocean Economy. ICMA. Published 6 September 2023. icmagroup.org/News/news-in-brief/new-guidance-on-blue-themed-bonds-to-help-unlock-finance-for-a-sustainable-ocean-economy

and GLP[668] and the UNEP FI Sustainable Blue Economy Finance Principles, which set ocean-specific standards to guide banks, insurers, and investors investing in blue projects.[669]

Blue Financing Examples (simplified)			
Project category	Example projects	Project category	Example projects
Water supply	Clean water treatments, rehabilitation of existing water infrastructure, and desalination.	Ocean-friendly chemicals and plastic-related sectors	Prevention of runoff chemical and plastic waste, reduction or replacement of phosphate- or nitrogen-based synthetic fertilisers, and recycled or reused plastics for manufacturing.
Water sanitation	Water treatment infrastructure and wastewater treatment.	Sustainable shipping and port logistics sectors	Ballast and bilge water treatments, black and greywater treatments, and oil spill prevention.
Ocean-friendly and water-friendly products	Aquatic environment-friendly household products and low carbon and biodegradable packaging materials.	Fisheries, aquaculture, and seafood value chain	Land-based aquaculture, pharmaceutical and cosmetic algae, and biorefineries.
Marine ecosystem restoration	Insurance products, information systems, and restoration techniques.	Sustainable tourism services	Certified tourism in marine conservation areas and marine visitor centres.
Offshore renewable energy production	Offshore energy facilities, wind, solar, tidal, wave, or ocean thermal energy farms.		

[668] International Finance Corporation. Guidelines Blue Finance. International Finance Corporation. Published January 2022. ifc.org/content/dam/ifc/doc/mgrt/ifc-guidelines-for-blue-finance.pdf?-MOD=AJPERES&CVID
[669] The principles. UNEP FI. unepfi.org/blue-finance/the-principles

ADDITIONAL DETAILS: FIRST SOVEREIGN AND CORPORATE BLUE BONDS

The Seychelles created the first sovereign blue bond in 2018 to finance marine projects, raising USD 15 million. The aim was to protect marine areas, improve fisheries governance, and develop the blue economy in one of the world's biodiversity hotspots.[670]

In 2021, Brim, an Icelandic seafood company, issued one of the first corporate blue bonds, raising EUR 16.7 million. Its framework covered traditional green categories such as eco-efficient and circular economy products, renewable energy, and pollution prevention and control but with a higher focus on maritime and ocean impact. According to Brim's impact report, the bonds helped avoid 1,157 tCO2e emissions.[671]

Social Financing

As the name indicates, social financing focuses on projects and assets that contribute to social justice and the well-being of society and on defined target populations. A target population usually consists of marginalised groups, individuals living in poverty, unemployed, women, people with disabilities, children, and more.[672] Social KPIs often include workforce diversity and gender equality, which are easy to measure. Sustainable procurement can also be a KPI, considering environmental and social factors in procurement decisions. Social targets should include global supply chains and issues like working conditions and pay.

The ICMA's Social Bond Principles (SBP) outline what types of projects are

[670] Seychelles launches World's First Sovereign Blue Bond. World Bank. Published 29 October 2019. worldbank.org/en/news/press-release/2018/10/29/seychelles-launches-worlds-first-sovereign-blue-bond

[671] Brim hf. Sustainable Financing. Brim hf. brim.cdn.prismic.io/brim/1f390906-89f7-4336-921c-f303aa667ec7_Brim+sustainable+bonds+framework.pdf

[672] ICMA. Social Bond Principles. ICMA. Published June 2021. icmagroup.org/assets/documents/Sustainable-finance/2022-updates/Social-Bond-Principles_June-2022v3-020822.pdf

social. They provide issuers with guidance on the key components involved in launching a credible social bond, thereby helping investors by promoting the availability of information necessary to evaluate the positive impact of their social bond investments. Social finance funds broad objectives such as education, healthcare, inequality, and poverty projects. The ILO social finance programme promotes decent work and social justice.[673]

The EU had begun developing a social taxonomy to improve transparency on the social aspects of sustainability. It aimed to provide shared, comprehensible definitions of what a socially sustainable activity, directing capital flows to activities that promoted human rights and improved living and working conditions, among others.[674]

It proved less straightforward than hoped for and was postponed indefinitely in the middle of 2022 due to political disagreements over what should be included. In 2023, a group of European financial institutions and industry associations called for it to be put back on the EU's agenda to ensure a positive contribution to social goals and a fair and just transition towards climate neutrality.[675]

Criticism of social bonds includes the difficulty in measuring their true impact or seeing immediate outcomes. While some social investments might provide traditional returns, some might not have immediately obvious benefits due to a lack of data that measures the desired outcome.[676] Often, the goal is to improve the quality of the community by reducing its dependency on government assistance such as welfare, which in turn has a positive impact on the community's economy.[677]

---

[673] ILO. Social Finance - Annual report 2021. ILO; 2022. ilo.org/wcmsp5/groups/public/---ed_emp/documents/publication/wcms_851884.pdf

[674] What is the European Union's social taxonomy for sustainable finance? BBVA. Published 1 April 2022. bbva.com/en/sustainability/what-is-the-european-unions-social-taxonomy-for-sustainable-finance

[675] Gambetta G. European financial institutions call for social investment framework. Responsible Investor. Published 12 October 2023. responsible-investor.com/european-financial-institutions-call-for-social-investment-framework

[676] Social Impact Bond (SIB): Definition, How It Works, and Example. Investopedia. Published 12 April 2022. investopedia.com/terms/s/social-impact-bond.asp

[677] Guide to Socially Responsible Investments. Investopedia. Published 21 November 2022, investopedia.com/terms/s/sri.asp

Social Financing Examples (simplified)

Project category	Example projects	Project category	Example projects
Affordable basic infrastructure	Improve water and waste management, transportation, and energy systems.	**Employment generation, including SME financing**	Support micro-businesses run by low-income individuals, elderly people, and female entrepreneurs.
Access to essential services	Build and improve schools and health-care centres and offer financial services to underserved populations.	**Food security and sustainable food systems**	Create new farms, teach sustainable agricultural practices, and improve small-scale producer productivity.
Affordable housing	Provide affordable housing, low-interest loans, and rental projects.	**Socioeconomic advancement and empowerment**	Improve education for underserved populations, housing finance systems, and support senior social integration.

Sustainability-Linked Financing

Sustainability-linked bonds (SLBs) and loans (SLLs) incentivise borrowers to achieve predetermined sustainability performance targets.[678] Unlike green, social, and blue finance, SLBs/SLLs are based on performance and linked to ESG targets. They offer more flexibility in how to use funds and allow companies outside of traditionally green industries to access sustainable finance and a more comprehensive range of investors.[679]

SLBs have focused mainly on carbon-emissions-related KPIs, but social and environmental topics are interconnected. Most issuers choose two to four KPIs that combine environmental and social indicators, such as GHG emissions reduction and gender ratios at the management level. Sustainability performance targets (SPTs) are then set under each KPI.

---

[678] Murphy D. What are sustainability-linked bonds and how can they support the net-zero transition? WEF. Published 11 November 2022. weforum.org/agenda/2022/11/cop27-sustainability-linked-bonds-net-zero-transition

[679] Chase M. Simplifying Sustainable Finance—Explaining Green Bonds... Sustainalytics. Published 5 November 2021. sustainalytics.com/esg-research/resource/corporate-esg-blog/simplifying-sustainable-finance-green-loans-vs-green-bonds-vs-sustainability-linked-loan-and-more

The strength of the KPI and the ambitiousness of the SPT may then be determined by whether it is categorised as advanced or highly ambitious. The KPI strength is assessed through its sustainability alignment and materiality. The SPT ambition is determined by comparing it to historical performance, science, and peers. Issuers need to have credible strategies for these topics and robust environmental commitments to access capital that rewards sustainable performance.[680] In 2023, the LSTA (Loan Syndications and Trading Association) published the first draft guidance for SLLs, focused on US practice.[681]

Following are the main guidelines for SLBs and SLLs and also serve as a structure for a framework describing sustainability-linked financing.[682, 683]

1. **Indicator selection:** Choose industry-specific and measurable indicators that can be verified externally and included in sustainability reports.

2. **Sustainability-performance targets (SPT) calibration:** Set realistic and ambitious targets for each KPI before bond issuance that align with scientific or official benchmarks.

3. **Bond/Loan characteristics:** Document whether KPIs meet SPTs and consider potential events impacting their calculation.

4. **Reporting:** Annually report KPIs and SPTs in an accessible way and explain how performance affects bond/loan structure.

5. **Verification:** Third parties should verify KPIs and performance in annual reports.

With SLB issuance comes the risk of greenwashing and setting hollow goals

---

[680] Social KPIs Matter, Setting Meaningful Indicators for Sustainability-Linked Finance. CommDev. 8 February 2023. commdev.org/publications/draft-for-discussion-social-kpis-matter-setting-meaningful-indicators-for-sustainability-linked-finance

[681] LSTA published drafting guidance. LSTA. Published 21 February 2023. lsta.org/news-resources/lsta-publishes-sll-drafting-guidance

[682] ICMA. Sustainability-Linked Bond Principles. ICMA. Published June 2020. icmagroup.org/assets/documents/Regulatory/Green-Bonds/June-2020/Sustainability-Linked-Bond-Principles-June-2020-171120.pdf

[683] LSTA. Sustainability Linked Loan Principles. LSTA. Published March 2022. lsta.org/content/sustainability-linked-loan-principles-sllp

for companies to access capital.[684] Companies have taken advantage of flexible financing tools, which raises concerns about greenwashing. A study from 2022 found that most SLBs worth over USD 70 billion were tied to weak, irrelevant, or already achieved climate targets.[685]

Around a third of SLB issuers aren't on track to meet their targets. At the time of writing and as reported, Enel SpA, a top issuer in the USD 250 billion SLB market, risks a trigger event as it looks highly unlikely to meet its key emission goal on its USD 11 billion SLBs, causing investors to brace themselves for a wave of trigger events as a result.[686] Researchers found that SLBs were being issued at a significant premium for issuers, even when not meeting their set goals, resulting in lower cost capital.[687]

This causes concern for the market as the use of SLBs continues to expand, particularly among issuers with different maturity levels regarding their sustainability approach. Harmonisation is crucial to maintaining the market's integrity. There must be a shared assessment approach to KPI materiality and the ambitiousness of targets to ensure investor confidence and achieve the desired impact over time.[688]

ADDITIONAL DETAILS: NORDEA'S SUSTAINABILITY-LINKED LOANS ISSUANCE INNOVATION

Nordea Bank has created a new framework using green bonds to fund SLLs, which allows them to capture a larger pool of sustainable lending. The framework is designed to fund highly sustain-

---

[684] Murphy D. What are sustainability linked bonds and how can they support the net-zero transition? World Economic Forum. Published 11 November 2022. weforum.org/agenda/2022/11/cop27-sustainability-linked-bonds-net-zero-transition

[685] Rocha PA et al. Empty ESG Pledges Ensure Bonds Benefit Companies, Not the Planet. Bloomberg. Published 4 October 2022. bloomberg.com/news/features/2022-10-04/greenwashing-enters-a-22-trillion-debt-market-derailing-climate-goals

[686] Ritchie G. Top issuer in $250 billion ESG bond market risks trigger event. Bloomberg. Published 20 October 2023. bloomberg.com/news/articles/2023-12-11/cop28-uae-s-presidency-floats-reduction-of-fossil-fuels-by-2050

[687] Kölbel JF, Lambillon AP. Who Pays for Sustainability? An Analysis of Sustainability-Linked Bonds. SSRN. Published 12 January 2022. doi:10.2139/ssrn.4007629

[688] Mylläri SM, Ray D. Sustainability linked bonds, a status check. Nordea. Published 3 March 2022. nordea.com/en/news/sustainability-linked-bonds-a-status-check

able projects aligned with relevant KPIs, actively reducing GHG emissions and mitigating climate change. Companies participating in the framework can receive a discount on interest paid once they meet the set goals rather than paying a premium.[689]

Sustainability-Linked Examples (simplified)			
Issuer	Bancolombia[690]	Norsk Hydro[691]	Sunny Optical Technology[692]
Region	LATAM	Nordics	Asia
- KPI 1 - Target - Baseline	The number of individuals accessing credit increased by 531% by 2025 1.5 million underserved low-income individuals given access to credit 2021 baseline	Scope 1 and 2 absolute GHG emissions intensity 30% reduction by 2030 and 10% by 2050 2018 baseline	Scope 1 and 2 absolute GHG emissions intensity 20% reduction by 2025 2021 baseline
- KPI 2 - Target - Baseline	CO_2 financed emissions reduction intensity 0,0238-tonne CO_2/COP million 2021 baseline	Postconsumer scrap aluminium recycling capacity (tonnes) Increase green sourcing and produce metal with a lower carbon footprint to 660,000 tonnes by 2025 2021 baseline	n/a

[689] Nordea issues innovative bond to fund sustainability-linked loans. Nordea. Published 14 September 2022. nordea.com/en/news/nordea-issues-innovative-bond-to-fund-sustainability-linked-loans
[690] Sustainability Linked Financing Framework. Bancolombia. Published September 2022. grupobancolombia.com/wcm/connect/9ce29fd5-a988-412d-80b8-16d2879539c6/SLB+Framework.pdf
[691] Green and Sustainability-Linked Financing Framework 2022. Norsk Hydro. Published 2022. hydro.com/Document/Doc/Green%20and%20Sustainability-Linked%20Financing%20Framework.pdf?docId=584561
[692] Sustainability-Linked Financing Framework. Sunny Optical Technology. Published December 2022. https://www.sunnyoptical.com/webfile/temps/20230104841029284.pdf

Transition Financing

Transition financing emerged in 2017 as a form of funding for projects that contribute to a sustainable future and want to transition towards net zero but cannot get funding under the other, more traditional labels.[693] [694] To avoid greenwashing concerns and to help investors avoid companies giving a false impression of transitional activities, a common requirement is that the borrower has a credible 1.5°C transition plan in line with the Paris Agreement.[695] Examples of projects are aviation fuel reduction, decarbonisation projects, and retrofitting transportation fleets or buildings to make them more energy efficient.

The Climate Bonds Initiative (CBI) published a white paper that defines transition financing and establishes a framework for the transition label. To prevent greenwashing, the CBI outlines five transition principles.[696] The ICMA's 2020 Climate Transition Finance Handbook provides issuers additional guidance with suggested disclosures that are less comprehensive than GBP and SLBP. The recommendations include having a clear transition strategy aligned with the 1.5°C goal, disclosing efforts to reduce carbon emissions, setting interim targets, and demonstrating a broader sustainability strategy that addresses environmental and social impacts, contributing to the UN SDGs.[697]

There is no universal definition of transition finance, nor is there a consensus on the acceptable minimum degree of transition required.[698] This may be why the financial market seems to have favoured sustainability-linked products to

[693] Transition bonds: Could 2023 be the year we see them take off? Environmental Finance. Published 20 February 2023. environmental-finance.com/content/the-green-bond-hub/transition-bonds-could-2023-be-the-year-we-see-them-take-off.html

[694] NZBA Transition Finance Guide. UNEP FI. Published October 2022. unepfi.org/wordpress/wp-content/uploads/2022/10/NZBA-Transition-Finance-Guide.pdf

[695] OECD. OECD Guidance on Transition Finance. OECD. Published 3 October 2022. oecd.org/environment/cc/policy-highlights-oecd-guidance-on-transition-finance.pdf

[696] Climate Bonds Initiative. Financing credible transitions. Climate Bonds Initiative. Published September 2020. climatebonds.net/files/reports/cbi_fincredtransitions_final.pdf

[697] Climate Transition Finance Handbook. ICMA. 2020. icmagroup.org/assets/documents/Regulatory/Green-Bonds/Climate-Transition-Finance-Handbook-December-2020-091220.pdf

[698] Tandon A. Transition Finance: Investigating the State of Play: A Stocktake of Emerging Approaches and Financial Instruments. OECD; 2021. doi:10.1787/68becf35-en

finance transition activities.[699] Transition bonds' popularity is uncertain,[700] and this label may soon fade out. A clear definition could encourage the market to finance transition and help create instruments that incentivise better performance in reducing emissions.

The EU taxonomy's definition might help transition financing develop further by defining transitional activities as activities for which there are no technologically and economically feasible alternatives but that support the transition to a climate-neutral economy consistent with limiting temperature rise to 1.5°C. Transition bonds represented USD 3.5 billion in 2022, an increase from USD 1 billion in 2019. They still represent by far the smallest share in the GSSSB market.[701]

Transparency and Disclosures: Allocation and Impact

Reporting validates the credibility and authenticity of labelled instruments when addressing specific sustainability issues. Generally, reporting on labelled instruments is divided into allocation and impact reporting, usually in one document. Sustainability-linked instruments involve KPI reporting. These reports then provide investors with information on the tangible sustainability benefits of their investment. Because no monitoring exists for issuing labelled instruments, reporting is essential to provide insights for investors and the market about the activities under the issued framework.

Allocation reporting: Discloses how sustainable investment proceeds are used. This helps investors know how their money supports the sustainability ambitions set out in the framework.

Impact reporting: Reports on funded projects or assets' actual or expected sustainability impact. This assesses their effectiveness in achieving objectives.

[699] Webb D. The death of transition bonds. Responsible Investor. Published 29 March 2022. responsible-investor.com/the-death-of-transition-bonds

[700] Transition bonds: Could 2023 be the year we see them take off? Environmental Finance. Published 20 February 2023. environmental-finance.com/content/the-green-bond-hub/transition-bonds-could-2023-be-the-year-we-see-them-take-off.html

[701] Sugrue D, Popoola B. Sustainable Bond Issuance Will Return To Growth In 2023. S&P Global; 2023. spglobal.com/_assets/documents/ratings/research/101572346.pdf

In 2015, a group of Multilateral Development Banks (MDBs) created a handbook, Harmonized Framework for Impact Reporting. This widely used guide provides principles and recommendations for impact reporting for green projects under GBP categories. The framework outlines sector-specific guidance, references, and templates, as well as core principles, indicators, and recommendations for impact reporting.[702] In a 2021 study, 66 percent of leading green bond investors stated that a third party should audit impact reports, compared to only 20 percent in 2020, signifying that third-party verification is becoming necessary.[703]

Currently, the consistency and quality of post-issuance reporting vary greatly. This makes comparability and data aggregation difficult. Issuers report on the proceeds allocation but omit the actual output and outcome metrics. Increasing consistency in this area will demonstrate the actual impacts of sustainable debt instruments to investors.[704] The ICMA provides resources and guidance on impact and allocation reporting.[705]

---

[702] ICMA. Harmonised Framework for Impact Reporting. ICMA. Published June 2022. icmagroup. org/assets/documents/Sustainable-finance/2022-updates/Harmonised-Framework-for-Impact-Reporting-Green-Bonds_June-2022v2-020822.pdf

[703] Green Bond Funds - Impact Reporting Practices 2021. Environmental Finance. environmental-finance.com/assets/files/reports/green-bond-funds-impact-reporting-practices-2021.pdf

[704] Baas D, Ho J. Navigating sustainable bond opportunities. Allianz. 15 November 2022. allianzgi.com/en/insights/outlook-and-commentary/navigating-sustainable-bond-opportunities

[705] Databases - Guidelines and mapping. ICMA. icmagroup.org/sustainable-finance/impact-reporting/databases-guidelines-and-mapping

Example of Allocation and Impact Reporting (simplified)					
Project category	Actual project	Share of total issuance	Allocated amount	Impact	Additional information
Green financing Renewable energy Lenovo[706]	Solar energy	1.3%	USD 8.1 m	920 MT CO$_2$e of GHG emissions avoided annually	Solar hot water facilities in Beijing and solar electric generation plants in Hefei, Wuhan, and Morrisville, North Carolina.
Social financing Affordable housing Morgan Stanley[707]	Affordable housing	99.7%	USD 996.5 m	47,737 affordable housing units 123,762 beneficiaries and USD 151 m tenant cost savings	This project supports families and individuals across the US who faced housing cost challenges after the pandemic.
Blue financing Fisheries, aquaculture, and seafood Íslandsbanki[708]	Eco efficient, MSC-certified seafood processing plants	9.2%	EUR 11.9 m	8,000 tonnes of sustainable seafood produced	Akraborg, a recipient of the financing, has become one of the world's largest canning companies for fish liver, which would otherwise be unsuitable for traditional cod liver oil production.

[706] Green bond post issuance report. 2022. Lenovo. investor.lenovo.com/en/sustainability/Green%20 Bond%20Post%20Issuance%20Report%2020221213.pdf

[707] Social Bond Impact Report. 2022. Morgan Stanley. morganstanley.com/content/dam/msdotcom/en/ assets/pdfs/Morgan_Stanley_2022_Social_Bond_Impact_Report.pdf

[708] Allocation and Impact report 2021 for Íslandsbanki's Sustainable Financing Framework. Published 28 July 2022. cdn.islandsbanki.is/image/upload/v1/documents/Allocation_and_Impact_Report_2021_ FINAL.pdf

Labelled Equity

Equity signifies ownership in a company or property through shares, entitling holders to a share of profits and assets, including cash, investments, and property. Equity labels, such as green or transition equity labels, address growing concerns about the authenticity of companies' investments. In recent years, methodologies have been developed to include equities, the assessment of companies' investments, and revenue streams. This led to the first Green Equity framework, launched in 2020 by the real estate company K2A.[709]

Nasdaq launched a Green Equity Designation Program in 2021. It provides green or transition equity labels to companies listed in its European Main Markets and First North Growth Market. This helps investors find sustainable investments and enables eligible companies to access financing.[710] Similarly, the London Stock Exchange launched its Green Economy Mark in 2019 for listed companies and funds that generate over 50 percent of their revenues from products and services contributing to environmental objectives. It uses FTSE Russell's green revenues taxonomy.[711]

In March 2023, the World Federation of Exchanges (WFE) also published Green Equity Principles for all industries to determine if stocks and shares should be considered green. The five principles of revenues/investments, tax-onomy, governance, assessment, and disclosure are used as a framework for green activities. At the time of writing, this framework is being developed.[712] Investors should expect more green equity classifications as more exchanges adopt the WFE's green equity principles. This makes it easier for institutional investors to categorise their equity exposures as green and meet their portfolio allocation goals.

---

[709] Casabianca, P. Cicero and K2A pave the way for a new green-labelled equity market. NATIXIS. Published 12 June 2020. gsh.cib.natixis.com/our-center-of-expertise/articles/cicero-and-k2a-pave-the-way-for-a-new-green-labelled-equity-market
[710] Nasdaq green designations. Nasdaq. nasdaqomxnordic.com/learn/nasdaq-green-designations
[711] Green Economy Mark. LSE. londonstockexchange.com/raise-finance/equity/green-economy-mark
[712] EGreen Equities Principles and guidelines: Public call for comments. WFE. Published 14 September 2023. world-exchanges.org/our-work/articles/wfe-green-equity-principles-and-guidance-note-call-for-comments

GREEN EQUITY REQUIREMENTS

Nasdaq green equity labels are:

- Green equity designation—50 percent or more of turnover derived from green activities and continuing to invest a significant share in green activities. Turnover derived from fossil fuels must be less than 5 percent.
- Green equity transition designation—with the ambitions to transition to green and have more than 50 percent of their investments (not turnover like for the green designation) allocated to green activities. There is no minimum threshold for turnover from activities considered green, but the company's turnover derived from fossil fuel activities must be less than 50 percent.

Additional approval criteria for the labels are:

- Investments: More than 50 percent of the company's investments must be allocated to activities considered green.
- Taxonomy: The company must state its alignment with the EU Taxonomy for sustainable activities.
- Assessment: To maintain the designation, the company must commit to an annual limited assessment by an approved reviewer and make annual updates of key environmental data to be shared in the ESG Data Portal.
- Disclosure: The company must provide information on its relevant environmental targets and KPIs in the Paris Agreement, such as science-based targets and climate.
- The World Federation of Exchanges (WFE) Green Equity Classification criteria are:
- Revenues: Listed issuers must generate over 50 percent of their annual revenue from green activities. Pre-revenue stage

issuers must allocate over 50 percent of their investments to green activities or expect 100 percent of their revenue to come from green activities.

- Taxonomy: The issuer must disclose, in an assessment report, the taxonomy used to classify activities as green, along with any other criteria and definitions used in the assessment.
- Governance: Issuers must meet existing listing requirements for corporate governance.
- Assessment: If required, an exchange-approved reviewer must assess the activities and related revenues annually.
- Disclosure: Listed issuers must disclose how they meet the criteria, the methodology used, and the assessment report's outcomes.

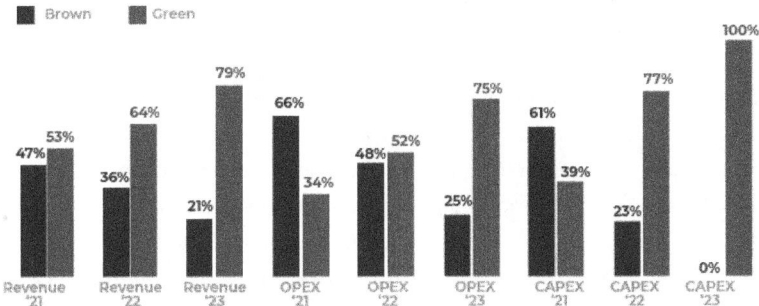

Image 8.4. By examining a company's income, expenses, and investments, we can determine green equity, revealing a story of progress. Source: Author.

Sustainable Insurance

Sustainable insurance comprises policies and practices prioritising ESG considerations to contribute to a more sustainable future. This includes integrating ESG criteria into the design, underwriting, and management of insurance products and services. Integration improves identifying, managing, and monitoring related risks and opportunities, fuelling innovation and improving company performance.

The UNEP FI Principles for Sustainable Insurance (PSI) was launched in 2012. The initiative comprises four main principles and is largely inspired by the UN PRI Principles. It is the largest collaboration between the UN and the insurance industry. As of early 2024, there are 159 signatories to the initiative and 106 supporting institutions.[713] Like the UN PRI, adherence to the PSI principles is voluntary, and signatories have no legal obligation to implement the principles. However, organisations face reputational and other ESG-related risks if they do not adhere to these principles.

Insurers are seeing higher-than-average losses associated with natural disasters. In 2022, insured losses were around USD 120 billion compared to the 2017-2021 average of USD 97 billion. Hurricane Ian was the costliest disaster in 2022, responsible for half of the insured losses globally. This was on top of a year characterised by high inflation and rising interest rates. With climate change exacerbating extreme weather events, financial protection, such as insurance, is imperative.[714]

Sustainable insurance is progressing via the UN's Net-Zero Insurance Alliance (NZIA), which launched its first protocol to help members set science-based targets for the net-zero transition. However, the NZIA lost a fifth of its members in 2023 for fear of being sued for antitrust violations. This included major insurers such as Munich Re, AXA, Allianz, and SCOR, following an accusation by the US Republican Party of NZIA of breaching antitrust laws.[715] Despite a promising start, as of February 2024, the alliance is left with only 17 members, down from around 30 previously, showcasing that not all initiatives are made to last.[716]

---

[713] Signatory Companies. UNEP FI. unepfi.org/insurance/insurance/signatory-companies
[714] Climate change and La Niña driving losses: the natural disaster figures for 2022. Munich RE. Published 10 January 2023. munichre.com/en/company/media-relations/media-information-and-corporate-news/media-information/2023/natural-disaster-figures-2022.html
[715] Wilkes T. More insurers desert net-zero alliance as U.N. climate group sounds alarm. Reuters. 30 May 2023. reuters.com/sustainability/political-attacks-are-damaging-insurers-climate-efforts-gfanz-2023-05-26
[716] Gangcuangco T. Who are still members of Net-Zero Insurance Alliance. Published 31 May 2023. insurancebusinessmag.com/us/news/environmental/who-are-still-members-of-netzero-insurance-alliance-447631.aspx

The insurance sector is addressing climate change through innovative products that bolster the resilience of vulnerable communities, like WTW's cyclone payouts aiding Pacific islanders in reef repairs and debris cleanup.[717] Other insurance companies are ceasing to provide the coal industry with underwriting services. "Insure Our Future" is a campaign that tracks and scores insurance companies' commitments to stop supporting fossil fuels. According to their 2022 report, forty-one issuers have either removed or reduced cover for coal. This corresponds to over 39 percent of the primary insurance market and 62 percent of the reinsurance market. Coal has essentially become uninsurable outside of China.[718]

Pension Funds

Pension funds, with their long-term investment horizons and diversified strategies, are fundamentally designed to serve the interests of retirees, who often reflect the diversity of our society. Their core responsibility includes safeguarding the future well-being of pensioners, making it imperative to ensure a sustainable and prosperous society for members to retire into. With pension assets surpassing USD 60 trillion in 2021, the potential for pension funds to contribute to this future is immense.[719] Another group of asset owners with the same long-term and diversified investment approach are life insurance companies, subject to similar challenges and opportunities as pension funds.

The debate around pension funds and their mandate to engage in sustainability investments often centres on the perceived trade-off with financial returns, traditionally seen as their primary fiduciary duty. Critics argue that sustainability investments may not always serve members' best interests, especially when fossil fuel investments offer better short-term gains. However, there's an evolving consensus that fiduciary duty encompasses more than financial profitability. It includes long-term sustainability and ethical considerations, reflecting a broader interpretation of acting in members' best interests and

---

[717] WTW launches first ever coral reef insurance policy in Fiji. WTW. 5 February 2024. wtwco.com/en-au/news/2024/02/wtw-launches-first-ever-coral-reef-insurance-policy-in-fiji
[718] Hapgood HR, Bosshard P. 2022 Scorecard on Insurance, Fossil Fuels and the Climate Emergency. Insure Our Future; 2022. insure-our-future.com/scorecard
[719] Pension markets in focus 2022. OECD. Published 11 December 2023. oecd.org/daf/fin/private-pensions/Pension-Markets-in-Focus-2022-FINAL.pdf

considering their sustainability preferences.[720]

This shift acknowledges that sustainable investments can align with, and even enhance, pension fund beneficiaries' long-term financial health and security. The Norwegian Sovereign Wealth Fund views working towards net-zero 2050 as being in the long-term financial interest of the fund.[721] Another example is CalPERS (The California Public Employees' Retirement System), which has set a 2030 sustainable investment strategy in which it commits to managing its portfolio efficiently and sustainably, including doubling its climate-focused investments to USD 100 billion to generate risk-adjusted returns to pay benefits now and into the future.[722]

Globally, not only are regulations compelling pension funds to weave sustainability into their investment strategies but also members themselves, resulting in an increased mandate by pension funds to engage in sustainable investing. This indicates a shift from the traditional "black box of investment", where pension fund members rarely interact with their pension managers. This shift is marked by a growing trend among individuals who proactively engage in their pension investments, setting ambitious targets like making 30 percent of their portfolio "green" by 2030 or channelling investments into sustainable funds and projects.

Pension funds are not only adopting green mandates but are also utilising their voting power to promote corporate actions that favour ESG principles. This active stance is further supported by the expanding sustainable finance market, allowing pension funds to increase their investments in green bonds and other sustainable financial products.

A prime example of this commitment was showcased at COP26 in Glasgow. Nordic and UK pension funds pledged to invest USD 130 billion in clean energy and climate initiatives by 2030. Facilitated by The Climate Invest-

---

[720] Consultation on the technical advice for the review of the IORP II Directive. EIOPA. Accessed 9 February 2023. eiopa.europa.eu/consultations/consultation-technical-advice-review-iorp-ii-directive_en

[721] Responsible investment Government Pension Fund Global 2022. Norges Bank Investment Management. Published 9 February 2023. nbim.no/contentassets/5804b35ea1e24063a79fca44a945e390/gpfg_responsible-investment-2022.pdf

[722] CalPERS' Sustainable Investments 2030 Strategy. CalPERS. November 2023. calpers.ca.gov/docs/board-agendas/202311/invest/item06d-01_a.pdf

ment Coalition (CIC), this initiative underscores a significant pivot towards sustainability, with an added promise of annual progress reports on climate investments.[723] This restructured approach highlights the evolving dynamics of pension fund investments, emphasising the transition towards sustainability and active management as integral to future investment practices.

Central Banks

Central banks manage countries' monetary policies and maintain financial stability. They try stabilising prices, regulating the money supply, controlling interest rates, and overseeing the financial system. While there is widespread agreement that climate change significantly affects the economy and price stability, there's a debate on whether central banks might exceed their existing mandates by addressing these issues.

On the one hand, acting on climate policies could be seen as central banks taking a stance and impacting economic resource allocation, potentially undermining their political independence without a clear democratic mandate.

On the other hand, climate change and environmental degradation present significant risks to the economy and financial sector, necessitating the evaluation of their impacts and the transition to a carbon-neutral society on economic stability. For central banks, understanding these influences is inherent in maintaining price stability and ensuring the safety of banks.

In response, central banks and regulators are refining how they better manage climate-related risks, including enhancing climate risk disclosure and classification standards, conducting stress testing, and applying capital requirements. These measures aim to provide clearer insights for financial institutions, investors, and regulators, aiding in the assessment of individual and systemic exposures to climate change.[724] [725]

It is unclear how effectively central banks can account for both environmen-

[723] 2021 Announcements - Nordic & UK. CIC. Access 9 February 2024. climateinvestmentcoalition.org/announcements
[724] Green Finance. IMF. imf.org/en/Topics/climate-change/green-finance
[725] Climate change and the ECB. ECB. ecb.europa.eu/ecb/climate/html/index.en.html

tal risks and financial stability, as well as how existing mandates should be interpreted.[726] A study from 2021 showed that 12 percent of 135 central banks worldwide had sustainability mandates. Also, 40 percent of mandates stated the need to support government policy, which often included sustainability goals.[727]

Institutions such as the International Monetary Fund (IMF), the European Central Bank, and the Bank of England are taking steps to address climate change. The Bank of England has prioritised climate risk following a stress test on Britain's financial system, warning that more research is needed on how climate risks could affect banks and insurers before changing capital requirement rules, i.e., to have sufficient capital to absorb unexpected losses. Addressing the issue now would reduce costs in the future.[728]

Is Sustainable Finance at a Crossroads?

Let's examine the evolving narrative on sustainability and ESG from one of the most influential figures of finance, Larry Fink. Changes in his letters should be monitored as they wield significant influence over the decisions and priorities of a vast financial audience and operators of companies, shaping the trajectory of sustainable finance development.

---

[726] Volz U. On the role of central banks in enhancing green finance. UNEP. Published February 2017. wedocs.unep.org/bitstream/handle/20.500.11822/16803/Role_Central_Banks_Green_Finance.pdf?

[727] Dikau S, Volz U. Central bank mandates, sustainability objectives and the promotion of green finance. Ecological Economics. 2021; 184:107022. doi:10.1016/j.ecolecon.2021.107022

[728] Bank of England. Bank of England report on climate-related risks and the regulatory capital frameworks. Bank of England; 2023. bankofengland.co.uk/prudential-regulation/publication/2023/report-on-climate-related-risks-and-the-regulatory-capital-frameworks

ADDITIONAL DETAILS: LARRY FINK[729]

Larry Fink, the CEO of BlackRock, a leading asset manager global-ly, is considered an influential figure in financial markets. He owns companies and invests in projects and assets, influencing how they manage their ESG approach. In his previous five letters to inves-tors, summarised here, an interesting observation emerged: "net zero" was mentioned 19 times in 2021 and zero times in 2023 and "trust" was mentioned once in 2021 but 19 times in 2023. Larry Fink has also faced criticism of hypocrisy and greenwashing as BlackRock is quite exposed to coal and other fossil fuels.[730]

- 2018: "A sense of purpose"—emphasised purpose in driving long-term growth, stakeholder engagement, ESG integration, and less focus on proxy voting and wars.
- 2019: "Purpose and profit"—linked purpose and profit, stating that profits are required to serve stakeholders, provide for employees' retirement, and achieve sustainable growth.
- 2020: "A fundamental reshaping of finance"—saw a significant reallocation of capital to sustainable strategies and stressed thinking of climate risk as investment risk and purpose as an engine of profitability.
- 2021: "Climate Change"—discussed Covid-19 accelerating deeper trends, the net-zero transition presenting an invest-ment opportunity, and called on companies to disclose their net-zero plans.
- 2022: "The power of capitalism"—stressed BlackRock's fidu-ciary duty to act in the best interest of its investors, provide

[729] Posts from: Larry Fink. Harvard Law School Forum on Corporate Governance. corpgov.law.harvard.edu/contributor/larry-fink
[730] Helmore E. BlackRock CEO faces call to step down amid claims of hypocrisy. The Guardian. Published 7 December 2022. theguardian.com/business/2022/dec/07/blackrock-ceo-faces-call-to-step-down-amid-claims-of-hypocrisy

value to all stakeholders, and focus on sustainability as capitalists, not environmentalists.

- 2023: "Music and returns"—commitment to making investing more accessible, affordable, and transparent, fiduciary duty, persistent inflation, trust, investing in the energy transition, and commitment to serving clients and making outsized returns.

CEOs of some major companies are withdrawing money from ESG investing or have even called it a scam. Large asset managers, private equity firms, and brokers have warned that ESG focus might threaten financial performance. In the US, Florida's treasury reportedly divested USD 2 billion from BlackRock, citing BlackRock's ESG investing and lack of focus on maximising returns as a reason.[731] Some states are introducing legislation to limit ESG investing, called Anti-ESG Bills.[732] Recent ESG-related backlashes and increased anti-ESG sentiment have encouraged the upgrade to ESG 2.0 to stay both competitive and relevant to issuers and investors.[733]

This "backlash" represents a healthy debate on the best way forward and how to best integrate ESG in companies and investments. I believe the people pulling money out would want to see a sustainable future for their grandchildren and the following generations. I believe that they are concerned about their responsibility for financial returns, and as we have learned, ESG cannot serve as a cure-all for weak business fundamentals. This is spurring the transition of ESG from 1.0 to 2.0 and further even. Who knows if we could potentially leap to EGS 3.0 shortly or even ESG 0.0, where the acronym is killed?

In most investor presentations, listing documents, or prospectuses of green financial instruments and ESG funds, a clause similar to the one in the following paragraph captures the market's current state. People want to play

---

[731] CFO Jimmy Patronis: Florida treasury divesting from Blackrock. MyFloridaCFO. Published 1 December 2022. myfloridacfo.com/news/pressreleases/details/2022/12/01/cfo-jimmy-patronis-florida-treasury-divesting-from-blackrock

[732] Dial L, Goldberg E, Mann R. The challenge of investing in the face of anti-ESG legislation. Reuters. Published 24 August 2022. reuters.com/legal/legalindustry/challenge-investing-face-state-anti-esg-legislation-2022-08-24

[733] Temple-West P, Masters B. Wall Street titans confront ESG backlash as new financial risk. Financial Times. Published 1 March 2023. ft.com/content/f5fe15f8-3703-4df9-b203-b5d1dd01e3bc

along but are also trying to manoeuvre and create value and impact without taking on too much liability. Sanctions and penalties for non-compliance are often not clearly defined or established, making enforcement sometimes challenging. However, with new and updated legislation and regulations, these are increasingly being specified. Despite this progress, reputational risks for non-compliance continue to be a significant concern for organisations.

ADDITIONAL DETAILS: DISCLAIMERS TO SUSTAINABLE FINANCE ACTIVITIES

The issuer gives no assurance that the use of proceeds for the funding of any Eligible Green Projects will satisfy, in whole or in part, any present or future investor expectations or requirements regarding any investment criteria. There is no clear definition (legal, regulatory, or otherwise) of, nor any market consensus as to, what constitutes "green" or similar labels.

Another consideration is that despite global efforts to dissuade lending to fossil fuels, oil and gas companies currently face minimal additional borrowing costs compared to less polluting companies. Environmental concerns seem to carry limited weight in funding decisions for these companies, as evidenced by the absence of a "premium" for issued bonds. Over 40 percent of banks, financial services firms, and insurers have committed to reducing direct and indirect emissions (Scope 1 and 2); only a fifth have pledged to address Scope 3 emissions tied to their investment and lending activities. This may affect the oil and gas sector's future financing, but a decline in new bonds since 2021 reflects their strong cash flow rather than financing challenges, indicating that fossil fuels remain a significant part of the energy and financial landscape, albeit with a diminishing share.[734]

Oil, gas, and coal still represent around 80 percent of the world's energy

---

[734] Johnston I. Oil and gas firms face virtually no extra borrowing costs, S&P finds. Financial Times. 17 November 2023. ft.com/content/830e3ae6-0c3c-4da9-87e7-4ff72aa3e249

consumption.[735] Some investors are placing big bets on the green transition, hitting major roadblocks, such as global conflict, and are buying up assets in and around fossil fuel and high-emitting industries at low prices, like the EPH Group, a Czech investment firm, building a "fossil fuel empire."[736] By managing lock-in risks, one reduces the risk of stranding assets. It took us hundreds of years to build the industries and societies that rely on these energy sources. It will take us a while, hopefully a shorter time, to re-design them for renewable energy.

Sustainable finance is arguably at a crossroads. However, there are good reasons to be optimistic about the role of financial markets in sustainable development. There is growing awareness and demand from investors for sustainable and responsible investments, which has increased the availability and variety of sustainable financial products and also forced their further streamlining. Governments and regulatory bodies also create frameworks and standards to encourage and incentivise sustainable investments.

However, we see a stronger narrative in the financial markets that investors demand risk-adjusted returns as many sustainable investments have yet to pay off financially. Perhaps we need to readjust our expectations for growth-oriented, risk-adjusted returns.

Endnote

In this chapter, we have looked at sustainable finance, the size of that market, and the investments needed to achieve a sustainable future. We have further explored different financing labels and their unique frameworks and principles, including green, social, blue, transition and sustainability-linked bonds, that aim to ensure credible and trustworthy progress. Before diving into labelled equity and sustainable insurance, we also explored taxonomies, specifically the development of the EU Taxonomy and EUGBS. The roles of pension funds and central banks in sustainable finance were discussed, and

---

[735] World Energy Outlook 2023. IEA. Published October 2023. iea.org/reports/world-energy-outlook-2023

[736] Naik G, Sorge P. Elusive Billionaire Bets Against Europe's Green Plans—And Mints a Fortune. Bloomberg. Published 6 April 2023. bloomberg.com/news/features/2023-04-06/daniel-kretinsky-eph-group-builds-17-billion-fossil-fuel-empire

CONCLUSION

lastly, we addressed some concerns regarding ESG investments.

However, I trust that there will be more evidence indicating that investing in a sustainable future can deliver strong financial returns. The increased corroboration would attract more investors to this market, creating a positive investment cycle—and a better future for our planet and its citizens. This was the final chapter of the book, and now we'll explore the question of whether 2050 will be brighter or not.

CONCLUSION

A Brighter 2050?

In this book, we have explored the significant challenges we face as a global community, including climate change, biodiversity loss, inequality, and trust. These challenges are interconnected and require a collective effort from various sectors, regions, and individuals to address them effectively. A concentrated, coordinated, collaborative push must accommodate diverse needs and perspectives.

Furthermore, this book emphasises the role of companies in shaping society and impacting people's lives and opportunities. It underscores the importance of democratic societies where elected officials set the legislations and regulations that govern us. We need active engagement in local, national, and global politics and international cooperation between nations and regions. Achieving a sustainable future requires voluntary actions by individuals and companies and robust regulations promoting responsible practices.

Several key factors will influence our future progress, including how we measure change, address climate change impacts, protect biodiversity, and handle social issues. Developing effective policies, embracing technological advancements, responding to global events, and balancing growth with sustainability are necessary. Businesses must proactively adapt by making sustainability a core principle and embracing opportunities for innovation and long-term value. When the business world recognises the interconnectedness of these challenges and opportunities, it can drive positive change and build a more sustainable future for everyone.

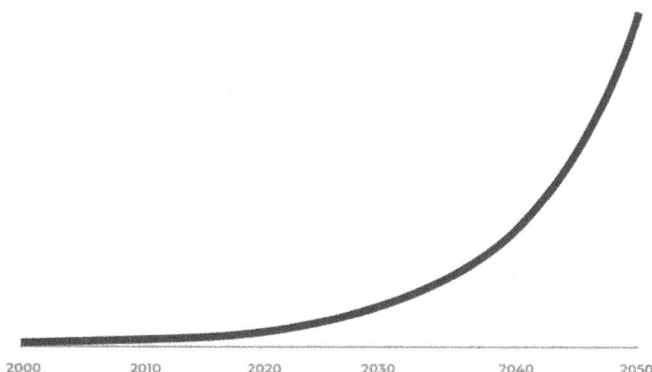

Image C.1. I imagine a future where environmental and social solutions converge and mutually reinforce each other driving exponential growth towards sustainability with prosperity at its core and underpinned by solid governance. All without the confines of a Y-axis as this vision transcends conventional measurements. Source: Author

It was courageous leadership that took early-adopting companies on a path to modern corporate sustainability in the absence of modern standards, legislation, and regulations. Today's legislative landscape forces most companies, at least larger ones, to integrate sustainability across the ESGP spectrum and doesn't necessarily require much additional courage. I believe courageousness will lie in leaders taking their companies on a path of hyper-materiality—cutting through all the noise, clutter, and non-value-adding metrics and initiatives, hyper-focusing on their business's core financial and operational fundamentals, and what really moves the needle for their company's success and significant contributions to a sustainable future.

Capital allocation may drive the transition to a sustainable future. Despite the current investment gap of what is needed to finance a sustainable future, there is an opportunity to bridge the divide by reassessing practices and identifying projects aligned with long-term value creation and positive environmental and social outcomes. The shift from ESG 1.0 to ESG 2.0, influenced by regulations like the EU Taxonomy and the CSRD, presents a turning point for sustainable finance. By demonstrating the financial viability of sustainable investments, we attract more investors and create a positive cycle of impact and returns.

Our world is a complex mix of progress and challenges. We have made strides in reducing poverty, improving healthcare, and expanding education. However, we must also recognise the hurdles we face, such as extreme weather, inequality, and political instability. Maintaining a balanced perspective and understanding that progress in one area doesn't solve all problems is essential. Each region has its unique trajectory, and measuring progress requires careful consideration of different metrics.

In my years of working with sustainability, I have met many excellent, forward-thinking executives who genuinely want to understand how sustainability impacts their organisations. They see it as more than just compliance; it's an opportunity for growth and long-term value creation. Although we have made progress, more people need to realise that investing in sustainability can also lead to risk-adjusted returns. However, we may need to discount our yield expectations in places to push through projects that progress us faster to desired outcomes.

I felt I had considerable knowledge and experience in corporate sustainability and sustainable finance when I started writing this book. However, the journey has humbled me and shown me how much more there is yet to learn. Sustainability infuses the intricate web of our environment, society, economic growth, and governance. It can be overwhelming to grasp the interconnectedness of everything amidst an overflow of fragmented information. However, by recognising the holistic nature of sustainability, we gain a deeper understanding of how these aspects intertwine and influence one another.

Conflicting information and multiple truths exist simultaneously. The complexity of reality, subjective perspectives, and varying interpretations can give rise to different valid truths. Personal experiences, cultural backgrounds, and individual biases shape our understanding of the world, and the truth itself can evolve with new information and perspectives.

This book aims to inform and empower us to make a difference. It's not about offering quick fixes or rigid rules but providing a deeper understanding of the challenges and opportunities ahead. Now, armed with this knowledge, it's time to act. Remembering that sustainability involves various disciplines, so collaboration and integrating diverse perspectives will enhance our prospects of success. Let's embrace this opportunity to create positive change. Together, through collective action, we can make a lasting impact.

As we conclude this book, our thoughts return to the cover image—the once mighty Ok glacier. Now stripped of its glacial status, it mirrors the vulnerability of our world in the face of relentless climate change. The disappearance of Ok is not just the loss of a glacier; it represents a deeper, more pervasive threat to our collective existence and the sustainability of our planet. As we reflect on Ok's fate, let it ignite a commitment to foster a resilient and sustainable 2050 future and beyond within us.

Thank you for joining me on this supercharged journey. I hope my words have inspired you to make a difference and shape a better world. I would love your feedback and thoughts. Together, let's forge a path to a brighter future.

Reach out and engage at bjarniherrera.com.

ACKNOWLEDGEMENTS

I extend my deepest gratitude to everyone who has contributed to bringing this book to life—my friends, family, colleagues, fellow experts, publishers, staff, proofreaders, editors, and students, for their invaluable feedback and support. Special thanks for the continuous support of those who believe in me and inspire me on my personal and professional journey. My first publisher went bankrupt, causing a nearly year-long delay in the process, but that ultimately worked to my advantage and contributed to the improvement of the book. This book would not have been possible without the help and contributions of all these individuals; I am genuinely thankful for that. Finally, I'm grateful to my readers!

Name	About
Senior collaborators, researchers, and reviewers	
Anna Jia	Sustainability Manager at Accrona. BSc in Engineering Management with a focus on Global Health and Social Justice. Certified patisserie chef and passionate foodie.
Anna Bryndís Zingsheim Rúnudóttir	Manager in Sustainability Consulting, KPMG. MSc in Sustainable Energy Engineering. Animal adorer who loves hiking and yoga.
Hildur Th. Armanns-dottir	ESG Analyst at Swedfund. Master's in Human Geography and Environmental Social Science. Second-hand bargain hunter and retired swimmer.
Knut H. Alfsen, PhD	Semi-retired Senior Advisor at Accrona and CCICED (look it up!). PhD in theoretical physics. Loves music and good books.

Tim Axtmann	Associate Director, S&P Global Ratings, Sustainable Finance. LLM in International Environmental Law. Keen amateur footballer and despairing Vålerenga IF fan.

Collaborators, researchers, and reviewers

Bernhard Schiessl	Director of Sustainable Solutions at S&P Global. MSc Physics. Passionate about the climate, the outdoors, and triathlons.
Catherine Rothacker	Associate Director, S&P Global Ratings, Sustainable Finance. Master of Environmental Management. Aspiring urban farmer and avid art, theatre, and global fiction appreciator.
Hildur Karen Haraldsdóttir	Senior Legal Counsel and Project Manager at Corporate Finance, Íslandsbanki. Master's in Law. Ardent about skiing, golfing, and embracing nature.
Ina Tuomala	Manager at Accrona. Sustainability communications specialist with a Master's in Research. Rock climber and owner of too many potted plants.
Isha Gupta Waghmare	Sustainable Finance Manager at Accrona, former Big 4 ESG Advisory Manager. MBA with a major in Sustainable Finance and Financial Technology. An amateur painter, kitchen gardener, and passionate fur mother.
Joëlle Amram	Investment Specialist in Sustainable Equities at J. Safra Sarasin Asset Management, with a background in fund selection for impact funds. MBA from Yonsei University, S-Korea. Fervent foodie and travel enthusiast.
Keith Lee, PhD	Buy-side green bond analyst. PhD in City and Regional Planning with specialisation in urban sustainability. Family man.

ACKNOWLEDGEMENTS

Kent Hanson	Undertaking an MSc in Sustainability Management student at Columbia University. Former professional basketball player in Portugal, Iceland, Canada, and Kazakhstan.
Kevin J Dillman, PhD	
Lena Schwenke	Sustainability Specialist in Supply Chain at Porsche AG. MSc in Sustainable Management. Passionate about the mountains and skiing through deep powder.
Petter Moger	Associate at Kron and pursuing an MSc in Business Analytics. An amateur sports athlete and passionate about mountain hiking.
Petar Madjarac	International Markets at Pivot Bio. Passionate about empowering farmers around the world to grow food more sustainably.
Remi Bonnet	Operations Supervisor Intern at Cascades Recovery+. Bachelor in Business Administration from HEC Montreal, specialising in Logistics and Sustainable Development. Passionate about the environment and a gym lover.
Sara Hemrajani	Business Journalist and Multimedia Producer. Master's degree in International Journalism and BSc in Politics with Economics. Music aficionado who enjoys Muay Thai training.
Sara Júlía Baldvinsdottir	Sustainability Specialist, KPMG and a UN Youth Delegate for Sustainable Development. Master's in Sustainability Management. Amateur upcycling-interior designer and hobby baker.

Snjólaug Árnadóttir, PhD	Associate Professor and Director of the Centre for Law on Climate Change and Sustainability at Reykjavik University. Doctorate in Law from the University of Edinburgh. Mum and aesthete, passionate about climate resilience, music, and spirituality.
Sverrir Falur Björnsson	Economist of the Icelandic Farmers Association. Master's in Economics from the University of Iceland. A sports enthusiast, a father, and a Swifty
Þorsteinn Kári Jónsson	VP of Sustainability & Community Engagement at Marel. Believer in the human spirit and the delight of connecting with others.

Editors, proofreaders, reviewers, publishers, and publishing advisors:

Amanda S. Coffin, Anna Dorfman, Hasara Nishshanka, Jim Symcox, Jordan Grenadier, Kevin J. Dillman, PhD, Linda Alila, Meghan McCracken, Miles Rote, and Robert Reddin.

ABOUT THE AUTHOR

Bjarni Herrera's diverse and international career lies in senior management and leadership positions in banking, finance, ocean transportation, and professional services with boutique firms and big global corporations. He has contributed to growth and value creation by building strong teams, creating robust operations, and working closely with customers to understand their needs.

His Nordic upbringing and Latin American heritage have encouraged him to explore the world and see things from unique perspectives. He enjoys long walks in nature, skiing, running, cycling, reading, immersing himself in good company and new cultures, and roaming in huge cities where he often finds peace.

Bjarni is a practitioner, leader, listener, advisor, talent developer, and now an author—who is unafraid to tackle big questions and challenges. He holds a corporate law degree from Bifrost with an exchange at Arkansas State University and an MBA from Yonsei in partnership with the Asian Institute of Management. He also holds certifications in securities trading, sustainability and climate risk, and board memberships.

In banking, he started his career in bankruptcy law. Then in the aftermath of the 2008 financial crisis, Bjarni served as the Secretary of the Board of Directors of Arion Bank while the bank was being restructured, including its corporate governance, under new leadership and later listed in Iceland and Sweden. He then immersed himself in Asia, living in Seoul, Singapore, Manila, Taipei, and Hong Kong, where he studied and later worked for Expeditors, an American Fortune 500 company.

As CEO and co-founder, he led the creation of Iceland's market-leading corporate sustainability and sustainable finance consulting firm, which helped transition the market from CSR-based to ESG-based. He further played a pivotal role in creating a market for sustainable finance instruments, where he led the design of the first green, blue, social, and sustainability financing frameworks. This company was later acquired by KPMG, Iceland's largest Big 4, where he served as its inaugural Head of Sustainability.

Later, Bjarni served as the COO of CICERO Shades of Green, a multi-award-winning provider of second opinions on green and sustainable finance instruments. When S&P Global acquired it in late 2022, Bjarni ensured seamless operations and sales integration. He then founded Accrona, an international sustainability and sustainable finance service firm, where he serves as CEO and is joined by some of his former brilliant colleagues. He also manages his own venture firm, where he helps the next generation of entrepreneurs solve sustainability and sustainable finance challenges. He participates in various board roles and NGOs and travels worldwide for speaking engagements and panel discussions.

Bjarni has gained a broad overview of working globally with companies across sectors, municipalities, and sovereigns on most sustainability challenges: strategies and policies, reporting, life-cycle assessments, target setting and action plans, risk management, coaching executives, and more. Despite his broad experience, he is painfully aware of how much he has yet to learn. This book represents his willingness and dedication to learning more, sharing, and contributing to designing a sustainable future.